Just Add Water

KATIE LEDECKY

SIMON & SCHUSTER

New York   London   Toronto   Sydney   New Delhi

100 YEARS
SIMON &
SCHUSTER

1230 Avenue of the Americas
New York, NY 10020

First Simon & Schuster hardcover edition June 2024

SIMON & SCHUSTER and colophon are registered trademarks of Simon & Schuster, LLC

Simon & Schuster: Celebrating 100 Years of Publishing in 2024

For information about special discounts for bulk purchases, please contact Simon & Schuster Special Sales at 1-866-506-3049 or business@simonandschuster.com.

The Simon & Schuster Speakers Bureau can bring authors to your live event. For more information or to book an event, contact the Simon & Schuster Speakers Bureau at 1-866-248-3049 or visit our website at www.simonspeakers.com.

Interior design by Wendy Blum

Manufactured in the United States of America

1   3   5   7   9   10   8   6   4   2

Library of Congress Cataloging-in-Publication Data has been applied for.

ISBN 978-1-6680-6020-9
ISBN 978-1-6680-6022-3 (ebook)

IMAGE CREDITS
Insert pages 10 (top) and 11 (bottom): Spencer Blake;
page 16: Mike Lewis/Ola Vista Photography;
all other images courtesy of the Ledecky family

*In honor of my grandparents and to my mother and father,
my brother, and everyone in my family and all others
who have been a part of my life.*

CONTENTS

Just Add Water

INTRODUCTION

I'm in the pool.

I'm always in the pool. Hours a day, nearly every day, since I was a toddler perched on the side ladder, blowing bubbles and kicking my feet. The pool is and has always been my refuge. It functions as my playground, my hobby, my passion, my workplace, my lifeblood.

Not too long ago, a reporter asked one of my coaches for estimates of the kind of mileage I would've logged in different years in my career. He figured I would've easily swum from Bethesda, Maryland, where I was raised, to Tokyo, where I competed at the most recent Olympics. It was wild to imagine that all the lanes I've swum, added together, could've led me across the sea.

When I review the stats that get posted about my swims, it opens my eyes to just how long I've been at this sport. Take the 800 free, for example. Right now I have twenty-nine of the top thirty times in history. There are a lot of my competitors who I don't think have even swum twenty-nine 800 freestyles in their lives. I've swum, probably, the most 800 and 1500 freestyles of anyone, ever.

Seeing those numbers, just comprehending the mileage on my body, makes me appreciate the longevity of my career. When I look up how many occasions I've swum any given event, year after year, I'm left with the same conclusion: *Wow, that's a lot of swim meets.* On average, across my swimming career, I'd estimate I swim nine meets annually. It's been twenty years now. That's 180 meets. That means 180 multi-day meets of waking up with the unique excitement that fills me on race day, going through countless warm-up and warm-down laps, and waiting through heats for my turn to dive into my race. And somehow it still feels like yesterday that I first dipped my feet in the pool.

I am many things—daughter, sister, Stanford graduate, Olympian—but the architecture that grounds and supports all those roles is my identity as a swimmer. Which is why, should you ever need to find me—you should first look in the pool.

Today the pool hurts. Well, I hurt. My arms and legs feel like they're filled with cement. I'm ramping up training to try to qualify for the Paris Olympics, which would be my fourth Olympic Games.

My story is unique in that I did not set out early on with the goal to become a professional athlete. I've been swimming in races since I was six years old—more than twenty years now—but I began as a truly mediocre swimmer. My initial ambition as a competitor was simply to make it across the pool without stopping. In my very first swim—a 25 free—I literally stopped on the lane line about ten times. It became a race between me and the girl next to me to see who stopped the least. We kept stopping to wipe the chlorine from our faces and check that we hadn't drifted into another lane. It was hilarious.

I've heard a lot of my swimming peers say that when they were young, they always knew they wanted to go to the Games, but that wasn't my experience. Back then I looked at Olympians and thought you had to be a superhero to reach that level. I couldn't relate what I was doing in the pool to what I saw them do on television. They seemed to be so fast, so focused, so otherworldly.

And yet here I am, entering what we swimmers call our "Olympic Year," a season that brings with it a rush of promise. The Olympic Year begins on September 1, when we start back after the summer break. College swimming runs through the fall, then the championship meets begin in February and March; that's all short-course yards. During that time, people are still training for Olympic Trials, and as a professional swimmer, I don't compete in the collegiate meets anymore. Throughout the fall and winter, training and racing may include short-course yards, short-course meters, and long-course meters. From March until the end of the summer, it's only long-course racing. Once the final summer competition of the pre–Olympic Year is over (for me, that was World Championships at the end of July 2023), that's when it's like—*Oh, it's time*. The Olympic Year has begun.

When I turn that calendar page to begin the Olympic year, I can feel the excitement. A sense of urgency descends. The clock begins ticking louder. Every swim counts.

I'm experiencing it as I write this, in fact. I'm doing a bit more than I normally would in the pool, escalating every facet of my training so I can shave slices of seconds from my prior times. I know I need to be in better shape than I was last year, faster than I was during the last Games. I want to be ahead of myself.

Maybe I've always wanted that.

I'M PICTURING MY FIRST summer-league pool. The temperature, the scent of the chlorine and how it mixes with the air. Sharp, enveloping. I *love* that smell. When I was three, my mom would take my brother and me to a neighborhood pool close to our house. My brother could already swim, and I remember doing bobs, where you hold on to the ledge and dip up and down in the water. My mother was the one who taught me how to float on my back, how to hold my breath.

Humans are not natural-born swimmers. Unlike most animals, we must be taught. We don't enter our lives swim-ready. Quite the contrary. Many of us possess a natural fear of the water, a caution that makes sense, given the consequences of not knowing how to stay afloat.

I never had that fear.

It's not that I'm fearless. I love dogs, but certain animals freak me out. I worry about people I love dying. I find horror movies unpleasant. But the pool never frightened me. You see videos of babies yanking their feet up when they dip into the wet or kids bawling during swim lessons. But I couldn't wait to submerge myself in the water. It was love at first plunge.

I remember playing sharks and minnows, Marco Polo, the sensation of jumping into the pool before I learned any strokes. I felt more at home in the water than on land. I felt free.

Swimming hit me differently than other sports. It provided resistance. That elemental shift from moving through air to moving through water was the heart of my relationship with the pool. That and the inherent paradoxes water offered. Water made me feel weightless even as it forced me to pull more weight while I swam. In a pool, I was unencumbered and able to flip and turn and spin my body in every direction. I was also hemmed in by a pen of concrete. It represented creativity within bounds. When I wasn't in the pool, I yearned for the buoyancy. I craved the resistance. I wanted, more than anything, to test my limits in the water. So I did. Starting at age six. And never once stopping since.

I swam my first race on June 25, 2003. I got assigned lane three. Like I said, I was not some prodigy who dove into the water and was able to zoom to the end. There I was, bobbing around in bug-eyed goggles, wiping my nose when I stopped on the lane rope, which was often (the stopping and the nose wiping). During one of these pauses, my eyes landed on the other swimmers cruising by. And something sparked. I let go of the rope and swam, plowing ahead, arms spinning like windmills till I hit the wall. I managed to come in second in the eight-and-under 25-yard freestyle.

My dad filmed the race on his camcorder, and when I finished, he did an interview with me from the pool deck.

"Tell me about your first race. How was it?" he asked.

"Great!" I answered, my heart beating like a drum in my chest. He asked what I was thinking about in the pool.

"Nothing!" I said.

Then he said, "Just trying to finish, huh?"

"Just trying hard," I replied, grinning the whole time.

I always smile when I think about that video. Not so much because it was my first race but because of the way I answered my dad. My observations as an eager, exhausted six-year-old have become the template for my whole swimming journey. *Great. Hard. Just trying to finish.*

In the twenty years since that day, swimming has not ceased being hard. Uniquely so. It tests my body and my psyche equally. It challenges me like I imagine a marathon would—a marathon with the added burden of the force of water reminding me with every stroke what I'm up against. But to my mind, the *hard* is kind of what makes swimming great. Giving your best effort has been baked into my DNA for generations. Trying hard is the whole point. It's what makes something as simple as swimming laps meaningful.

I realize I didn't grasp the significance of this when I was a kid. But some part of my brain or my body understood that happiness would result from being in a space where the mind can run quiet, and the body can try hard. Swimming is an unusual career in that it comes down to the will of the swimmer, in this case me. I am the only one who has been there in the pool with me every stroke of the way. I had the incredible luck of being mentored by a series of devoted and wise coaches willing to lift me up without making swimming my sole raison d'être. My family did the same. I was never pressured to perform by anyone but myself. Of the many twists of fate that lead to greatness, this support system was the one for which I'm most grateful. It's what I credit with keeping me sane and grounded all these years.

My goal was to better myself through swimming. To discover who I was and what I was made of. The pool provided the ideal instrument for that journey. The Olympic medals, the world records, those are incredible achievements. But I'm more gratified by how swimming has shaped me. How the pursuit has molded me into the best version of myself.

One thing I've learned, maybe the most important thing, is that you are who you are in the moment only because of all the moments that came before it. Past is prologue in swimming. Same goes for life. Swimming has rendered me into someone I wouldn't be otherwise. Long after another swimmer breaks my records, I'll still have the benefit of being raised in and by the pool. I hope my tenacity outlasts any blip of athletic fame. That would be the gift of a lifetime.

For as long as I've been swimming, I've had people asking how I got where I am. They speculate about my physiology, analyze the geometry of my body, comb through my training. For a lot of people in the sporting community, I am a puzzle to be solved. A code that, if cracked, will enable them to replicate my results. When I was young, they asked my parents. Then my coaches. Now the inquiring minds come to the source.

This book is my answer. My attempt to lay out all the ingredients of my swimming life.

Becoming a successful athlete isn't accomplished without the help of many others. And as I now reflect on my childhood, teenage years, and early twenties, I can begin to grasp and understand how and why I developed into the person I am today. The people who influenced my character. The places that welcomed me. The life experiences that molded me into the dedicated swimmer I am today, opening my eyes and heart to every possibility until all that was left was to just add water.

Chapter One

PALISADES

I grew up in Bethesda, Maryland, a northwestern suburb of Washington, D.C. The kind of place with a small-town feel and big-city access. The house I was raised in is a modest Colonial where my parents still reside. I lived there with my mother, Mary Gen, a hospital administrator; my father, David, a lawyer; and my older brother, Michael. We were a close-knit family.

We lived on a street that had a lot of kids my age. Our house was walking distance to a park. We went every day. Shooting baskets, playing on the swing, running around with the neighborhood pals. I attended Little Flower School, a Catholic pre-K-through-grade-eight school about a half mile from our house. I was a good student with a knack for math. My life was so full. I sang in the school chorus, learned to play the piano, joined the soccer team and the basketball squad. And, of course, there was the swim team.

Swimming in our leafy-green suburb was both popular and fiercely competitive. The local league had approximately eighty different pools. When my parents moved to Bethesda, they didn't know anything about the Montgomery County Swim League. But it quickly became clear to them that the area they had chosen was an incubator for dedicated swimmers.

Around twenty thousand kids swam during the summer. Many of them were quite serious about the sport. Michael Phelps came from

Maryland. The great female distance swimmers Katie Hoff, Kate Ziegler, and Debbie Meyer are also all from the D.C.-Maryland-Virginia (DMV) area. We were assigned "buddies" at Little Flower School, and my very first younger buddy from fourth grade was pre-K student Phoebe Bacon, who ended up on the 2021 Tokyo Olympic swim team with me, competing in the 200 backstroke. There must be, forgive the pun, something in the DMV water.

I was three years old when we got on the waiting list for Palisades, a club with an outdoor 25-meter pool surrounded by trees. The summer I turned six and my brother was nine, they finally had room enough for us to join. Because of the large concentration of swimmers in the area, these wait-lists were common. In fact, the closest pool in our neighborhood had a multi-year wait. I would've been in college by the time we got in.

That said, it was not my mother's mission to put us on a swim team. Nor was there some master plan to turn me into a future swim star. What Mom wanted when she put us on the Palisades wait-list was a way for me and my brother to enjoy swimming in the summer and make friends. She'd already taught us the basics of swimming at the Sport & Health club pool in McLean, Virginia. Safety, floating, stuff like that. Then one day she saw a bulletin board at Palisades advertising a swim team, turned to us kids, and asked, "Do you guys want to join this? Could be fun." And just like that, we were Palisades Porpoises.

If you're not familiar with summer swim leagues, they have an interesting dynamic. It starts with a swim meet once a week. It's boys and girls, young and older kids all the way through high school. A great mix of ages and abilities. All the parents are involved. Then slowly, little by little, before you realize, swim league takes over every spare minute of your life. More practices, more meets, more responsibilities for the parents.

Put plainly, swimming is a lifestyle. The deeper in you get, the more commitment it requires. My school and college experiences were not typical, because swimming demands payment from every corner of your life. I went to bed early. I used my weekends to do homework. I ate the right things, not the fun things. I rarely wavered. But what other people would see as burdens, I viewed as opportunities. These sacrifices were steps on a ladder to success.

My swimming routine did take over the family. My parents schlepped me to practice, traveled with me to meets. They put in a lot of hours on the road and racked up impressive mileage on their vehicles. As time went on, it meant passing up other things. For example, we couldn't visit my grandma's farm in North Dakota as frequently because of my training and my schedule. Plus, everywhere we went needed to have a pool nearby. And not just any pool; I needed a big one. Even as a kid, I knew that this was a sacrifice.

We did the Palisades summer-league team, and then we joined a year-round swim team, now called Nation's Capital Swim Club. We had the same swim meets every year. There was the Pilgrim Pentathlon. There was the Fall Gator Mini Meet. There was the Winter Gator Mini Meet. There was the Mini Champs. There was the JOs, Junior Olympics, basically the fourteen-and-under championship meet for the area. Eventually I qualified for the Potomac Valley Swimming Zones team, which competes in a meet against the whole Northeast. On and on, rinse, repeat, until eventually I was an Olympic and World Champion and every single day meant being at the pool.

And to think I owe all of that to my mom signing up my brother and me for the swim team so we could make friends at our pool. Imagine if she'd decided to enroll me in ballet instead? Or the drama club? I'm sure I would have enjoyed both of those activities, but neither would have likely become my passion or taken me so far around the world.

One reason I believe I've kept my wits about me through the many ups and downs of being a professional athlete is that my swim career started in a super-low-key environment. Palisades was not an expensive, exclusive swimming club. It was built in 1969, and it doesn't have any neighborhood limitations on its membership.

Instead of a fancy country club restaurant, there was a picnic area with grills and tables. We'd have team barbecues after the swim meets. Or we'd throw team pep rallies the night before the swim meets, like the pasta pep rally or the poster pep rally. (Upon reflection, there were a lot of alliterative themes.) We'd have Fun Fridays where, at the end of morning practice, we would play a game of sharks and minnows or water polo and the eight-and-unders would sit on the fifteen-to-eighteens' shoulders. There was such camaraderie between the age groups, all the way from six to eighteen years old. We'd make posters Saturday morning, then dress up in crazy outfits for the meet. There was one summer when I decided to wear a black wig that I had from Halloween to every single event. It became a game to work it into every theme. All to say, this was not a stuffy, well-heeled country club pool affair.

What Palisades really provided was community. It was family-oriented and emphasized fun. The fact that Palisades was unpretentious and welcoming meant the members were largely that way too. I understand that this is not everyone's swim league experience. Many people who go into the sport are driven, or they see swimming as a constant competition, and the vibe is more intense. Palisades was maximum chill.

I have such fond memories of that pool. I remember sitting on the ladder, one of those big stepladders that dip into the water, and my coach teaching me how to breathe to the side in freestyle. Her name was Catherine Pitcher. Most of the coaches of the summer-league team were eighteen or nineteen years old, maybe even younger. Kids themselves, really. Catherine stood in front of me in the water and taught me how to tilt my head from side to side.

Every weekend during the summer, there would be a swim meet and my parents would attend as timers, hang with the other parents, get to know all the families. There were a lot of very nice teenage kids who took interest in us younger swimmers, helping us learn how to race.

I remember getting an ear infection the night before my last meet of my first season. We went to Spring Valley Pediatrics, and when the doctor told me I shouldn't go in the water, I bawled like a toddler. I was devastated that I might not be able to swim. The doctor eventually relented, telling my parents, against his better judgment, "Okay, fine, put a swim cap on her." Which, incidentally, is when we bought my first ever cap at the local shop next to the grocery store. It had a frog on it.

I swam the next day. And for the first time, I made it across the pool. No stops, no nose wiping (that frog must have been lucky). When I hit the wall on the other side, I was so exhilarated I felt like I could fly. My body was weary yet energized at the same time. I wanted to swim the length of the pool again, right away. Instead, my mom reminded me I had an ear infection, and any additional swimming was off the table until I healed. She drove us to Panera, and we drank hot chocolate. A solid consolation prize.

When you swim competitively, you end up revisiting the same pools season after season. You can end up failing spectacularly in the same pool where, years later, you set a world record. You also develop favorites. Pools that, for whatever reason, bring out your best. For me, one of those locations is the Rosen Aquatic & Fitness Center pool in Orlando, Florida. It was the site of many of my Junior National meets, one where I won the 1650 free in March 2011, at age fourteen. I was in eighth grade, competing against eighteen-year-olds. That same pool was where I broke my 1650-yard freestyle American record in 2023. I clocked in at 15:01, narrowly missing becoming the first woman to swim that length in under fifteen minutes.

There are dozens of different pools I've developed affection for over all these years, like the American University pool, where I swam every day when I began to get serious; the Fairland Sports and Aquatics Complex (the site of many meets, and many family renditions of Bruce Springsteen's "Badlands," with the lyrics tweaked to "Fairland" during the car ride there); Swimming Stadium Podolí (in Prague, Czech Republic, where my brother and I swam while visiting with our grandparents in 2007); Stone Ridge School of the Sacred Heart (my high school pool, where I have countless memories of my high school teammates and coach Bob Walker); the University of Maryland pool, where I watched Michael Phelps swim in the summer of 2003, and also the pool where I broke the 1000 free American record twelve years later, the first woman to clock in under nine minutes.

I broke more records at the Woodlands' Conroe ISD Natatorium (two world records in 2014), Irvine's Woollett Aquatics Center (the 400 free world record), the University of Texas (reset the 800 free world record in January 2016), Germantown Indoor Swim Center, Ohio State University, the Natatorium at IUPUI (broke the 1500 free long-course meters [LCM] world record in 2018, broke the 500 free American record in 2017, broke the 800 free short-course meters [SCM] world record in 2022), and the Toronto Pan Am Sports Centre pool (set the 1500 SCM world record in October 2022).

And yet, even after all those pools and all those years and all that history, Palisades remains my most meaningful place to swim. It's been a constant, a North Star. It's the pool where I came of age as a swimmer. It's where coaches first invested in me; where I screamed the Porpoise cheer with my teammates, all our voices echoing off the walls; where I learned how to win and how to lose with equal amounts of grace.

We still belong to Palisades. I love that I can go back there whenever I want. My brother swims at Palisades when he's in town. My mom does too. My dad socializes with the people he met when we were competing there. Our whole family benefited from Palisades in ways far more meaningful and far-reaching than just joining a swim club.

After the last World Championships in July 2023, I was advised to take one full week off from exercise, no running, no dryland, no weight training, no swimming. My coaches knew this would be a tough pill to swallow. I miss the water after even just one day off. They said after seven days I could ease back into the pool. When that day came, I was visiting home in Bethesda. Which meant that my first official swim of my Paris Olympic Year was at Palisades, in the very pool where I learned how to be a swimmer. It fills me with pride and emotion just thinking about it.

The morning I went for that first Olympic training swim, I drove to Palisades with my mom. She had her water aerobics class, and I took part in the early-bird swim. There was one lifeguard. I was the sole swimmer doing laps. The scene was low-key and normal as could be.

I'll admit, there are times when people get excited because they spot me at the hometown pool. But it's not because of "who I am," it's because they haven't seen me in a long time. It's down-home week when I return to Palisades. Catching up with everyone's lives while I've been away. The friends my mom does water aerobics with have known me since I was a child, and some are the parents of swimmers I grew up with.

The closest thing to any celebrity status is the fat-head photo of me in the Palisades lifeguard office. It's a cardboard cutout of me holding an inflatable porpoise, the club mascot. I've been told they bring the cutout to swim meets. Which means I'm always on deck with the team. I can't imagine a better place to be.

There's also a plaque on a bookcase that says something like "Katie Ledecky, London 2012 Olympian, Palisades Pool," indicating that I made it all the way from Palisades to the Games. I think they put that there because, well, I mean, they're proud. But what I love is that it's next to the record board, where I still hold a lot of bests from eight-and-up. My mom has attended some Palisades meets in recent years, and she tells me a lot of the little kids look at the record board and talk about breaking my records. I'm happy to say several of them have already succeeded.

I love stories like that. It makes me feel like I'm motivating the future generation, making young people excited about swimming. I remember doing the same thing as a kid, looking at the boards and chasing records. The Montgomery County Swim League produced quite a few Olympians. Whether it was seeing their names on the boards at local pools or hearing about their accomplishments, I was inspired by those swimmers. And now I get to inspire others.

On July 5, 2014, when I was seventeen years old, I went back to Palisades to swim one last meet. Until I was fourteen, I'd swum every summer at Palisades. Then, the next year, I made my first Olympics. Two years after London, I had some time at home in Maryland in the summer before the National Championships and Pan Pacific Championships, and it coincided with a chance to swim with my old league team, which I hadn't done since 2011.

Two weeks prior, I'd broken two world records at a meet in Texas. I didn't really belong at the summer-league level anymore, but all my friends were still there. Those were my people, and they all wanted me to come. For my part, I longed to return to the community that had profoundly influenced my life. I missed the feeling of being there. I'd always felt the support of Palisades when I was at the Olympics and other high-pressure meets. That day I wanted to show up for them.

Surprising no one, I won all my events that day. But being there wasn't about the swimming. My dad was timing, my mom was helping run the races. The families I grew up with were all in attendance, occupying their usual spots. Everything felt so familiar. It was trippy, like traveling back in time.

I did all the old things—the warm-up with the team, the Palisades Rip Ram cheer, the Porpoise team barbecue after the meet. I signed a ton of autographs for both Palisades swimmers and the opposing team. I smiled for selfies at the pool.

I remember there was a new crop of eight-and-unders. I watched them swim and imagined myself. I saw a familiar joy in their swimming and splashing. They were around the same age I was when I started in the sport. My entire history in that pool flashed before me, how far I'd traveled since.

Looking back on it, I think that was the one meet where my times didn't matter to me. Where I didn't focus on my performance. After every other summer-league meet in my history, I'd rush home and compare my results with all the other times around the county, figure out what my ranking was. Which sounds crazy, right? I was such a swim nerd. (Still am.) But I loved it. It was part of my Palisades routine every Saturday.

Since then, I've only gotten bigger, older, and wiser. I've racked up more experiences in more pools than I can recollect. A ton has changed. But what remains is my love of Palisades. It is as intense now as it was during my first race—when I flailed across the pool, head barely above the water, unable to contain my happiness.

Chapter Two

MICHAEL

According to my mom, my older brother, Michael, was thrilled when she told him she was going to have another baby. Apparently he even said he wanted a little sister. (A preference he may or may not have regretted when, five years later, I repeatedly belted the musical lyric "the sun will come out tomorrow" into his face during a flight home from one of our family trips to North Dakota.)

When my mom got pregnant with me, the family moved from a small townhouse rental in D.C. to a house in Bethesda. Michael says his earliest boyhood memories include settling into our new home and then me entering the frame. When I arrived, he allegedly ran laps up and down the maternity ward, so excited to finally meet me.

From then on, we were inseparable. I was the typical little sister and adopted his interests as my own. We agreed that we loved dogs and didn't trust cats. We compiled long summer reading lists, and I tried to keep pace with him on the latest *Harry Potter* book. I staunchly supported him when he held a mock presidential election for his tenth birthday (he ran against Dad and won in a landslide). We also learned piano and sang in the school choir together. The one time we entered a talent show, we performed matching British pop hits (Michael performed "Let It Be," while I performed "Can You Feel the Love Tonight"). *School of Rock, Miracle,* and *Monsters, Inc.* were some of the movies we'd play on repeat. We had different opinions on *Annie* (see above).

I trailed Michael by three years in school. We both went through eighth grade at Little Flower School, run by the Sisters, Servants of the Immaculate Heart of Mary. It was a tight-knit community with twenty-five or thirty students per graduating class. Michael often took on the role of teacher's pet, but he also frequently annoyed teachers with mid-class fact-checking. He decided in fourth grade that he would get straight A's and earned only two or three non-A grades through high school. We never had classes together, but Michael and I hung out during recess. Sometimes he played touch football with the boys in his class, but he hated the idea of getting injured. When touch football turned into tackle football, he could rely on me to shoot hoops with him instead. Sometimes I'd convince another classmate or two to join. I'm not sure we ever successfully completed a game of H-O-R-S-E, but I just enjoyed that small window in the day when we could catch up and joke around.

Neither of us was the coolest kid in our class, but I noticed that Michael had little interest in being the coolest kid. He didn't worry about what his friends thought of him hanging out with his little sister or skipping team sports. In seventh and eighth grade, he certainly didn't worry about showing up to homeroom smelling like chlorine. While he probably should have showered more, he made me feel like it was okay to be a bit different, or nerdy, or quirky. I found that perspective empowering in my own awkward girlhood years. I followed Michael's example and didn't spend much energy on what people thought of my wet hair and off-trend fashion choices as I juggled practices and school. I saw the joy that Michael took in setting big goals for himself and reaching them. And I saw that Michael had no problem making friends just by being himself and treating people with kindness.

I think Michael's friends like how he blends goofiness and intensity. In his graduate school years, he poured hours into writing comedy bits he'd perform at his classmates' request. As kids, we found plenty of goofy things to be intense about. We squared off in Scrabble, Monopoly, and chess. We'd compete over who could eat the most pancakes or who could spy the Palisades pool sign first as we were driving on MacArthur Boulevard. I did my best to keep up with him academically and embraced his competitive spirit in the classroom. When my elementary school math teacher started timing my class on multiplication drills, I made sure to assign myself extra homework.

Michael and I didn't take our sibling rivalry much further than that. We rarely fought, and there was no roughhousing or hairpulling or anything I saw other siblings do. Okay, I did bite him on the hand once when I was five years old. We were on our grandma's porch, blowing soap bubbles, and I wanted the bubble wand. He wouldn't give it over. To his credit, he didn't cry or scream or retaliate. He had a strong protective instinct and took his older-brother mentoring responsibility seriously from the very start. Especially when it came to swimming.

When we joined the Palisades Porpoises at the ages of nine and six, Michael had already taken many swim lessons. Unlike me, he could swim a full length of the pool without stopping. That said, neither of us had ever competed on a team. Michael decided to pour his energy into making the "A" team, the group that competed on Saturday mornings. In the preseason time trial, he placed seventh in the 50-meter free with a time of just over a minute, one place outside of making the "A" team. You can see on home video he didn't know how to do a flip turn yet. After he placed last in his heat, he tapped the water in a spasm of disappointment. But as luck would have it, Mom received a call from the coach four days later. The fifth-place finisher was unavailable for the first Saturday meet. Michael had made the "A" team, and he never relinquished his spot from there.

He dropped twenty seconds in the 50 free that summer and earned the team's "most improved" award. I was there on the pool deck every Saturday morning, cheering him on. At the season's end, our coaches selected Michael to swim on a relay in a county-wide all-star meet. It was the biggest meet and biggest pool we had ever seen at the time. We all thought it was the coolest thing. In our family home video, Michael is in his all-star T-shirt. I'm there hopping around in the background in my little-sister all-star T-shirt, and Michael elatedly shouts to the camera, "It's almost like the Olympics!"

This memorialization has become part of our family lore. Who knew that animated girl goofing off on the pool deck would be going to the real Olympics only nine years later? And that her whole family would be there to support her, just like we were all there to support Michael on that all-star day?

By the end of that first summer, Michael was hooked on competitive swimming. He insisted on joining a year-round swim program, and our parents found a successful team at the American University pool. I, of course, went with him. That next summer, we both made the "A" team, and we started winning races. Our second swimming summer conveniently coincided with another Michael winning his first gold medals at the Athens Olympics. My brother liked that they shared a name and a home state. I liked that someone from our area was making waves. During the August break before the indoor season, my brother decided he would swim 2400 meters daily. Sounded good to me. I was methodical, planning step-by-step to reach my goals. Whatever Michael wanted to do, I wanted to do.

From there, swimming became a bigger and bigger part of our routine. We went to the same swim meets. We did our homework and ate dinner together after swim practice, often with a pencil in one hand and a fork in the other. The wake-up times for practice crept earlier and earlier. There were many mornings when Michael had a swim practice that started a half hour before mine, like around 4:45 a.m. I would go early and watch him swim. This routine began out of convenience for our chauffeurs (read: our parents), but I quickly began to enjoy it. I genuinely liked seeing Michael swim, and we developed a habit of soft-coaching each other. We were able to spot minute tics and habits other folks might miss, like our hand positioning under the water in freestyle or how to execute a faster flip turn.

My early summer-league swimming memories with Michael are some of the best that I have. The summer weeks had a special rhythm to them: Outdoor morning practices. Donuts and games after. Wednesday-evening "B" meets. The occasional cozy thunderstorm delay. Friday pasta pep rallies. Saturday-morning "A" meets. New pools to visit across the county. Extended post-meet barbecues. Everybody knew each other and supported each other, boys and girls, ages five to eighteen, all on a single team. It didn't matter if you were the worst swimmer on the team, people would still scream your name.

There was a silliness to it, but the community made Michael and me feel special. As Michael and I started to compete for spots on the league leaderboard, the fun would continue well into Saturday night. We would post up around the family computer, waiting for results to trickle in from around the league. We'd pass the time dancing to music, telling stories from the meet, and quoting our favorite Will Ferrell or Chris Farley sketches from *Saturday Night Live*.

Our parents were alongside us, willing to join in the antics. For as long as I can recall, the Ledecky family ethos has been oriented around doing your best. Mom and Dad never told us, "You've got to get straight A's" or "You have to qualify for this swim meet." But once they knew that those were our goals, they were committed to helping us achieve them. They put us in the best position to succeed, and then let us take ownership of our ambitions. They matched our energy and enthusiasm and made sure we had fun along the way.

Michael had his own dreams of swimming in college and competing at a higher level. He finished near the top of the local age-group rankings in butterfly as a twelve-year-old. He was one of a few freshmen selected for his high school's championship team, and he helped his school win multiple team titles. But by then he had hit somewhat of a ceiling with his swimming. I observed how he spread himself thin during high school: chasing perfect grades, becoming editor in chief of the school newspaper, and pursuing other writing and journalism projects. He put a good deal of pressure on himself and probably didn't get enough sleep. Looking back now, he knows he was often burnt out going into practice. He wasn't rested or ready.

Despite his challenges in the pool, Michael never contemplated quitting. He was stubborn, and he loved the pool and his teams too much. He took pride in pushing his limits in practice, even as his technique broke down. We agree that it's hard to match the feeling of a challenging workout or a breakthrough personal-best swim. When things clicked, he felt great. As if he were flying through the water. For those moments, he found it all worthwhile. And he'll still tell you that his happiest place is between the lane ropes of an outdoor lap pool.

Michael has always taken pride in my swimming, motivating and encouraging me. He celebrated my earliest wins. He never compared our trophies or medals. But when I began beating his times in the pool, I know it had to be a blow. He wrote an essay for his junior-year English class about how difficult it was to perform worse than me in a meet. "Each event burdened me with new layers of exasperation that gradually crushed me. By the final day of the meet, only a brittle shell of a swimmer remained in my spot on the pool deck. How Katie managed to surpass me in my primary sport baffled me . . . Why can't I beat my younger sister?"

He went on to describe a 200-meter free we swam against each other: "As we prepared to push off the pool wall, I held a deep desire to prove that I was better, faster, and stronger." When I beat him, he ripped his goggles off, breaking them in half. Something that embarrassed him almost as soon as he'd done it. As he explains now, he was freaking out because the race showed his lack of personal progress. He thought that he needed to be faster than me to do well for his high school team and earn a spot on an Ivy League team. He felt a good deal better (and, at that point, proud) when he noticed several months later that my times were faster than everybody else's at his all-boys high school. He eventually transitioned from longer distances to sprint freestyle, a discipline in which he could (temporarily) keep up with me.

While Michael struggled to top his class in swimming, he found another area in which he could lead: journalism. He created a website for his school newspaper, and he created a short-lived network of D.C.-area high school newspapers. In fact, he ended up in the press section as a credentialed reporter for the 2012 Olympic Trials. He frequently tells stories of watching me compete, there with the other journalists, who had so many questions about this young teen named Kathleen. When I missed qualifying by just one place in my first swim, various seasoned journalists congratulated him. "Third at Olympic Trials! What a great swim for a fifteen-year-old." But Michael had a pit in his stomach. He knew how hard I worked, and four years felt like a long time to him. Michael recalls riding in the car with me between the hotel and the pool after the 400 free. He says my eyes were wide, as if I were shell-shocked.

When I was able to pivot during my next races, to pick myself up from that disappointment and crush it enough to win a spot on Team USA, Michael confessed he never would have been able to recover that quickly, and told me he'd never been so proud of me. When I won the 800 free five days later, Michael flashed his press pass, walked onto the pool deck, and gave me my first family hug as an Olympic qualifier. It was a huge moment for both of us.

My brother left home when I was entering my sophomore year of high school. I'd just won a gold medal in the London Olympics. He'd graduated and made his way to Harvard, just like he'd dreamed. The house felt empty without him around. I felt empty too. The person who'd been my closest friend my whole life wasn't there anymore. At the exact period when I was weathering these huge social, psychological, and biological transitions, growing rapidly into young adulthood in what seemed like a million ways, my confidant and sounding board and touchstone was gone. It dawned on me that I really, really missed him.

That I missed who I was with him. Swimming is largely an individual sport, but I realized I was missing my best teammate.

In college, Michael found a better balance between swimming and his other interests. He tried out with the Harvard varsity team for a month before joining the school's club team. He threw himself into sportswriting and radio. In the summers, he coached at Palisades and interned for various sports teams and companies. He always made sure to organize his internships around my international championship meets, where he returned to his role as public relations agent. He bought a fancy camera for those trips and kept my Facebook fan page up to date with his photos from the stands.

I notice that Michael is careful not to place unnecessary burdens on me. He defers to my schedule, my commitments, and even my state of mind. I can talk to him about swimming, but he also understands when I want to talk about anything *besides* swimming. He doesn't want to disrupt my training or derail my path. I appreciate the care. But again, I sometimes miss the carefree days—running around the playground, shooting baskets, and being geeks together.

When I was nineteen, Michael took me to the park to learn how to ride a bike. It was a week after the Rio Olympics and a week before I was due to head out to Stanford. I should say I knew the basics of how to ride a bike, but it wasn't routine for me. Whenever I tried, there was something *lacking* in my technique. I knew biking would be my main mode of transportation around the Stanford campus, and I hadn't biked much since my training-wheel days.

Michael had volunteered his expertise, not knowing the time and energy he'd need to spend getting me road-ready. There I was, riding around on the park's basketball court, hanging on to my bicycle for dear life, with my big brother trying to keep me from falling off. I was great with speed. My main problem was stopping. (Which a psychologist could probably have a field day dissecting.) Michael was teaching me the proper way to dismount, but I struggled to go from two wheels back to two legs. It was a balance issue. Or maybe it was an I-was-on-land issue.

After hours of his help, I learned to ride a bike as well as your typical nine-year-old. We ran drills like we used to in the pool, and I could feel my confidence rising as my skills improved. My brother looked out for me, just as he always had from the start. He reminded me to trust myself. He helped me find my balance. Then he sent me on my way.

Chapter Three

YURI

Around March 2008 I broke my first two Potomac Valley Swimming records for nine-to-ten-year-olds. I remember watching the 2008 Beijing Olympics that summer, the big one with Michael Phelps's eight golds. I was at my Grandma Berta's apartment in New York City and had to excuse myself from the dinner table to catch the famous men's 4x100 free relay on the television. My brother and I screamed in excitement from the other room, while Grandma Berta wondered what all the fuss was about.

By the time I turned eleven, I'd entered Coach Yuri Suguiyama's elite swimming group at the Curl Burke Swim Club (now Nation's Capital Swim Club), following my brother's lead. Yuri was in his twenties and had been a standout swimmer both locally, as a youth in D.C., and then later, in college at North Carolina. As a senior, Yuri was a first-team all-American. By the time he graduated in 2004, he was the school record holder in two distance events. He'd long harbored a dream of coaching, and back at home, he found himself working at Curl Burke, an organization that in 2016 was ranked the top club in the nation by USA Swimming, having produced several Olympians, including Mike Barrowman, Tom Dolan and, well, me.

When I joined Yuri's group, I was on the younger end of the spectrum, which only drove me to try to keep up with the older swimmers (including my brother). Yuri managed the wide-ranging squad

27

dynamics well, finding ways to motivate each swimmer in a unique way. He encouraged team bonding and scheduled activities away from the pool. Once, we did a scavenger hunt through downtown D.C., running through the various museums and monuments in our nation's capital. He was consistently energetic even when we weren't, instilling in each of us an important lesson: we had to put in the extra effort if we wanted to improve, moods included.

When I was around twelve, Yuri started having me come in for extra workouts with a few teammates my age. He wanted us to start doing additional dryland training. We would jump rope and concentrate on shoulder exercises. His focus was preventing injury down the road. He saw our potential and wanted to make sure that, as we were moving into this new training with greater intensity, we were taking care of our bodies and gaining strength on land that would transfer over to the pool.

I give Yuri a lot of credit for recognizing how vital it was for me, even as a young girl, to train to avoid overuse injuries. So many swimming prodigies go too hard, too soon. They don't balance their routines, and they wind up with damage that shortens their careers or causes them unnecessary pain. I was beyond lucky that Yuri invested in my overall health as a swimmer, not just for the short term but for the long term. Before we even knew what "long term" would mean.

Shortly after we started our twice-a-week dryland workouts, when I was around thirteen, Yuri added a swim session each week where he could focus more attention on my stroke. I had this habit in my freestyle then where I would swing my arm. Basically, one of my arms would flap to the side and straighten, which created a lot of torque on my shoulder. When Yuri spotted this tic, he was concerned that, over time, the swinging would eventually erode my shoulder. When multiplied across thousands of strokes, this bad form could damage the muscles and tendons in my shoulder and lead to a rotator cuff injury—a worst-case scenario for a swimmer. Every session, he kept harping on me to bend my elbow, bend my elbow. After maybe a year of riding me to quit swinging my arm, there was one practice where he said sternly—and Yuri was never this stern to me, which is why I vividly remember the moment—"Katie, don't come crying to me in ten years if your shoulder is wrecked."

I don't know if it was his admonishing tone or the seriousness underneath the message, but that was the moment when I stopped swinging my arm forever. It finally clicked. Not only did I never swing my arm again, but his words also made such an impact that they've rung in my head ever since. Like, *Oh, man, I really hope I don't ever have any shoulder problems. I don't want to have to tell Yuri!*

At some point during that new regimen, I started doing an extra swim on Sundays where it would just be me. I was now logging around 40 miles a week in the pool. Multiply by the number of practices a week and you get to 2,700 laps a week, 135,000 a year, or around 1,920 miles annually. And I was still a teenager.

I remember Yuri had us doing a set of 125's—five lengths of the short-course-yards pool, and the main set would be eight 125's one week and then ten the next week, then twelve the next week, fourteen the next week. We would either add repeats or he would change the interval, so I was getting varying amounts of rest each week. The goal was to hold my time and my stroke count no matter how far or long I was swimming. Yuri also had me count my strokes each lap. It was nice to focus on something as straightforward as counting, and it was helpful in reorienting my focus. I needed to prioritize my stroke efficiency in the long term, rather than just hitting goal times in the short term.

The overall objective was to improve the time and reduce the stroke count. That individual training set, as punishing as it was, ushered in a lot of progress. My stroke count dropped. My time dropped. But most critically, that was the practice set where we stumbled upon my new form. The trademark "loping stroke."

It happened one afternoon in 2011. I was fourteen, and Yuri was challenging me with a tough set. I wanted to finish strong, so I kicked super-hard at the end. When I did, my body galloped a little in the water. When Yuri saw that, he nearly jumped up and down.

"What you just did, try to swim the whole lap like that!" I did, with only a few reversions to my previous stroke. Yuri and I were both pleasantly surprised when the new stroke clicked into place. Yuri beamed. "That's it! That's the stroke you need to swim with all the time!"

It was a true eureka moment. It was as if Yuri had been waiting for that stroke to come out of me. And then he finally saw it. A serendipitous adjustment that ended up refining my whole approach to swimming and ushering in a new realm of potential achievement. It was also very different from what other female distance swimmers were doing at the time. The stroke was immediately viewed by the swim community, erroneously, as a "men's technique." Which is silly. Technique has no gender. Technique is technique, and this modification was the best thing that could have happened to my swimming style.

After that recalibrating session, Yuri emailed me a video of Michael Phelps swimming, which showed a similar galloping form. Yuri often sent out videos of World Championship or Olympic races to our whole swim group, usually with some notes about certain swimmers' styles or race strategies. Swim geek that I am, I loved watching those videos of races online. I had this one video downloaded on my iPod Video that compiled Michael Phelps's eight races from the Beijing Olympics, including his 200 free gold, which was the world record. I would watch it on repeat in bed as I fell asleep.

Unlike Michael Phelps's physique, which is widely considered genetically predisposed for swimming, my body is not tailor-made for the water. As far as physical proportional advantages go, I have zero. To compensate, Yuri and I worked together to continue refining my stroke. We wanted to create a quick connection to the water. Using a high elbow catch, we made sure my arms were never up in the air for long. As for the "gallop," all that meant was I would glide on one side a blink of an eye longer, which propelled me forward like a sailboat keeling.

With a galloping or loping stroke, there's a fine line between galloping that moves you forward with increasing speed and galloping that bobbles your body up and down so much you go slower (and look a bit goofy). My Stanford coach, Greg Meehan, used to explain my stroke to the media as one where I grab and hold a lot of water for the entire length of my pull. Do that enough times, and you travel through the pool much faster.

The day Yuri spotted my gallop, I logged one of my best sets. A new page had been turned, and we both felt the promise of the future.

Soon I was racing much older swimmers. At a 2010 sectional meet in Buffalo, New York, I swam against high schoolers four years older and managed to win five events—the 200, 400, 800, and 1500 freestyle, and the 400 individual medley. That was a wake-up call to a lot of swim folks. Maybe even to me. At my first ever Junior National meet the next spring, I won the distance event on the last day, racing against high school seniors who had been recruited by exceptional swim colleges like the University of Texas and Florida. I remember my teammates chanting, "She's in eighth grade! She's in eighth grade!" The combination of the new stroke and my work ethic was proving to be a winning formula. I began to suspect that I was more ahead of the curve than I realized. At least in the pool.

On land, I still had a long road to travel. The year I turned fourteen, Yuri told me now that I was growing up, he expected more open communication from me. For context, I've always kept a tight lid on my emotions. It's not that I try to be elusive or unduly private. I don't even have secrets. If you ask me something, I'll answer as honestly as I can. That said, I am perhaps naturally guarded. Not in a defensive way. More in an I-prefer-to-be-private way.

My personal preferences didn't matter to Yuri. He wanted access to bits of my interior life to do his job more effectively. He needed me to step up and out of my comfort zone so he could reach me, and thus coach me, better.

In the fall of 2011, we sat down for my goal meeting at a casual restaurant in downtown Bethesda. I'd won some Junior National races but hadn't really swum in a Senior National–level competition yet. We talked about what meets I was going to attend, what technical things I wanted to work on, certain race strategies or times that I wanted to hit in various events, things like that. Then we got to talking about Olympic Trials, which were eight months away, that next summer, in Omaha, Nebraska.

"Now, Katie, what would be the ultimate goal at Olympic Trials?" he asked.

I was quiet.

He asked again. "What would be the ultimate goal at Olympic Trials?"

I was kind of like, "Um, I don't know?"

Yuri tried a third time, emphasizing the word "Olympic," and on that third ask, I whispered under my breath, almost like a question, "To make the Olympic team?"

"Say it again!" Yuri urged.

I repeated it more strongly. "To make the Olympic team!"

And then he said, "Okay, Katie, we don't have to tell anyone else this goal. We don't even need to talk about it the rest of the year." But he had made it clear that he believed I had a real possibility to earn a place on Team USA. Yuri planted the seed. He just needed me to water it. This was harder in some ways than you might expect.

While I had always been driven and gung ho about swimming, there was absolutely no thought or strategy that I would become an Olympic swimmer. I hear a lot of my peers say, "Oh yeah, of course. Being an Olympian is the first thing I thought about when I was seven years old." Well, not me. And not my mom and dad. The Olympics was not something that our family had on our radar or that my folks even necessarily desired for me.

There was one story I remember when an announcer at one of my meets said, "I'm sure we're going to see Katie at the Olympics someday."

I was twelve. And my father went up to him and said, "Come on, don't put that kind of thing out there, don't put that into her head." He felt it was reckless to mention this when the odds were so slim. Why put that kind of pressure on a kid who hadn't even qualified for Junior Nationals yet? The American system for selecting Team USA athletes is ruthless, and different from almost everywhere else in the world. In swimming, the only way to make the team is to go through Trials a few weeks before the Summer Games. Either you make top two in each race or you're out. Your involvement is not based on a series of wins or an evaluation of your overall success. You're judged on a discrete moment in time. It's a lot of pressure for a kid.

My ambivalence about the Olympics wavered when I entered my mid-teens and started beating college-level swimmers. By the time I had that meeting at the restaurant with Yuri, there had begun to be some inevitability to the fact that I was going to be swimming at the higher and higher levels that eventually lead to the Olympic Trials. But there was a problem.

A few months after our conversation, Yuri reiterated that he didn't feel like I was communicating with him enough. I'd had a couple of bad practices. I seemed tired. After practice one day, he handed me a composition book. The standard notebook you would use in school.

"Katie, I want you to keep a journal," he said. "Write down the main set from practice. And write down something special you did that day." That was kind of his tag phrase, "something special." He wanted his swimmers to do something special every day. I was to write how I did in practice, the total yardage. And he wanted me to rate on a scale of 1 to 10 my wellness, my nutrition, and my sleep. Then he added that I should feel free to jot down anything else I wanted to write. Which I took to mean the personal-excavation stuff.

Oh boy.

My first journal entry was January 9, 2012. Right above the date, it said 168 with a circle around it. That was the number of days until

Olympic Trials, a countdown I scribbled atop every entry. I wrote my total yardage, 8,000. Wellness 10, nutrition 10, Granny Smith apple and English muffin with peanut butter before practice. I wrote sleep 10, about eight hours. And then, because I was a teenager eager to make my coach feel like I was doing my job, I added a passage that I probably googled, under "inspirational quote" (Yuri really liked quotes): "Excellence is the result of caring more than others think is wise, risking more than others think is practical, and expecting more than others think is possible."

Full cheese plate.

But as I continued writing, I realized the journaling practice was worthwhile. It pulled stuff from inside me that I wouldn't have confronted otherwise. Journaling kept me centered and my coach in the loop at a time in my life when I couldn't do that verbally. I mean, I couldn't even verbalize that I wanted to make the Olympic team.

The journals quickly became our way of communicating about the Olympics without having to talk about it out loud, something Yuri sensed was difficult for me. I didn't want to make my feelings about the upcoming Trials that big of a deal. I was hesitant to dwell on them. And Yuri, in turn, wanted to relieve any pressure on me. He didn't want me to feel like it was all or nothing, that if I didn't make it, it was going to be the end of the world.

Every week, I would give Yuri the notebook, and he would look it over and jot back one page of notes to me, or sometimes just make comments on individual pages, like, "This was a great practice." And as we got closer to Olympic Trials, his notes got a little bit longer. Pumping me up. Reassuring me I was performing well.

One of Yuri's strengths is the subtlety of his influence. He instilled in me a belief that I could compete with the very best. Well before we had that meeting in the fall where I reluctantly admitted I wanted to make the team, we did small things in training that not just physically prepared me for Trials but, without my realizing it at the time, mentally prepared me.

For example, we practiced doing the same set on back-to-back days. The idea behind it was that at Olympic Trials and the Olympics, for the 800 freestyle you swim both the prelims and finals of the event. Swimming that event two days in a row was something I'd never done before at a competition, because in most national meets, you only swim the 800 free once. Yuri wanted me to feel physically prepared to handle swimming the same distance two consecutive days—with the same intensity, or even better the second time. He was baking it into my mind that if I could get there, make the final of the 800 free at Olympic Trials, my body would know what to do.

Nothing Yuri did was by accident. Leading up to trials in 2011, I'd qualified for Senior Nationals, but Yuri wanted me to go to Junior Nationals instead because I'd never been. Even though I could have gone to Senior Nationals and probably qualified for the USA Swimming National Team there, Yuri didn't think it was wise for me to skip that step. He believed it was vital for me to learn what it was like to compete at that level, to learn how to win or lose, how to manage one race into the next—all the knowledge you can only glean from firsthand experience.

His insistence on process was in service of a larger goal. What he wanted to avoid was an inexperienced me being thrown in with a pack of apex athletes and coming away feeling confused, or less than, or out of my depth. Yuri intuited that I needed to work my way through, so when I did arrive, I would know in my bones that I had earned my spot among the best. That I would recognize my success wasn't a fluke.

Part of this instinct derived from his own swimming trajectory. In a moment of touching vulnerability, Yuri confessed to me that regardless of what he'd achieved, he felt like he never belonged at the elite competitions. He saw the faster and more accomplished swimmers and didn't always realize that he'd had to go through the same things they did to secure his spot. Because of his own experience, he wanted me to always feel like I was meant to be there. That I deserved my place at the table.

In February 2012, at the start of the London Olympic Year, we went to my first national-level meet, the Missouri Grand Prix. There, Yuri kept reminding me, "You earned your way here, you belong here, you should feel like you belong here, you qualified for these big meets."

In Missouri, I cut nearly six seconds off my lifetime best in the 800 free, swimming 8:30.14 to win the race, and become the fourth best in the world at that point. An amazing feat, and yet it wasn't until the Charlotte UltraSwim Grand Prix in May when Yuri and I got confirmation that our stealth goal of my making Team USA was viable in the real world, outside the pages of my journal and our shared imagination.

Early in the Grand Prix, I broke two minutes in the 200 free. In the 400 free, I got second place in a time of 4:05.79, prompting longtime NBC Sports swimming analyst Rowdy Gaines to tweet, "The swimming world might want to keep an eye on Kathleen Ledecky."

Then came the 800 free. I swam a lifetime best by almost four seconds: 8:25.85. The fastest time by a fifteen-year-old in at least fifteen years. After the race, I was interviewed by veteran swim commentator Ted Robinson. "This weekend here in Charlotte is almost like your arrival," he said.

"I don't know about that," I responded. "I'm just trying to do as best as I can."

The whole meet seemed otherworldly. Yuri and I were stunned. When you work toward an objective, then find yourself on the cusp of realizing it, sometimes your brain can't process the reality. Yuri had sensed my potential, but really, he was coaching a regional all-ages group swim program. He was as surprised and delighted by my success as I was.

Yuri was never too proud to learn from other coaches, relying on them for advice, studying their methodologies. He wasn't like some coaches can be, pushing their young athletes to chase results, to compete with the top people right from the get-go. But Yuri was methodical in terms of planning my progression. His approach was intentional. He didn't want me to do too much yardage too early in my career. He wanted me to train all four strokes. He didn't want me to start weight training too young. He always wanted there to be room to improve. Basically, he didn't want me to peak too early. He saw the future. And suddenly, the future was upon us.

A lot of national teamers and coaches came up after that Grand Prix meet to offer their congratulations, telling Yuri that I had a real shot next month at the Trials.

I want to note here that even when all signs pointed to my making it to the Olympics in 2012, my parents stayed skeptical. My mom called the Trials "Katie's Olympics," meaning she doubted there would be an actual Olympics afterward. My folks weren't naive. They knew only two people make it to the Games from each event. My chances in their eyes were slim. I'd go and do my best and not make the team, and that would all be perfectly okay because I was, after all, still a kid.

Because of this operating philosophy, my mom invited a bunch of relatives to come to the Trials. More than sixty people from my family came to watch. Not one of them even tried to reserve Olympic tickets. My brother had just graduated from high school and was headed to Harvard. He wanted to write for *The Harvard Crimson,* so he asked if they wanted him to cover the Harvard swimmers at Olympic Trials. They said great, that'd be super. He got a media credential. Amy Shipley from *The Washington Post* was in the press pool, and she asked my brother for my dad's phone number. Put on the spot, Michael gave it to her.

The Trials did not begin auspiciously for me. I missed making the team in the 400 freestyle, and finished third. After I finished, Shipley called my father, asking for a comment about what she expected would be his devastated reaction to his daughter finishing third. My dad said he wasn't disappointed at all. I had broken Janet Evans's age-group record, and he was proud of that. He reminded her I had other races I was looking forward to. These were not the answers Shipley wanted, so she hung up while he was still answering the question.

Shipley wasn't out of bounds. I missed the 400 free Olympic spot by eighty-two hundredths of a second. As Yuri would later remark to reporters, "What can you say to that?" For most swimmers, coming in third and missing out on your dream is devastating. But I was not most swimmers. And my parents were not most parents. Their investment was in my well-being. For them, it was almost like, Olympics, Schlympics.

Even with the "losses," I pressed on. Yuri kept me positive. The 200 free, I finished ninth. And then came my third event, the 800 freestyle. That one, I won.

I owned the race start to finish, coming in at 8:19.78. I went out hard and barreled forward for the duration of the race, never letting up and earning myself the title of the youngest swimmer to qualify for the 2012 U.S. Olympic swim team.

After touching the wall, I looked at the giant scoreboard and pumped my fist in the air after I registered my time. Michael, on his feet in the press gaggle, was equally shocked. In the stands, my parents and relatives couldn't contain their elation. There was hugging and crying and hollering and disbelieving grins all around. Yuri was beside himself.

To be honest, I'd gone out faster than I intended, against coach's orders. But all's well that ends well. I was a newcomer to the international swimming scene, but thanks to Yuri, unbelievable as it all seemed in the heat of the moment, I still felt like I deserved my spot on Team USA.

When I think back to this time period in my swimming career, from ages eleven to fifteen, neither Yuri nor I knew that I was going to be an Olympic champion so soon. His ultimate goal was to create an environment for each of his athletes to improve. He could see that I had all the tools in my toolbox in terms of work ethic and family support. He could tell that I loved the sport. I arrived early to practice. I was engaged. So we talked about the ins and outs of race strategy. We talked about how some of my national competitors swam their 800 frees. We would look at splits and analyze them. We discussed Janet Evans's American record, and even though I was ten, fifteen seconds off that at the time, he'd still have me study her. When I was fourteen, he emailed me videos of Rebecca Adlington and Lotte Friis racing each other.

I never assumed he was preparing me to compete against them.

I knew he was sending the videos for inspiration. Yuri would say to me, "Watch how Adlington makes her move." Or "See how Friis bursts off the wall." At the time, I understood it as trying to learn from the very best. These are the most incredible swimmers in my event in the world, why not try to learn from them how to execute my race better? Watching their races, I thought, *How can I be creative or energized in my own technique?*

But I think again, in Yuri's sort of sly way, he was psychologically preparing me for the fact that I could swim a race of this caliber and compete against these people should the moment ever come. That's part of what made it so easy to race them when the time did arrive. I'd studied inside and out how they swam. I knew about their strengths and weaknesses, and that gave me confidence going into the 800 in London, having that knowledge in my back pocket.

The fall after the Olympics, Yuri took an assistant coaching job at Cal Berkeley. He moved, and I got a new coach, Bruce Gemmell. After Yuri departed, I didn't journal for three years. That had been our thing. It felt odd to think of doing it on my own.

Then, in 2015, I entered another Olympic Year. I found myself thinking about Yuri and how he'd introduced me to the practice of writing and the value of examining my thoughts and feelings leading up to such a demanding event. I was training for Rio at home, having graduated high school. I'd be heading off to Stanford after the Games. There were myriad, significant life changes to wrestle with, multiple pressures to process. So I channeled my inner Yuri, picked up a pen and notebook, and got to writing. I wrote right up to and through the Olympics. I still do it today.

I don't do the wellness, nutrition, or sleep scores anymore. Nor do I give my pages to any coach to review. One, because I'm older and less reserved. Two, because writing has evolved into something I do for myself. I find being able to look back over the pages a real confidence booster. They provide a clear way to take stock of where I've been, to keep both my past achievements and pitfalls top of mind. They remind me of the work that I've put in, what I was feeling in the past, and how I managed to make it through. It's comforting to recognize patterns in my emotions. To jog my memory that none of what I'm going through is unknown territory. If I handled it before, as a young adult, I can surely handle it now, as a full-grown woman.

I didn't realize it when I started, but journaling was the genesis of taking ownership of my practices and my path in swimming. I got better at communicating. I got better, period. I owe Yuri more than I can say for that.

I owe him for other things too. Much of his advice has stood the test of time. Thanks to him, I remain a student of the sport. I learn from all the former greats. I also hear his voice in my head to this day. I remember him telling me, well before I was even thinking about the Olympic team, "You can be not just one of the best distance female swimmers ever. You can be one of the best swimmers ever." Yuri believed I could be a world-class swimmer. When you give a kid hope that they can become something, it is a unique and indispensable kindness. Yuri believed I could compete with the very top in the country and the most seasoned in the world. And because Yuri believed it, I did too.

I remember this one practice when we were refining our finishes, the last five to ten meters of our races, and Yuri wanted us to celebrate at the end, to pretend like we'd just had the best race of our life. We were all being timid with our celebrations, not doing much beyond a few half-hearted "yeahs." Yuri was like, "Guys, come on. You've got to *celebrate*." Then he whooped real loud and jumped in the pool fully clothed.

He didn't plan it. He wanted to get across the point that you need to have a good time. That if you're going to survive in this sport, you need to enjoy yourself. Yuri created an environment for me to train to be a champion but stay a kid.

Yuri has two children of his own now. Two boys, a one-year-old and a three-year old. If we see each other at meets, he shows me their pictures on his phone. We chat about the past, all the swimmers from the group, who is doing what and where.

There's a photo I have that Yuri took of me in 2011, practicing in the Georgetown Prep School pool, my gear scattered on the deck. It was during an extra training session that I'd come in for, and I was by myself in the water. He gave me the photo right before the Olympic Trials. On the back he'd written: "The vision of a champion is someone who is bent over, drenched in sweat, at the point of exhaustion, when no one else is watching. —Anson Dorrance." (Once again, he never met an inspirational quote he didn't love).

Underneath he added: "Let's have fun next week. This is your stage now and I have no doubts whatsoever that you're ready to go and shine! I've always thought of someone's swimming career like a book with each year or step like a different chapter. You've been able to write some pretty exciting chapters thus far, but I've got a really neat feeling that the best ones are yet to come! Seize the moment. Dream, believe, achieve. You're ready! Yuri."

I keep that photo framed on my bookshelf in Bethesda. It reminds me of who I was.

And who Yuri knew I could be.

Chapter Four

LONDON

I was six the first time I met Michael Phelps. It was the summer of 2003, and my older brother (then nine) and I decided to wait outside the Eppley Recreation Center Natatorium at the University of Maryland for a chance to interact with one of the most prolific young swimmers in the country.

Our family had been at the pool all day, watching some of the biggest names in American swimming competing at the U.S. National Championship meet. Even though I was a young girl and a novice swimmer, I'd noticed Phelps and was captivated by his presence in the water. He was only eighteen then, another Maryland native, and a swimmer who was busy redefining what was possible in competitive swimming. Two weeks before, at the 2003 World Championships in Barcelona, Phelps had won four gold medals and two silvers. He'd also set three world records—in the 200-meter butterfly, 200-meter individual medley, and 400-meter individual medley. (Phelps would go on to earn twenty-eight Olympic medals, twenty-three of them gold.)

My brother and I stood in the parking lot outside the back door. Sweating. For hours. Eventually, Phelps emerged, alone, no coaches, no entourage. He noticed the line of fans waiting and ambled over in that trademark chill way of his. When he got to me, he bent down and signed a swim cap I'd been clutching in my hand. I can't remember if I said anything. I'm sure I wouldn't have known what to say. I do know I smiled so hard I felt it in my jaw.

Swimming is a small world, and swimmers tend to stay swimmers for life. The sport is a little like the Hotel California: you can check out any time you like, but you can never leave. Nine years after I met Michael Phelps in the parking lot as a guileless fan, I was stepping onto the blocks at the 2012 London Summer Olympics, competing alongside him as part of Team USA. In that brief span of time, I evolved from admiring observer to one of the gang. To say that experience was surreal is to do a disservice to the word.

Being at any Olympics is a wild experience. Being a teenager at the Olympics feels like you've been transported into a different world. And I wasn't just the youngest American swimmer—I was the baby of the entire 530-athlete USA delegation.

Prior to London, we had training camp in Knoxville, Tennessee, before traveling to Vichy, France, to adjust to the five-hour difference from Eastern to British time. I was in disbelief early on in Knoxville, when I had the opportunity to swim a practice with swimmers like Phelps, Tyler Clary, Connor Jaeger, Allison Schmitt, and Andrew Gemmell. We were doing a set where we were supposed to hit specific times for different distances. I was not only meeting the times I was being asked to meet but surpassing them. I got through the set with flying colors, until the end—when I hit a wall and tanked. Frank Busch, who was the national team director, pulled me aside and said, "Katie, just do the times, you don't have to go any faster."

The truth was that I was keyed up to be swimming with people like Michael and Allison, who were heroes to me. Who wouldn't be? Besides, I believed I had something to prove. Who was I? A wide-eyed kid from Bethesda. I didn't even have a driver's license yet.

A big part of my Olympic journey was coming to terms with my place on Team USA. I was so quiet during the initial days of camp that breaststroker and team captain Brendan Hansen was worried about me. He said he was concerned about whether I was fitting in and feeling comfortable with the rest of the team. He was kind of right. It was a major shift from my local teams. I was away from home, a Catholic schoolgirl among seasoned young adults with no shared experience to speak of outside the pool. I knew literally nothing about what to expect in training camp, to say nothing of the Olympic Games. I remember getting all my racing suits and caps with the flags on them, taking a picture, and thinking, *Why am I getting twenty white caps and twenty black caps for a maximum of two races?*

Brendan asked if I could join him to chat over a breakfast of eggs and toast. He took the time to check in with me, which was kind of him. He let me know I wasn't on my own, even if it sometimes felt that way. Everyone feels out of their depth around the Olympics. It's the big leagues. Nerves and discombobulation are the order of the day.

Thanks to that talk, I calmed down. I began to ease into my surroundings. I learned about the caps. (American swimmers race in white caps in the prelims and semifinals. The black caps are for the finals. You get plenty in case they rip, and they are fun to share with family and friends post-competition.) I clued into the other Olympic rites and rituals. I loosened up. So much so that by the end of camp, as part of another tradition, I didn't hesitate when asked to imitate a teammate as part of the "rookie skits." I got assigned Tyler Clary in my group's skit, and I did such an uncanny impression that the whole room was in stitches. They hadn't known I had it in me.

Ridiculous as it sounds, that off-the-cuff imitation freed me from my protective shell. After that, I was fully in the mix of the team. I recall sitting at the end of a long table with a bunch of the swimmers, right next to Michael Phelps, who was telling—well, let's call them *colorful* stories from his college days in Ann Arbor. He'd forgotten I was there, and when he turned and spotted me at the end of a particularly sensational anecdote, he blanched.

"Katie, I'm so sorry," he said. "I apologize. You shouldn't have to hear all that." I smiled, told him I didn't mind. I may have been inexperienced and somewhat sheltered, but I wasn't a complete shut-in. It would take more than Michael Phelps telling a typical college story to shock me.

As I headed into the final camp days in France, any prior awkwardness had all but evaporated, and I was assured enough to make the most of my adventure. My roommate, Lia Neal (who was sixteen at the time), and I connected as newbies around the same age. We had a lot of innocent fun, like scrounging in Vichy for Nutella at two in the morning. How does one ask for Nutella in France? Lia had taken Spanish and Chinese; I had taken French at Little Flower. But the only French phrase I could recall in the middle of the night was: *En Anglais?* We managed to work it out, procuring Nutella and laughing ourselves silly in the process.

By then I'd realized that Ryan (Lochte), Matt (Grevers), Missy (Franklin), Allison (Schmitt), Rebecca (Soni), and, of course, Michael, whose autograph I had waited for in the parking lot all those years ago, were not distant stars out of reach in the swimming firmament. That I was not just *with* them, I was one of them. I felt I truly belonged.

This sense of belonging culminated in the filming of a viral "Call Me Maybe" video, a montage of vérité footage of Team USA lip-syncing to Carly Rae Jepsen's pop hit. We weren't Justin Bieber and Selena Gomez, but our take was charming in its own right, and people loved getting to see our goofy side. The video was a sensation, netting eighteen million views.

The whole idea came to be when a few of the girls on the team started filming us at practice around 2012, collecting mini clips of us pretending to call someone on the phone, mouthing the lyrics, or dancing underwater. We had one of USA Swimming's videographers capture the underwater bits. No one knew it was going to be a big thing, so we were all unguarded and hamming it up. Every day at training camp, they shot a bit more. Then, during our charter flight from Vichy to London, we filmed the choreographed dance scene. Missy, Natalie Coughlin, and Kathleen Hersey strut and sing down the aisle, and you can see everyone on the plane bobbing in unison. I wasn't a huge part of the final cut, but I am in the background in a few shots, grooving along.

There was so much excitement and anticipation among the team the day before we posted the video on YouTube. We were trying to keep it low-key. We didn't want NBC to scoop it and release it first. We all wanted the video to come straight from us as a team. I remember emailing or texting my family like, "Hey, you can't tell anyone about this, but . . ."

When the video dropped, we were giddy, watching the views and likes tick up and up. We knew it was cute, but we hadn't thought the whole world would champion it the way it did. The video humanized us athletes in an organic way, the opposite of those glossy, super-produced network packages you see every Olympic season. This was a love letter from Team USA directly to the fans, and the fans embraced it wholeheartedly. It also served as a reminder to me of how many people were paying attention to what we—even me, a fifteen-year-old kid—were doing in and out of the pool.

On July 23, 2012, we arrived in London. When I got to the Olympic Village, I was in awe of the athletes I was rubbing shoulders with in person for the first time. Around every corner was a competitor who was the best at their sport, all the international pros and veterans I'd marveled at on TV or at fields and stadiums. *Boom!* Like magic, I was standing next to a gold medalist in line at the omelet bar.

I pinched myself every day. The opening ceremony parade was giant, and I got to walk with the USA delegation. Most swimmers don't get that chance because of the schedule. The ceremony is always on a Friday night, lasting four hours and ending well after midnight. The swim meet commences the next morning, making it all but impossible for swimmers to take part in the ceremony. The coaches advise you not to go because it is miles of walking and could interfere with your performance. In Rio in 2016, for instance, after Michael Phelps led the U.S. team into the stadium, he was immediately whisked away.

In London, I got lucky. The heats of the women's 800 free weren't scheduled until day six. I was able to fully immerse myself in the festivities, dressed head to toe in my Ralph Lauren Team USA–issued uniform of navy blazer, beret, and red, white, and blue scarf. Walking among the other athletes, bumping shoulders with my teammates, I was bowled over by the sheer number of people present. Every athlete had worked so hard to be there, many overcoming obstacles we would never hear about. The pride, elation, and camaraderie are almost impossible to describe, and that marks the beginning of eight days of mind-blowing competition.

The opening showcase was entitled *Isles of Wonder* and orchestrated by the famous British director Danny Boyle. After the spectacle of Beijing's 2008 ceremony, the media was making a big to-do out of the pressure on London to match that extravagant pageantry. From what I witnessed firsthand, the ceremony was a triumph. The highlight was watching Paul McCartney close the show. Seeing Queen Elizabeth escorted by "James Bond" was no small potatoes either. As I emailed my coach at the end of the night: "Highlight of my life!!!! So freakin' cool!!!"

My race being so late in the swim schedule worked to my advantage in other ways as well. For one, I had time to adapt to the atmosphere of being in the Village and at the Olympics. The Village is an exceedingly cool place to be. It's almost like a video game. You're dodging Olympic-level speed walkers doing their training exercises with their hyperflexible knees. You're strolling beside weightlifters and towering basketball players and demure gymnasts. All shapes and sizes of athlete, speaking in every language you've ever heard. Representatives from every country, mingling and chitchatting. Especially in the cafeteria.

Each athlete is trying to get a glimpse of his or her personal idol, while loading up a tray with grub. At the same time, you're cheek by jowl with your competitors. The mix gives rise to a palpable buzz. It doesn't feel tense so much as like you're floating in this exclusive, singular bubble. There's pin trading, like at Disney World. You get on the bus to go to the venue, and you find yourself in conversation with a diver from Italy or a water polo goalkeeper from Germany. Everyone is over the moon to be there because they've all worked incredibly long and hard and consistently to earn a spot in the Village. We're part of a joyful club. When you're there, among so many talented people, you feel like you've already won.

A second benefit of my late start time was I got to be a fan for the first five days of the Games. It gave me a chance to focus less on competition and more on the beauty of swimming at that level. No one is a bigger swimming dork than me. I attended every prelim and finals session. I got comfortable with the flow of the meet, observed how to walk out for races, learned little details about the run of show. More, I had a front-row seat at all the races. For the men's 400 individual medley, I was on the deck when Ryan won. Same for the women's 200 freestyle and Schmitty's gold. Cheering the other swimmers cemented the fact that I was teammates with these gifted athletes and made me even more determined to do my best for the group.

Yuri came along to London too, but unfortunately, he wasn't one of the official USA swimming coaches at the Olympics, and he wasn't able to obtain a credential to come on the pool deck. I had kind of expected that he was going to be right there with me in the moments before the race, but because of regulations, he ended up stuck in the stands like any other fan attending the Games. I didn't even get to connect with him before my prelim, which fell on day six of the games, the third of five heats that morning.

I remember my legs were shaking as I mounted the blocks for my first go, my nerves punching through. Despite that, I managed to win my heat, but I fell to third overall behind Lotte Friis of Denmark, and England's Rebecca Adlington, who had taken gold in Beijing and was lauded as the hometown heroine of the games. Rebecca beat my time by more than two seconds.

To me, the only thing that mattered was that I had made it to the finals. My time of 8:23.84 was near what I'd done at the Trials, which boded well. Officials assign lanes by race times, fastest in the middle, slower on the outside. My time put me in the middle of the pool, in lane three.

I met Yuri outside the spectator entrance as soon as I could after my prelim. It was as if he was being kept behind the velvet ropes of a nightclub or something. I have this picture of the two of us meeting that one of my family members took. We're huddled together whispering in the public area—among fans and competitors alike—about my stroke and my race strategy.

Despite the odd circumstances, Yuri was reassuring and focused. He emphasized how proud he was of me for making the final. I told him something along the lines of "I believe I can do it" and "I have nothing to lose." Which was the truth. And that's when he gave the last-minute advice that changed everything.

Yuri told me to breathe more to my right side and less to my left. In swimming, I'd been doing what's called breathing bilaterally, which means you breathe to a mixture of your left side and your right side. Yuri didn't say breathe *only* to the right. Just less. He wanted me to reduce the number of times I breathed left because he noticed that it was slower for me, and he wanted me to swim as fast as I could. That was his final technical instruction. Oh, and not to take the race out so hard and fast. To be more controlled. (This was not a new suggestion, but I appreciated the reinforcement.)

Last, as a warning, Yuri told me, "It's going to be loud. You're going to be in lane three. Rebecca is going to be in lane four. The place is going to erupt for her. I want you to get behind your block, and when it gets loud, channel all that energy down your lane. All that energy is for you. Don't let it be more than that."

Then he smiled and added, "You're going to be great."

After the prelims, I emailed a news story to my mom that read, "Rebecca Adlington Sets Up Nail-Biting Final in 800m Freestyle." The story pitted Rebecca against Lotte. "It has always been us two," declared Rebecca. As far as the press was concerned, I didn't exist.

In reading the Olympic press, it became clear how big a race this was going to be. The Olympic Committee had scheduled the race toward the end of the night. It was advertised as two huge swimming giants, local sweetheart Rebecca and rising star Lotte, pitted against each other in lanes four and five. The two were viewed as rivals who had been in many prior tight battles and knew exactly how the other swam. I was next to 100 percent certain neither Rebecca nor Lotte knew anything about my racing style.

The upside of the media's hyper-focus on Rebecca and Lotte was that I could exist in the shadows with zero notice from the greater swim world. Being an underdog gave me space to concentrate on my own game. Invisibility would be my superpower.

That night I emailed my mom: "Going to nap, will call around 3:45. Good swim this morning. Nerves forced me out fast, but now I have the first race nerves out of the way. Saw Yuri and we talked and he gave me good advice. I was breathing too much to my off side . . . need to get into rhythm on good side . . . that's my bread and butter. I noticed I was doing that too. Should be easy fix :)."

Seeing Yuri had left me calmer than I'd felt in the prelim race. I knew I was ready, come what may. In a way, all these factors combined—my race time, my age, it being my first Olympic rodeo— enabled me to, if not relax, then feel zero pressure. No eyes were on me. No one was sweating me to deliver anything but my best effort. Not even my folks.

I called my mom the day of my race. She and my dad were concerned between themselves about what they would say to me if I flopped in my first ever international showing.

When I rang her, I said, "When I make the podium, even though your seats are really high, you'll be able to move down for the medal ceremony." My mom said, "Oh, great. That's wonderful." Then she hung up, turned to my dad, and winced.

"She thinks she's going to make the podium," she said. He answered, "Well, if she doesn't, we will remind her that she's just fifteen. And that this was a good experience."

I smile, thinking about that conversation. And all the many other conversations when the topic was how to smooth over or assuage my devastation if I didn't win a medal. No one in my family could conceive of my winning a medal at my first Olympics. My parents always get asked, "When did you know Katie was gonna make the Olympics?" And they shoot back honestly, "When she touched the wall at the Olympic Trials."

To be clear, my parents were thrilled that I made it to the Games. But they were also realists, and they weren't in the business of filling my head with fantasies they had no way of knowing could or would come to pass. They supported me from a place of love and consistency, which was separate from my accomplishments. If there is such a thing as the opposite of stage parents, my folks are it.

As for my own mindset, I consistently saw myself winning gold. At that point I think I'd only lost one 800 freestyle race in my life. I'd won the Olympic Trials. I'd won Junior Nationals. I'd won Sectionals. I had read that Michael Phelps's coach, Bob Bowman, would have him visualize both the best-case and worst-case scenarios of every race. What if he forgot his credential, or sprained his ankle walking in, or his goggles fell off midswim? In 2008, in Beijing, the worst did happen. Michael's goggles filled up with water as he dove in for the 200 butterfly. Unable to see the walls of the pool until he was upon them, he had to count strokes. He ended up not only winning the race but setting a world record. I tried to visualize different scenarios, but I struggled to visualize anything but winning. Given my record of success in the 800, I was convinced the odds were in my favor to win this race. Anything, good or bad, could happen—and wasn't that the beauty of a competition day?

From my room in the Olympic Village, I sent an email to my parents that quietly shared that confidence. I reminded them again that if you win a medal, the family can come down to the swimmers-only section and throw flowers or take photos. My parents told me after the fact that when I wrote them this, they thought I'd lost my mind.

Looking back, I can understand that I was a young girl in my first Olympics, and the possibilities for less than wonderful outcomes were far higher than the odds of everything coming up roses. My parents were proud. And they were present—at meets, at practices, at awards ceremonies. But they kept their composure, even when my swimming career took off and the world of our family was forever altered. To borrow a phrase from the British, their keeping calm enabled me to carry on.

Before any race, I typically eat the same thing: plain pasta with olive oil and Parmesan cheese. In London, prior to my 800 free, it was no different. I wolfed down a plate of noodles at the Olympic Village before busing to the aquatic center early. By then the media coverage was at a fever pitch. Prince William and Princess Kate were going to be in the stands. As were LeBron James and a handful of other NBA players from Team USA Basketball.

I was in the pool warming up when my parents arrived. I waved to them, and one of the ushers noticed and asked who they knew swimming tonight. My mom said that their daughter was in the 800. The usher asked where they were seated, and my mom told her they were up in the nosebleeds, ten rows from the top of the arena. The usher explained that right before the 800, my folks should come down, and she would direct them to better seats.

My parents found their section, and my dad, ever practical, realized it might be impossible to find that same usher later. So they went back down, found her again, and volunteered to wait in the hallway until the 800, when she could retrieve them. The usher agreed to the plan, walked my parents to a side area, and said, "Wait here."

The meet began, and of course, other ushers approached my parents, trying to discern why they were idling alone and not seated. This went on for several races, until right before my swim, when a new usher approached, pointed, and shouted, "You two!"

My parents freaked out. They were positive they'd be ejected from the arena and miss my race. Instead, they were walked to the best seats in the house, ten rows up, dead center, a perfect view.

My race was the third, on the seventh night of swimming. First was the women's 200-meter backstroke, followed by the men's 100-meter butterfly. Then I was up, swimming the women's 800 free. We were told to be at the ready room (a private holding area for swimmers to wait before being called to the pool deck) twenty-five minutes before our race. I was early. I'm always early.

When I walked in, Michael Phelps was there. Hood up and deep in thought, he was preparing to go out and swim the 100 fly, a race the media was reporting would be his last ever individual Olympic event. His mind must have been reeling with the significance of that milestone. The best in the world, headed toward what was meant to be his Olympic swan song.

As he passed by me, he gave me a high five and said, "Good luck, and have fun out there."

For a moment, I was thrown back in time to when I was simply another young fan, clutching my swim cap, waiting in line for this swimming legend to acknowledge me and feeling elated when he did. It was a small connection, but one that was so meaningful to a kid whose dreams were only just starting to coalesce. That fate would find us on the same team less than a decade later, and that he would again choose to take a moment to connect with me, says a lot about the family you build in the sport of swimming—and even more about the kind of person Michael Phelps is.

As he left the ready room and walked toward a career-defining night, it hit me that who I was now—the youngest Olympian, minutes from her inaugural race—was not so different from the girl I had been in

2003, idling outside the Eppley Recreation Center Natatorium. Yes, I had leveled up beyond all expectations. But I was still swimming because I loved swimming. I wanted to win, yet I was still focused on the joy, the exuberance of doing the thing I loved most in the world. I believed I could bring home the gold medal. But even at the Olympics, I hadn't lost sight of what made me appreciate the sport. The community of swimmers. The common bond we all share. I was going to do exactly as Michael advised. I was going to have fun out there.

When I walked onto the London Aquatics Centre pool deck from the ready room, the crowd was riotous with collective anticipation for Rebecca. They were standing up to witness the coronation of their favorite swimmer. As the crowd screamed and shouted her name, I thought about what Yuri had told me—that the arena would be noisy, that the energy would be epic—and I told myself the chants of "Becky! Becky! Becky!" were actually "Ledecky! Ledecky! Ledecky!" I took a deep breath and assured myself that I would do what I had trained to do—take the lead and keep the lead. Attack and not look back.

Yuri, stuck watching me swim from just below the rafters, would later tell me I looked much more relaxed than I had in the prelims. He knew I'd listened to his counsel and stolen all that noise and enthusiasm to put into my own lane.

At significant meets, there's always a camera in front of each of the racers. Many swimmers smile or wave into the lens. I'm not that person. When it's time to go, that's it, and I'm not there to mess around. I keep my game face on come what may, camera or no camera.

Typically, before the call comes to take your mark, I do three claps. That night, it was so noisy, I had some concern I would not hear the starter. I decided to forgo the three claps and bent into position and waited for my cue.

BEEEEEEEEP!

When I dove in, my mind was clear—blank, really. I was on autopilot. My coaches wanted me to swim a controlled first half of the race. I started so eagerly that I took the lead by the 50-meter mark. It was as if the adrenaline made my brain black out.

I settled in my second 50 of the 800, and then my third 50 was faster than my second. Yuri recalled that's when he was able to sit back and enjoy the race, because he knew it was going to be something special. Yes, I was going out fast, but I wasn't spinning my wheels, I wasn't out of control. I was pacing myself, not putting it all into the first 100 meters.

If you watch video of the live broadcasts of the race, the British announcers remained centered on Rebecca, mentioning me only to comment that I was foolishly going out too fast. Same for Dan Hicks and Rowdy Gaines at NBC. The coverage consensus was that as an inexperienced competitor, I was surging ahead, but would soon tire out.

After 150 meters, I broke away. By 200 meters, I'd flipped at under two minutes, faster than the world-record pace. Even in the water, the noise in the aquatic center was deafening. When I would turn my head to breathe, I was hammered by a wave of sound. It was the crowd, still chanting, "Becky! Becky! Becky!"

At the 600 turn, I had an epiphany. I thought, *This is just a 200 free.* I thought, *I've done thousands of 200 freestyles in my life. I won't mess this up.* From that moment on, I felt vibrant, alive in my body, present. I registered every detail. The London Olympic signage. The crowd on their feet, waving pink and green "Becky" banners. The slosh of the water churning around me. I took a breath to the left, against Yuri's orders. I couldn't help myself. I had to see if anyone was sneaking up in lanes four, five, or six. They weren't.

For the last 200, I was on my own. Well ahead of everyone else, in my first ever Olympics. The kid leaving everyone else in her wake. I felt like I was on another planet. For eight minutes, I swam like my life depended on it. Then I touched the wall.

And just like that, I was an Olympic champion. I was the youngest athlete ever to have won the women's 800 free at the Olympics. I'd beaten Rebecca by more than five seconds, breaking the U.S. record set twenty-three years earlier by Janet Evans. One of the broadcasters said, breathless and in disbelief, "We may have just seen the making of the new long-distance queen for the United States."

Rebecca took third, losing to Spain's Mireia Belmonte García. (A fact I did not register, honestly, until the medal ceremony, because I was so overwhelmed by the win.) My mom told me when she watched me race, she was so anxious that her mouth went dry. She didn't know my competitors, the history of their races. While I was ahead, she didn't trust that I could keep the lead. She assumed the other swimmers were holding back. But when I turned at the last 200, she, like me, knew I had it. She began jumping up and down. The usher who had been helping them came over, glanced at me in the pool, and gave my mom a giant hug. She still has a photo of the two of them on her iPad.

I felt for Rebecca. In retrospect, videos of the London race reveal the pressure she was under. When she walks out to the deck, she quick-steps to her lane and yanks off her warm-up clothes. You can tell she's registering the gravity of the moment. The eyes and expectations of a nation were bearing down on her. The commentators relentlessly broadcasted how they'd never seen a crowd so amped as they were for her. The hype would be a lot for anyone to weather.

After I won, Rebecca was unbelievably gracious, far warmer to me than she had to be given the circumstances. The first thing she did was swim over and hug me, saying, "Well done, amazing." She kept telling me how incredible I was, how she thought I could break her record, maybe even as soon as the next year. Even saying she was looking forward to watching me break it. It was clear all the prior pressure had fallen off her shoulders. I'm sure there must have been a level of disappointment, but she was a study in class. Her country should have been as proud of that as any swimming medal.

When I caught up with my parents and my brother, they were all kind of in a daze. Almost like shock. Like I said, none of my relatives expected me to win a medal. Never mind the gold. My mom's uncle Red, who was eighty-six at the time, may have been the only true believer. He'd flown in from Washington State with his daughters. One afternoon he walked down to a little coffee shop near his Airbnb and started chatting with the locals there. He bragged that his grandniece was going to be swimming in the 800. They listened, offered good luck, but assured him I would never beat their Becky. Bullish, Red made the whole place a wager. If I won, he'd buy all of them breakfast. Apparently, he tried to make good on the bet the day after the race, but when Red went back to the restaurant, nobody was there.

While on the deck, I was handed a bouquet of flowers, which I threw to my brother to hold for me. In a strange twist of fate, our across-the-street neighbors in Bethesda, Dr. Kurt Newman and Alison Newman, had watched me swim from the second row. Ironically, they were the family who had originally recommended that my mom enroll us at the Palisades pool. None of us knew they'd be in London. While I was swimming my guts out, they were losing their minds, waving at my parents to join them near their seats. After the medal ceremony, they threw me an American flag. To this day, Kurt jokes that he wants his lucky flag back.

Next, Team USA took me to the International Broadcast Centre for press interviews. After the chaos of my upset, the media had a lot of questions.

"I don't think two years ago I could ever have imagined this," I said to a crowd of reporters circling me on the deck, noting it "was a great honor to be here" at all. I said that I'd known before I went out for the 800 that Michael had won that 100 fly and Missy the 200 backstroke. "Missy and Michael's performances got me pumped up," I told the gathered press. "I just wanted to see how well I could represent the U.S."

When a reporter asked Michael Phelps about me, he said, "Katie went out and just laid it on the line. It looked like she went out and had fun and won a gold medal and just missed the world record. So, I could say that's a pretty good first Olympics for a fifteen-year-old."

Eventually, I was reunited with my family and with Yuri. I don't remember too much besides giving everyone a big hug. I'm sure there were some tears. I showed Yuri the gold medal. He had to leave the next day to coach a swim meet in Buffalo. It was a sectional-level meet with the other kids in my local group, and he'd missed the first two days, being in London to support me. I asked him how my teammates were doing, what their times were.

Yuri had cried, watching me swim. All he wanted was to get closer to the podium so he could snap some pictures of me. He took off running down the stairs, trying to get through the door, his backpack strapped around his shoulders. A security guard clocked him, warning, "You are not going through there!"

For a brief moment, Yuri attributed this to my victory, thinking: *These people are really upset that Katie won.* He tried to explain who he was, that he coached me. Then he realized he was being held because Prince William and Princess Kate were sitting nearby with British security. Yuri jokes now that these guards nearly arrested him because they thought he was some crazed royal fan when all he actually wanted to do was celebrate my victory with me and my parents.

If you go back and watch my event, I breathe primarily to my right side, like Yuri suggested. But I do breathe a few times to my left, wanting to confirm that I'm still ahead. You can see as I take these covert breaths that I'm right on the world-record line. I ended up missing the world record by about half a second. I always think: *Geez, if I had only listened to Yuri and breathed to my right side instead, maybe I would've broken the world record.*

Though I didn't get to spend too much time with Yuri in London, knowing he was there was profoundly meaningful to me. I wouldn't have wanted him to miss that moment, the culmination of our efforts together. To be able to share that journey with him was crucial to me. I think both Yuri and I were able to embrace the experience and come away from it with a sense of belonging. We felt a sense of satisfaction, of a shared "mission accomplished."

The night I won gold, Yuri sent me an email: "Wow. What a night, huh? I can't imagine what you're feeling / thinking right now. Maybe one day soon we can sit down and talk about everything. In the meantime, just keep smiling and being yourself. Enjoy this moment, Katie. You've earned it :)."

The family photos of that time show me wiping away tears on the medal stand, my fingernails painted red, white, and blue. There's one photo I always think about. It's a candid of me getting out of the pool after my prelim swim. My cousin snapped the picture, then posted it with the caption: "The last time Katie walked away from a race where she wasn't an Olympic gold medalist."

In my room later, I found a handwritten note from my teammates Dana Vollmer and Rebecca Soni. Dana had won the 100 fly and Rebecca the 200 breaststroke. "We couldn't be any more proud!" they wrote. "No one deserves that more than you! We love you!" The next day, headlines in the British papers read: "Adlington sees her crown snatched by an unknown, aged 15."

After I returned home to Bethesda, there were dozens of invites to events and appearances, like one to throw out the ceremonial first pitch at a Washington Nationals game. Ize's deli, where I used to stop after swim practice, gave their tomato, cheese, and bacon omelet a new name: Katie's Gold Medal Omelet. Even with all this excitement, I had school summer reading assignments to finish and an essay due on the first day of my sophomore year. It was quite the juxtaposition.

In September, I joined other Team USA members to visit the White House. Both President Obama and the First Lady spoke on the South Lawn. Mrs. Obama had been in London as the lead of the U.S. delegation, and she'd had a great Olympic experience, even getting lifted up by one of the women wrestlers in a moment that went viral. The president joked that he was jealous she'd gotten to see us compete in person, but he had followed the coverage from home.

He continued, "One of the great things about watching our Olympics is we are a portrait of what this country is all about, people from every walk of life, every background, every race, every faith. It sends a message to the world about what makes America special. It speaks to the character of this group, how you guys carried yourselves. And it's even more impressive when you think about the obstacles that many of you have had to overcome not just to succeed at the Games but to get there in the first place."

And then he mentioned me by name, a shock I still haven't recovered from.

"Katie Ledecky may have been swimming in London, but she still had to finish the summer reading assignments for her high school English class."

Everyone laughed. Then he searched the crowd to find me. "Where's Katie? Yes, there she is."

After pointing me out, then–Vice President Joe Biden came over to me and quipped, "I bet you finished that reading, didn't you?"

There are pictures online of Vice President Biden speaking to me. I'm laughing as I stand there nervously in my Team USA jacket and khakis, hands clasped in front of my waist. I remember he and President Obama made a point of staying long enough to shake everyone's hand and meet all the athletes, even though I'm sure they had more critical and urgent obligations vying for their time.

This was all heady stuff for a teenager entering her sophomore year of high school. Thankfully, my classmates and teachers did a great job of making things normal for me at school when I returned. I mean, sure, I did an assembly and answered a lot of questions about the Olympics. Students, teachers, everyone could ask whatever they wanted. What was Michael Phelps like? (Just like you see on TV.) Ryan Lochte? (Same.) I did that for the upper school, the middle school, and the lower school. But after that, rarely did I spend a lot of time talking about London with my peers. The all-consuming feeling of having been a part of the world stage receded. At random times, I would feel somewhat overwhelmed, but I wasn't exactly sure why.

I did my best to push forward and inhabit my school universe, until at one point during the winter of my sophomore year, I was hit with the recognition that although I kept telling people I felt my life was still the same as it had been, maybe it actually wasn't.

Like it or not, I'd become a public figure. A professional athlete with an international audience. Being an Olympian, having that title and profile, was a massive adjustment. As was my brother leaving home and starting college. I was adapting to the fact that I was suddenly an only child in my house, and that my brother, Michael, the person who knew me best—and kept me levelheaded—was elsewhere. At school, it wasn't as if I was treated as a different person post-London. But I kind of felt like one.

When I'd started at Stone Ridge the year before, I'd entered as a new freshman, not an Olympian; just another student trying to make friends. When I returned from London, Bob Walker, my spirited high school swim coach, counseled me that though I was a gold-medal winner now, my other qualities were what made me who I was. Bob, my classmates, teachers, and administrators helped me traverse the bridge between regular fifteen-year-old and Olympic gold medalist.

In swimming, it can be easy to get stuck in your own head. After all, you spend most of your time facedown in the water, staring down at the black line at the bottom of the pool. Back at Stone Ridge, I was fortunate to be able to get back in the swing of things with my high school classmates on the swim team. We were all dedicated swimmers, but we also kept things fun and light. After London, I also took care to balance out my swimming with volunteering and committing to school service projects. I tried to maintain a connection to my community that went beyond the pool. By doing more, I filled my time, stayed occupied, literally spent more hours with my feet on the ground. I held on to who I always was while accepting who I was becoming. And I reminded myself every day that I was, like Coach Bob and Yuri and my parents so frequently said, so much more than a swimmer.

Chapter Five

DAD

There are probably three things to be said about my dad: he loves his family, he loves sports, and he *loves* Bruce Springsteen.

The love of sports started early. My dad and his older brother (my uncle Jon) grew up playing on the streets, sidewalks, playgrounds, and bowling alleys of Bayside, Queens, in New York. They came of age during an exciting time for New York professional sports teams and their fans— when the Knicks, Jets, and Miracle Mets all won World Championships circa 1969–'70. As kids, they would ride the subway with their dad, one stop from Flushing to Shea Stadium, to attend just about every Mets Sunday doubleheader. They would save up paper route money and milk bottle tops that could be traded in to attend baseball games in the upper deck as "Midget Mets." They were also big Yankees fans and got to witness the final few seasons of Mickey Mantle's career.

By the time my dad and Jon moved out of the city, they knew so much about sports that they were both able to get minimum-wage jobs with their town's newspaper and radio station, covering high school athletics in Greenwich, Connecticut. Jon led the way, becoming a radio announcer for the weekly high school football games. At age fourteen, my dad secured his own five-minute nightly sports segment on radio station WGCH. They were also sportswriting "stringers" for the *Greenwich Time* newspaper, and my dad took sports photographs and built his own photography business while still in high school.

The stories my dad and Jon told me about their childhood must have had some influence on me. If they were so obsessed with sports, there had to have been a good reason. Both my dad and my uncle carried their involvement with sports into adulthood. When I was around two years old, Jon became an owner of the Washington Capitals hockey team, along with Ted Leonsis. My family attended a lot of hockey games, and Uncle Jon introduced us to some of the players. Hockey is famously a contact sport, but I observed how some of the nicer professional athletes comported themselves, guys like Adam Oates, Peter Bondra, Ken Klee, and many others. They had a real sense of sportsmanship that was easy to see on the rink and instructive to admire up close.

I remember we'd sometimes run into Adam Oates at Starbucks. One of the best setup guys of all time. A Hall of Famer too. Yet he was invariably chill, crouching down to chat with me even though I was a kid. It was a small gesture but one I recalled years later when I started having encounters with my own fans. There's rarely a reason to be curt or unkind to an admirer. It costs you nothing to make their day.

I also was honored to meet Michael Jordan when he became involved with the Washington Wizards when I was two years old. My dad jokes now that there must have been at least an iota of transference of athletic ability when Michael Jordan played a much documented game of peekaboo with me.

Yes, I was super young. But I believe growing up around pro athletes humanized them for me. Elite sports were not exotic. Elite athletes were just people. Exceptionally talented people. But also people who played peekaboo and bought grande lattes with whipped cream.

At the various games and matches, my uncle Jon made sure I had snacks and a good spot to see all the action. My dad would point out when someone had made a particularly good move, or explain when a rule had been broken. Dad and Jon taught me what mattered in athletics. They were both measured fans. An underappreciated part of sportsmanship is approaching everything with a light touch. Of acknowledging that everything doesn't have to be so serious.

My dad made sure that we laughed a lot growing up. Music also played a big part in the levity. The Ledecky family loves music, and we always had some kind of music playing. Bruce Springsteen consistently received the most airtime. My dad's probably seen him perform live more than fifty times. That's a lot of "Dancing in the Dark." For my dad, like many Springsteen fans, seeing Bruce and the E Street Band live for the first time (for my dad, it was August 22, 1978, at Madison Square Garden, two weeks before Dad headed off to college) was an indelible experience.

Springsteen's song catalog is unrivaled in rock. He's been at it for more than fifty years. Springsteen's heart, hunger, and energy resonated with my dad when he was a young man growing up in the New York area. That's as true today with my dad as an older father, gazing into an unknowable future. My dad would say, "Katie, I could give you all sorts of sophisticated, intellectual reasons as to why I love Springsteen, but I just really like the music, his performances of the music, and his sense of humor." Springsteen's music has always been the soundtrack to my father's life, and because of that, it's been the soundtrack to mine.

My Springsteen education started early, when my father would drive me to and from swim practice. Dad would be up at 3:45 a.m. to get me to the pool on time. I'd shuffle out in my sweats and coat, climb into our family minivan, and settle in for the half-hour ride to Georgetown Prep. Dad would use the time to extoll the many virtues of Bruce Springsteen and the E Street Band.

In those years, my dad drove a silver 2008 Toyota Sienna. He still does. He says it's on its fourth Olympic cycle, and superstitiously, he won't give it up. The van has a six-slot CD player. At any given time, five of the six CDs feature Springsteen. The sixth would be *Hearts of Stone* by Southside Johnny and the Asbury Jukes, a group from the Jersey Shore fronted by longtime Springsteen friend and soulful lead singer Johnny Lyon. My evening practice would end around 5:30 p.m., which in D.C. meant rush-hour traffic. We'd be stuck cooling our jets anywhere from twenty-five minutes to an hour. My dad would pack a lunch box stocked with chocolate milk, Greek yogurt, and other recovery foods for me to snack on until we arrived home for dinner. Then he'd crank up the stereo, and Bruce Springsteen's raspy baritone would fill the air.

Starting when I was in ninth grade, Dad began making commuting playlists. Gone were the CDs, replaced by iTunes song compilations that started playing as soon as we climbed in the car. My family all used the same iTunes account, so we would see each other's song selections. It wasn't only Springsteen. My mom loved Broadway. When she drove me, we'd be singing along to show tunes the whole way. Sometimes I'd add songs that I was hearing at school. I remember Bon Jovi's "You Give Love a Bad Name" was a big pump-up song for me back in the day. My dad would add other artists to the mix. But there was never a doubt that Bruce was what he preferred.

I didn't get my driver's license until I was twenty years old. Part of the reason is that Maryland has onerous prerequisites. You must go to ten three-hour in-person driver's ed classes. You must log a certain number of hours with an instructor. You must drive a certain number of hours with your parents. Because I was busy with swimming, I never got around to ticking all the boxes on those requirements. But a deeper reason I never applied for my license, one I've only recently come to realize, is that part of me knew if I did, I wouldn't be spending that time with my dad anymore. I cherished our time in the car together, even in traffic. I loved hearing his stories of growing up in Queens, rehashing early Washington Capitals games, and listening to Bruce on repeat.

For my dad, Springsteen's message actually cut deeper than the music. It was about community and bringing energy to one's community. My dad wanted me to bring that approach to my own communities. Learn how to *do* things. Learn how to be a good classmate, be a good person. Participate. Be a good sport. Be of service and try to help other people if you can. This was the abiding ethos of our schooling and our family.

Though Springsteen music is a bond I share with my dad, I relate to Springsteen in my own way. Metaphorically, I identify with Springsteen's legendary endurance. He performs three- or four-hour shows. He breaks records for the length of his gigs, and he's been doing it for years. There's a correlation there for me in terms of how he pushes the limits of what he's done before, giving it everything he has, every time. His work ethic is incredible. Watching him sweat and run around decade after decade is impressive. He provides a model of what a career can be if you never stop trying, if you never cease growing.

In 2016, right after the Olympics, my family and I went to see Bruce Springsteen in concert together. Thanks to the generosity of his management team, we were fortunate enough to get to meet him. He was playing at Nationals Park. We arrived early and had to idle a bit before we could be let into Bruce's dressing room; we'd gotten there before his pre-concert meal. While we waited, Nils Lofgren, guitarist in the E Street Band (who—hometown pride alert—went to high school at Walter Johnson in Montgomery County, Maryland), was riding around backstage on a bicycle. Apparently, it was part of his warm-up routine. Every time Nils rode by us, he would honk his bike horn and wave. We were cracking up. It reminded us of a Harpo Marx comedy routine. He was wearing a Harpo-style hat too. A total character. After a few rounds of this, Bruce's colleague Wayne escorted my family and me to a door off the backstage corridor. As we waited a beat, I noticed Bruce's food tray with an empty soup bowl sitting outside on the floor. Soon enough, Bruce's manager/producer, Jon Landau, exited Bruce's dressing room, and we were cleared to go and meet Bruce.

The whole scene unfolded like a dream. We introduced ourselves, said a quick "hello" and "pleased to meet you." Bruce, keeping it chill, mentioned that his daughter, Jessica, was a champion equestrian. I remember we told Bruce how we listened to his music all the time, driving to swim practices and meets. We thanked him for his songs and told him what his work had meant in our lives. My dad told him that he has a friend, Anthony, who has seen Bruce live more than 120 times. Bruce smiled and said, "I've heard of people going to a lot of shows, but *that's a lot of shows.*"

I nervously showed him my Olympic medals. Bruce, who has won a Tony Award, an Academy Award, Grammy Awards, and every conceivable honor, held one of my medals and said, "I always wondered what athletes do with these things." Laughing, my dad chimed in, "They take them to show their favorite rock star." Bruce asked me what year I was in college, and I said I was about to start my freshman year. "Wow, you've accomplished a lot for a freshman," he said, and again we all laughed. That felt amazing in about a thousand different ways.

Then we took a photograph: Bruce and I each holding one of my medals, standing shoulder to shoulder, he's in a white dress shirt, I'm in my navy Olympic cardigan, my hair styled for the occasion, smiling wide.

As we left the dressing room, I got to see all the guitars backstage, the whole stage and video production setup, which was epic. We exited through one of the baseball dugouts and were shown to our seats, which were left of the stage, about ten rows back.

When the show kicked off, I was instantly enthralled. From the first notes, there was this wave of energy that rolled out over the crowd. We stood the whole concert. The entire audience was singing, dancing, screaming their heads off. Halfway through the show, one of the security guys took me and my dad up into the pit. We got to see Bruce work his magic close up.

The whole night was incredible for us. Meeting somebody whose creative work you've admired for so long. Getting to have a conversation with them. Being able to express gratitude. And the timing was fortuitous. When I'm training and competing, I never have time to go to shows or stay up all night dancing. Luckily, the concert fell during the weeks between when I got back home from Rio and when I had to start Stanford. I got to be a normal person for a night. And it was a beautiful thing.

Seeing Springsteen was both a way to celebrate Rio and to mark my heading off to college. My parents always had this routine with my brother and me when we were growing up: during the summer, we each got what we would call a "special day" when we could choose something unique to do with our mom and then separately with our dad. It might be going to a museum, or a movie, or our favorite restaurant. We did that most years before school started, which amounts to a ton of special days. But this one was far and away the most special.

To have the chance just to go to the concert with my dad was special, after all those years of car rides and the music education that he'd given me, which was actually "life education" in an E Street Band wrapper. Work hard, never quit, be a good person, show up for your team, remember where you came from, keep the faith. All takeaways from Bruce's storied career and legendary zeal.

Recently, my father sent me an article about Springsteen's birthday. The writer talked about growing up with Bruce's music, going to one of his first concerts when he was twenty-three, and the thrill of watching a musician you loved when you were younger grow up and change along with you. I think my dad wanted me to see the value of finding a voice that speaks to your deepest self. A touchstone that reminds you of what truly matters in life, a safe harbor that keeps you anchored and secure.

I hope my dad knows that, for me, the safe harbor has always been him.

Chapter Six

KAZAN

The 2015 World Championships in Kazan was my first and only time visiting Russia, an uncanny experience from start to finish. My parents remember packs of stray dogs roaming the streets and having to duck behind doors and kiosks to avoid them. The food wasn't anything to write home about. There were a number of unusual rules that had to be followed. My family members had to surrender their phones to the front desk at the hotel at certain times. Who knows what was done with them. Then there was the swimming.

I broke my first world record at the 2013 World Championships. Then more in 2014 in Texas, California, and Australia. By 2015, I was beginning to feel like a Team USA veteran. But I didn't expect how my week in Kazan would unfold.

My meet schedule was jammed. I was slated to race the 400, 1500, 200, and 800 frees as well as the 4x200 relay. My coach, Bruce Gemmell, and I had a strategy to survive the arduous lineup. Exert the maximum when I needed to, then pull back when I could, in order to conserve energy for the races to come.

I began the meet handily winning gold in the 400, four seconds ahead of my closest competitor. The 1500 was next on deck. I usually cruise through the 1500 and 800 free prelims. You don't need to go fast to make the final, and everyone kind of slow-walks the prelims of the distance races. Before the initial prelim, I reviewed the plan for the 1500 with Bruce. He reminded me how he wanted me to swim. "Go 900 easy, 300 where you can pick it up a little bit, and then the remaining 300 can be your choice." Meaning I could either continue gaining modest speed in those last laps, or I could slow it down and coast to the finish. When I shared this plan with my USA teammates, they kind of chuckled because, well, they know me. I had a reputation by this point. There was a lot of teasing, like "So what's it going to be, Katie? What are you going to do for the last 300?"

I was super-relaxed the afternoon of the race. I'd been enjoying my morning, not getting in my head. As a rule, I take my coach's instructions seriously. I know that sometimes I need to be pulled back so that I don't kill myself in prelims and jeopardize having a successful final the next day. The decision I made for myself was 900 easy, 300 a little bit faster, and then a comfortable 300. That's what I told myself: "Comfortable."

The Kazan venue was in a soccer stadium, the same location where they'd held the World Cup. They had installed two temporary pools, a warm-up/warm-down pool and the competition pool. At most World Championships, the scoreboards are at the far ends of the pool. Because it was in a stadium, the Kazan meet had huge scoreboards flanking the sides of the pool. Scoreboards I could clearly see *while* I was swimming. I was able to read the splits in real time. One board even played a live-stream of the race. This was new.

I dove in for my 1500 prelim. As I was swimming the so-called easy laps of the race, I could already see on the boards that I was ahead of the world-record pace, which was the record I'd set myself the previous year, in the summer of 2014. They'd put up a graphic of a red line, and from the pool I could clock that I was ahead of it. Knowing that fact was not conducive to abiding by my coach's caution to "take it easy."

At the top of the boards, the world-record split was displayed with a plus or minus sign of how many seconds you were on or off. If you're ahead of the world record, it's green. And if you're behind the world record, it's red. Again, I could see these graphics so clearly, down to the minus-one-point notation by my name.

In the beginning, I followed Bruce's instructions, but the scoreboards kept distracting me. It was like the cartoon with the devil on one shoulder and the angel on the other. I wanted to be prudent and swim as I'd been directed. But how could a competitor like me ignore the blinking pace line?

I was legitimately conflicted: *Should I pick it up because I'm under world-record pace and could break this record this morning? Should I slow down and do as my coach advised so I have more left in the tank for tomorrow?* I began giggling to myself as I mentally debated. The giggling made me feel further relaxed and comfortable.

At this point I was having the time of my life in the temporary Russian stadium pool. The stands were mostly deserted, so I could plainly pick out my family in their seats. I noticed my brother, Michael, watching me intently, like the old days when we trained together in Bethesda. I could sense he was aware of the back-and-forth happening in my brain. He probably intuited my decision before I did.

Suddenly, I was on the last 300, dealer's choice. I wanted to have an aggressive final the next day, but there was no shutting down the enticement of the scoreboards and their flashing minus signs. I'd swum ahead of pace the whole race. There was zero chance I was going to remove my foot from the gas now. I sped ahead.

I ended up breaking my world record by a second. When I touched the wall in 15:27, I was barely out of breath. I looked up from the water, and my teammates were all laughing hysterically. They knew that I wasn't supposed to go super-hard, but they also knew I'm not inclined to moderate my pace. They thought what I'd done was crazy, but they were unsurprised. Then I spotted Coach Bruce. I gave a small shrug, like, *Oops.* He gave a tight smile. What did he expect? If you give me the choice, I'm going to go fast.

The meet schedule had me swimming the 200 prelim the next

morning, then the 1500 final that night, with the 200 semifinal thirty minutes after that. Going into that session, I remember the USA women's team head coach, Dave Salo, announcing at our team meeting, "Well, Katie broke the world record yesterday, so she can have a comfortable final tonight and be ready for that 200."

The 200 was always going to be a harder distance for me. Then there was the added fatigue of going into it right after the 1500. Coach Salo was basically conveying that I could cruise through the 1500 final since I'd taken care of business yesterday, keeping my powder dry for the 200 heats. I nodded absently, but in my head, I was like: *Are you kidding me? Do you even know me?* I think Bruce and I smirked at each other. I understood why Coach Salo was concerned about the quick turnaround of the 1500 final and 200 semifinals, and I knew why he thought I could take it easy. But after the team meeting, I knew in my heart of hearts that his plan was not going to happen.

When it was time to race, I dove into the 1500 final with a private mission—to go out there and break the world record again. I wasn't done in Kazan yet. I wasn't going to phone in a race. I was going to do what I always did—go out fast and challenge myself to bring it home.

Two nights before the 1500 final, I dreamed about my grandfathers. I never dream during meets. But this time I did. Their voices and faces were so clear, even through the haze of sleep. Midway through my swim, the dream popped back into my head.

My mind flooded with memories of these two men who had sacrificed in profound ways simply to stay alive. My Grandpa Hagan had survived some of the most dreadful battles of World War II. My Grandpa Jerry came to the United States after defecting from Czechoslovakia to escape Russian rule. Being in Kazan had put him at the top of my mind. My uncle Jon had told me how, after my grandpa was allowed to return to the Czech Republic, he seemed so much lighter, so relieved to be among his people. These were the memories driving me as I swam. Faster and faster. Starting furiously and never losing the lead.

At the end of the final, I'd broken my day-old world record by 2.23. For the effort, my body ached a bit more than it had the day before.

When I climbed onto the blocks for the 200 a half hour later and just minutes after the 1500 medal ceremony, my legs were jelly. My thighs shook as I heard, "Take your mark." I'd never experienced exhaustion that profound in any prior meet. I remember thinking: *My ego and my stubbornness are coming back to haunt me. Maybe I should have cruised in the 1500.*

I dove in and was somehow able to take third in my semifinal 200 heat, sixth overall. You must be top eight out of the sixteen to move forward. I finished barely fast enough to sneak into the final. But I made it through.

I won the final the next day from lane seven. That was my first time ever doing that double, and it was my first time winning the 200 at that level of meet. Another Kazan miracle.

After that, on the fifth day of competition, I won gold in the relay along with Missy Franklin, Leah Smith, and Katie McLaughlin. Then the 800 final was my last race. The meet had been charmed thus far, and I was confident I could break my world record of 8:11. My goal for Rio the next year was to go 8:05 or faster. Breaking 8:10 would be a substantial step toward that.

I remember visiting with my family at my hotel on my one night off. We were sitting around talking, and it dawned on us that it was Grandpa Jerry's birthday the next day. August 8. I said, "Wouldn't it be cool if I go 8:08 tomorrow?" Now, as I've explained, I'm not someone who shares my goals, even with my family. I think they were a little surprised I said that. But the numbers were lining up—all those eights. My dear departed grandpa's birthday. Me swimming in a country he had history with. It seemed meant to be. In my brain, it was settled: 8:08.

I ended up going 8:07.

I set my tenth world record in two years with that 800-meter freestyle. I won by 10.26 seconds, chopping 3.61 seconds off my record from 2014.

After I touched the wall, I slapped the water three times. One slap for each world record I'd set in Kazan.

I finished the meet with five gold medals and became the first swimmer to win the 200, 400, 800, and 1500-meter freestyles in a major competition. I'd swum 6200 meters over seven days and broken the 1500 free world record twice.

When reporters ask me what I believe is the most amazing athletic feat, I answer: Michael Phelps's eight-gold-medal performance at the 2008 Beijing Olympics. After Kazan, *USA Today* called my performance "The sports feat of the decade!" I felt this was an overstatement. But I was charmed by the moniker that the media chose for the sweep: "The Ledecky Slam." Which is humbling and appreciated. And sounds a bit like the best burger on a menu.

I left Russia elated and excited for what was to come in my career. I personally wouldn't call what I'd achieved the sports feat of the decade, but I was genuinely pleased. I knew that streaks like that are few and far between. I got the job done. I showed up for myself, my team, and my family. I hoped if my grandfathers were watching over me, that they felt honored.

My achievement was worth a $175,000 purse from FINA, now known as World Aquatics, swimming's governing body. But I couldn't accept any prize money. I was still an amateur, readying to compete for Stanford. Instead, I flew home to Bethesda and did what every teenager does—got my wisdom teeth removed.

Such was the contrast of my life. One day I'm being hailed in the international press as a sports icon, earning my own nomenclature. The next, I'm curled on the living room couch, slurping milkshakes as I recover from oral surgery. I wouldn't have had it any other way.

Chapter Seven

TECHNIQUE, TRAINING, TENACITY, TEDIUM

I t's often said that distance swimming requires enduring an excruciating, mind-numbing tedium few other athletes experience. Hour upon hour, day after day, for months, years, decades, distance swimmers stare at the dark line marking the bottom of a pool, tracking and tracing it as we churn back and forth in our muffled bubble of virtual silence, plagued by a loop of our innermost thoughts, our bodies screaming in agony from the stress of pushing ourselves to the limits of exertion. For me, this is any given Saturday.

I'm kidding, of course. I, for one, have never viewed my chosen sport as a source of pain. For me, swimming has been a pleasure, even when—or perhaps especially when—it tests my limits. That said, I'm not here to argue with the common perception that long-distance swims can brutalize the body and mind. They absolutely can.

Water is 800 times denser than air. After a few minutes of swimming, your body enters aerobic respiration, which increases your heart rate and prompts your body to circulate oxygenated blood to your muscles. At the end of long distances, those muscles are flooded with lactic acid, which causes fatigue, cramps, and a host of other unpleasantries.

Maintaining a high heart rate over that long period of time can even cause the atria, or chambers of the heart, to stretch and result in a greater risk of arrhythmia. Distance racing is fully masochistic. You're going to feel pain in a unique and terrible way.

Coping with excruciating discomfort during an event is a distinctive mental challenge. Your body begins to pose questions to your brain. Questions like: *Seriously, how long are you going to make me keep doing this?* And: *Are you not noticing the pain cues I'm sending? Because I can turn up the volume if I need to.* For any distance swimmer, the only question that actually matters is: *How are you going to respond to the pain?* Are you going to shut down and throw in the towel, or are you going to hold steady, believe that you can survive your anguish, and carry on?

I'm at the point in my career when, during races I know, when I feel that little cramp in my side or that ache in the pit of my stomach, I can acknowledge it and change nothing: hold the stroke that I have, hold my rhythm, hold my pace, and, in some cases, go even faster, my body urging me to push past the pain. I've isolated that sweet spot between torment and success.

To thrive in distance swims, you have to train yourself to focus on nothing, or on something constructive, otherwise your brain will default to a self-preservation cycle of registering that your body hurts—signaling to you to stop doing whatever it is that is hurting your body and sending messages to all corners of your mind to *quit swimming already!* In short, if you can't harness your thoughts, you become your own worst enemy in the pool.

Repetition challenges your mental and physical game, and swimming is repetition to the nth degree. But for whatever reason—genetics, luck, stellar coaching, a particular physiology—I've been able to embrace the good and tolerate the rest. The predawn wake-up times. The cold, dark commutes to the pool. The eating in the car. The exhaustion. The rigor. The restrictive schedule that has me in bed at sundown. Rinse, repeat. I recognized, even as a little girl, that I had a level of focus and a competitive nature that other swimmers my age did not.

After that first summer at Palisades pool, I continued to play other sports, like basketball and soccer, but as I got older, I always chose swim practice over any other activity. Soon enough I realized that I wanted to give swimming my all and channel every bit of energy I could into it. I vividly remember my dad reviewing the results of one of my early races with me and teaching me about hundredths and tenths of seconds. He showed me on a stopwatch how blink-of-an-eye those winning margins are. This was a math lesson that I viewed as a personal challenge.

From the beginning I saw myself as my competition. My goal setting has never been "I'm going to beat so-and-so." Or "I want to break so-and-so's world record." Instead, starting at about age seven, I set specific objectives for myself that I called "want times." Scribbles on pieces of paper I kept by my bed or taped to my bathroom mirror. Like the 25 free: 15.99. The 25 back: 17.74. After a meet, I would pencil in my actual times to see how much faster I needed to be at the next race to make my goal. I didn't really share that I was doing this exercise. It was my own private project: mapping out ambitious goals that seemed unreasonable at first, then, as I worked toward them, became more realistic. These were goals I set for me and me alone.

I loved being in the water. I loved practice. When I wasn't logging laps, I thought about the next time I could. Twenty years later, that pattern remains exactly the same. I challenge myself to improve, to grow, to push. What everyone else is up to in the pool is not my business. The more far-fetched an objective appears when I come up with it, the better. If, when I say my goals out loud to my coaches, they sound unfeasible—that's when I know I'm on the right track. The impossible is what motivates me every day to go to the pool. It's so satisfying, so epically rewarding, when you start chipping away at those idealistic goals. Nothing has made me more committed to my training than choosing a scary goal and taking the steps to go after it.

Thankfully, when I was developing as a swimmer, I had coaches who held the reins in a bit. As determined as I was, they did me a solid by keeping my preliminary training reasonable, teaching me how to prevent injuries, emphasizing the proper stroke form. They allowed me to progress naturally as an athlete.

Not every coach takes this naturalistic approach. Many want to capitalize on the talent they have on the roster as soon as possible. They make training decisions based on the shortest distance to capture results. For example, there is a debate around bilateral breathing, the technique of breathing to both sides as you swim. When you advance to a certain level, it's more economical to breathe to one side only. But when you're younger, it's safer to breathe to both sides because it creates balance with your stroke. This prevents future injuries, along with creating a better overall stroke in the long term. Besides, it takes a few years to determine which side you're faster on. Coaches who skip that developmental stage may get their swimmer winning quicker, but it will cost them down the line.

Even after I reached Olympic level, my coaches ensured that I still had room to improve. I had a body that wasn't shredded from overuse. No torn rotator cuffs. No hip displacement. The only injury I've ever had is a broken arm, and that was from playing basketball in fourth grade. Well, not so much playing as tripping and breaking the bone when another teammate fell on top of me, if you want to get specific. I was ten and had a bright green cast on my arm through Christmas. I often cite this as a turning point in my life—it hit me that I loved swimming so much I didn't want to get injured again outside the pool. Even my cast couldn't keep me from the water. I sealed a plastic bag over my arm and used a kickboard so I could still be in the pool.

What people get wrong about swimming is thinking that it's every four years or so, when the Olympics or the Worlds come around. In fact, we're constantly training. It's every day, ten times a week. It's a lifestyle in more ways than one. We stay submerged, both physically and metaphorically, so that we can peak before critical meets. We're defined by the clock as much as anything. So much so that we call each other by our times. "She's a 54–100 freestyler." Our fastest times and our preferred races become our identities.

It comes down to how you're made. I've known I had an engine since I swam my first mile, when I was probably eleven. I remember swimming that distance for the first time and walking away from it like "That wasn't so bad." Then I realized that I'd sort of enjoyed it. And then I realized that a lot of my teammates who were also swimming that distance for the first time did *not* have that same reaction. They loathed the mile, dreaded swimming that far again. I had zero fear of another mile in the pool.

Each time I took the next step with a harder distance event, I got more and more confirmation that long swims were for me. Maybe it was as simple as the fact that those lengthy swims let me be in the pool for a longer period of time. In shorter events, if you mess up one thing, you're not going to have the race that you want. Whereas, in the distance events, there's wiggle room. There's also more time to think, more time to react, more time to strategize. By early adolescence, I began targeting distance races for my championship meets and long-term goals.

Mentally, I've learned that I'm wired as an aerobic swimmer. I embrace routine. I lean into the regularity. The endless laps become a kind of meditation. It's a bit like walking through those spiraling Zen gardens, a way to calm the noise of the world and let the consistency and predictability of swimming back and forth wash over you. I don't have as many fast twitches as the sprinters, and I don't have the technique to be a 50 freestyler. But psychologically, I'm built to endure.

I've known that I'm a distance swimmer for going on fifteen years now. If you compare that to the people I'm racing against, some of whom are eighteen, nineteen years old, well, they've only been doing it for six or seven years. I've been training at this level for so long I have a honed feel for the pool. I don't fight with the water. I don't battle its resistance. I allow it to lift me up. To torpedo me along. The water isn't foreign to me. It's home.

I'm often asked why I've never tried open-water swimming, Diana Nyad–style. There is a 10-kilometer open-water race in the Olympics. Talk about long-distance swimming! The truth is, I did try an open-water race once as a youngster, but I didn't like it. I'm not comfortable where I can't see the bottom, when there are fish swimming around, along with other scary creatures and the vast unknown. Hard pass on that. I like the *known*. I like clear parameters.

For example, with freestyle, there are observable rules. As strokes go, it's unfussy. It's also my preferred stroke. When I was six, I swam in this meet called the Pilgrim Pentathlon. It was in November, around Thanksgiving, and I swam the 25 butterfly, 25 backstroke, 25 breaststroke, 25 freestyle, and 100 individual medley. I should say, I *tried* to swim—I disqualified in the butterfly, breaststroke, and individual medley. In breaststroke I wasn't doing the kick properly, or the arms. In butterfly I didn't keep my feet together. And the individual medley turned out to be a *medley* of the same mistakes from the earlier butterfly and breast-stroke laps.

Now, I have to say proudly—knocking on wood—that's the last time I ever got disqualified. I've never false-started. I've never touched with one hand when I was supposed to touch with two. I've got a twenty-year streak going. And I am pleased with some of my individual medley performances over the years, including a few American record swims in the 400 IM while at Stanford.

Admittedly, I have swimming weaknesses. The aforementioned backstroke. A stroke I do not and have never enjoyed. With back-stroke, you can get water up your nose or accidentally swallow it. You can't see anything. There's a totally different dive. I will never get the appeal.

I often fail at practices. I swim at race pace even when I shouldn't. As I've said many times over the years, I'm a distance swimmer with a sprinter's mentality. I'm not good at conservation when it comes to energy. My reaction time off the blocks is often the fastest in the distance events, .66 to .73 seconds. My instinct is to replicate the race conditions at practice, which can lead to burnouts. I never want to leave the pool with too much left in the tank. But in my defense, it also prepares me. When I dive in at a meet, I know my stroke rate, I know I can handle my pace. I've practiced that pace thousands of times. And I have the advantage of knowing the discomfort won't kill me.

Another knock? I'm an average kicker. When we do kick sets, I'm very *meh*. I'm far more of a puller than a kicker. I'm better suited to sets when we're swimming with a pull buoy or paddles. If I'm doing a "lactate set," where you build lactic acid and let it sit in you like poison and then you swim fast again—after some rest, but with no warm-down in between—I'm hopeless. I mean, everyone hurts during those practices, but I seem to struggle more. I'll be humming along on the first swim, but on the later laps—not so much. There are swimmers who are experts at lactate sets. Freaks.

My best practices are "threshold sets," where you swim varying distances while holding fast paces for an extended period of time. My heart rate might be around 180 beats per minute for 45 to 60 minutes during those sets. I also shine on the days when we do super-long swims. As I said, most people despise long swims. The 1500 is the longest race that we do, so at practice we may swim a 3000, a 2000, and a 1000 and be asked by the coach to pick up our pace as the swims go along. That's only 6000 but a lot of straight swimming, which can be the challenge. Back and forth and back and forth. Swimmers dread those sets, but I like them. (Guess I'm the freak now.)

When I swim, I can almost hear my heartbeat. Audibly, there's a rhythm to the water. Especially with my stroke, because I breathe every two strokes. My same ear is going out of the water, back in the water, as I'm breathing. That creates a pattern, a drumbeat, almost. Whoosh . . . whoosh . . . whoosh. It's layered under the sound of my hands hitting the water, a sort of melody that can be fast or slow. I become a human metronome.

The dialogue in my head varies every race, but I almost always count the laps, the meters, or the yards. Just like I do in practice. It steadies the mind. Then I have different self-talk based on my race plan. That voice sounds like a motivational speaker. I'm very direct with myself. I'll say, *I've got to hit this turn.* Or *All right, 500 left, it's time to go!* If I'm really suffering, I try to keep in mind how little is left of the race. If there's 400 remaining of 1500, I say, *I've got eight 50's left.* I break it down so it seems shorter, kind of like eating a meal you hate in tiny bites.

Sometimes I'll think of something I've done in the past and compare it to what I'm doing in that moment. I'll remind myself how quickly I've done 100's in practice. I'll tell myself, the distance left to swim, *That's nothing.* All these tricks up my sleeve to fool my mind and my body to get through races and not just survive but excel. I avoid dwelling on any pain.

Those can be brutal moments, but I get off those thoughts as quickly as possible because it's better not to think of anything. Song lyrics help. Any song that has a good rhythm that matches the tempo of my stroke. Like "Beautiful Day," by U2. And, naturally, I've had a lot of Bruce Springsteen songs stuck in my head.

My technique has altered the way distance swims are raced, at least on the women's side. Especially in the 400 freestyle, which is now viewed almost as a sprint. When I was young, I would take that race out like lightning, and now a lot of other swimmers follow that pattern. There's a critical difference, though, especially in the 800 and the mile, between taking the race out too fast and taking it out too fast, too *soon.* You can be fast and keep your energy up, but if you expend too much energy—you're toast. There have been races that I've swum where I've taken it out too fast, too soon, even just the first 50 of an 800 where my tempo is too rapid or I kick too much. That's when I hit a wall I can't push through.

After I became the world's top female swimmer in the 200, 400, 800, and 1500 freestyles, there was feverish interest in studying my technique. It was like a fixation. The training required to excel in a 1500 makes shorter distances harder to master. The skill sets are at odds in many ways. Sweeping four events of varying lengths is like a runner winning a marathon, a sprint, and the hurdles. That accomplishment gave rise to so many articles examining me. Which is cool, I guess. I try to accept the compliments and disregard the remarks that make me feel like a lab animal.

In 2016 the Mayo Clinic in Minnesota said I was dominating by the widest margin in international sport, comparing me to runners, cyclists, and other endurance athletes. Bob Bowman, Michael Phelps's coach, told the press that was because I was "very connected," meaning my upper and lower body work in unison. Russell Mark, a college swimmer who later became a high-performance swim analyst, labeled my form as close to perfect as exists.

I mean, I appreciate the approbation and the acknowledgment, I do. But I didn't enter swimming to become some iconic figure, a yardstick by which my peers would be measured. I started swimming to measure myself. It's uncomfortable for me to reflect on my success or my alleged physical superiority. I can think of many other things I'd rather do with my time, like napping, or watching a romcom, or calling my grandma. My brother, Michael, calls me "extraordinarily ordinary," and that tracks for me.

All my coaches have had to answer query after query about what it was that made me able to swim the way I do. They all gave different answers, but the theme was consistent: hard work. I've never hit the snooze button. I take feedback eagerly. I implement change as soon as I can master it. I've always been a knowledge sponge. I thrive not on wins but on improvements. Bruce Gemmell frequently joked with me that I could swim in a dark cardboard box, by myself, and still perform at my best. An observation that, while peculiar to imagine, rang true.

When I started training with Nation's Capital Swim Club, I occasionally observed teammates showing up late or not going to every practice, not setting the kinds of goals I was setting. I recognized I wanted to be better than that. I wanted to be that person who got to practice early and swam every meet I qualified for. Who welcomed coaching and kept her cool. Doing those things, I could be better and I could get further. Even when I was young, I knew.

My mentality now is similar to how it was back then. If I get pulled from practice, if I'm having an off training session or meet, I remind myself tomorrow is another day. I stay involved with my peers in the sport. I check on teammates. I text coaches. I remember that this is meant to be fun, that the real payoff is the swimming family I'm part of. Not whether I got my stroke to work on a random Tuesday.

When all else is said and done, my favorite thing to do when it comes to technique and training is finish strong. Even in practice. That last 15 meters are everything to me. Grinding to the end, touching the wall—there's something almost sacred about the finish. I don't want to coast. Not even when I'm exhausted from the other endless meters I've swum. I know it only matters to me. For many swimmers, there is little to be gained from that last burst in a training session when nothing is actually on the line. But I see the final surge as being a bit like the old adage that you are your truest self when no one is watching. Who you are alone, with no consequences, no external pressures, is generally your authentic character.

Powering to the wall means something similar in my mind. No one cares, no one expects it. But it matters to me. I want to touch that wall. To end with effort. To leave nothing untapped. To do otherwise would mean letting myself down. Not because I tried and failed, which happens to everyone. But because I just didn't bother to try. I always have to try.

Chapter Eight

GRANDPA JERRY

I was thirteen years old when my Grandpa Jaromir (Jerry) Ledecky passed away. It was March 2, 2011, two weeks before my fourteenth birthday.

Grandpa Jerry was born in Czechoslovakia. He was twenty years old when he left Prague to come to America, with little money in his pocket. It was 1947, and he traveled aboard a ship with many other students of differing nationalities, all on educational visas. He was coming to study at Rutgers on a scholarship named after Jan Masaryk, then Czechoslovakia's foreign minister. Shortly after my grandpa arrived in New York, Masaryk was discovered dead beneath a second-story window, a likely victim of the Soviet takeover.

The new regime demanded that Grandpa Jerry leave the U.S. and return to Prague, but his father begged him to stay. He knew his son's only chance at an independent life was in America now. My grandpa listened to his father and remained in the States, a choice that had dire consequences for the family members still in Prague. Businesses were taken from them. Soldiers occupied the family home. His brother—who eventually became a physician—was sent to the mines to labor for a while. It would be seventeen years before Grandpa Jerry would see any of his family in person again.

The psychological effects of his decision to stay in America were devastating. There were times when he felt he had betrayed his loved ones. That he should have gone back, even though his return would not have changed the political landscape or the cruelty of the current policies. Being removed while his family suffered was difficult. But the circumstances also motivated my grandpa to achieve in all his endeavors. He decided if he was given this opportunity to live and live freely, he was going to wring the most he could from that blessing. He didn't want the sacrifices of his family to be for naught.

As such, Grandpa Jerry resolved to embody the American dream. I would often hear the story of how he worked at the Howard Johnson's restaurant in New Brunswick, New Jersey, when he was studying at Rutgers. He was a dishwasher and a soda jerk. In a fifty-four-hour work week, he made $35 plus one complimentary meal per day. At some point, he started saving quarters and coins with silver content, with the dream of buying a house. He believed that the silver coins would grow in value. Eventually, he was right. He ended up saving $8,000 for a down payment, allowing him to move his family out of their small apartment in Queens.

It's crazy to think of my grandpa finding his way in the U.S. by himself, going through school, at first navigating New York City essentially alone. His mother died from an ear infection when he was six years old. His father remarried a woman who gave her biological child food before her stepchildren when there wasn't enough to go around, meaning my grandpa frequently went hungry. To go from that hardscrabble beginning to earning a doctorate in economics from New York University is remarkable. I'm sure if he'd told anyone his goals, that he intended to go from dishwasher to the top of the education and business ladder, they'd have dismissed him as delusional. Kind of the way if I shared my goals, people would think they were impossible. I like to imagine I inherited some of my nerve and perseverance from him.

My grandpa was fundamentally scholarly, very much like his wife, my Grandma Berta. Grandpa Jerry wanted his kids to go to the best schools, the most elite colleges. They were expected to take their schoolwork seriously. When I would visit my grandpa, he was living in D.C. in an apartment at the Watergate. Every surface was piled with stacks of books. There were also reams of newspapers. Grandpa Jerry was fluent in eight languages by the time he died. I remember he was teaching himself Swedish on his deathbed.

Grandpa began service in the U.S. Army in 1950, during the Korean War. He worked as a linguist and then as a radio operator for the army, earning $100 a month. The army promoted him from private to corporal during his service. He became a U.S. citizen in 1954.

When he met Berta, Jerry proposed after two hours. He was sure this intelligent spitfire was the woman for him. She was less sure. He approached the challenge of wooing her as he did every other goal in his sights. He turned up the charm. He lost forty pounds. He made sure she arrived safely home from her dates with less zealous suitors. Eventually, she was won over by his persistence and ardor. They got married a year after he proposed. Soon they had my uncle Jon and then my dad.

After marrying Berta, Jerry felt even more pressure to achieve. He attended NYU night classes and earned a master's degree, then a Ph.D. After school, he would read seven Czech newspapers. He needed to stay connected back home, even if there was little he could do to change the circumstances. He was so grateful to be in America, a democracy, a place where he believed that if he put in the work, he would be rewarded. When he was able to earn more of a living, Grandpa Jerry moved the family to Greenwich, Connecticut. Which was quite a change of pace, to say the least. Queens was a multicultural melting pot of urban strivers and immigrants. Connecticut was . . . Connecticut.

But Grandpa Jerry loved his new neighborhood. It was as if he had raided and taken over the castle. He was living in the heart of old money, but he was proud that his family could hold its own. For Grandpa, there was the particular satisfaction of coming to America with nothing and making it to the highest rung. That pride and thirst for the traditional markers of excellence transferred to my dad and uncle, and later to my brother and me. But even with all of Grandpa's success as an economics consultant and professor, there remained a scrim of sadness beneath the surface. As is inevitable with anyone who has been cast out of their homeland and cleaved off from their past, he carried the weight of displacement with him. My dad grew up sensing the ennui. Uncle Jon said he never understood how melancholy his dad actually was until he was allowed to go back to his homeland. Uncle Jon saw him fill with light, as if his heart had been plugged in upon his return home. It was a side of his father Uncle Jon hadn't seen in America.

By the early 1990s, Grandpa was traveling home to Prague several times a year. As soon as he was able, he reclaimed a share of the family textile factory, which the Communist government had converted into mechanical chain production. He reconnected with friends and relatives. He did what he could to make up for lost time. Under his leadership, the family factory grew and became a thriving company again. Grandpa helped his Czech family reinvigorate the business that had been stolen from them. Together they rebuilt their world as best they could, healing wounds along the way.

For that and many other reasons, Grandpa Jerry always seemed so accomplished and sophisticated to me. He knew a ton about other cultures. He would sit me down and talk to me about foreign countries and far-flung lands. He had a distinctive voice: a lingering Czech accent delivered with a heavy rasp. To this day I can hear the exact way he would phrase something, even though it's been over a decade since I've heard his voice.

As he got older, Grandpa was frequently in the hospital, suffering with a congestive heart condition and other ailments. There was one point, a couple of years before he passed, when he fell into a coma. One of the young priests from my school came to perform last rites. Grandpa's eyes were closed. My whole family was there, stoic and sad. I was at the foot of the bed, listening, waiting for the grieving to begin. And then, halfway into the sacrament, a miracle! My grandpa's eyes opened, and he came out of the coma. I was stunned! He was such a solid presence, full of winning stubbornness and so much self-belief. Honestly, we all thought Grandpa Jerry was going to live forever. No one more than him. I think that's another characteristic I inherited from him. He never gave up on himself or on life.

For his eightieth birthday, we visited Prague as a family. I got to see where my grandpa grew up, where he went to school. I remember going out to dinner with him in the city, traveling around to the family neighborhood, visiting his childhood home. He talked about seeing Hitler in Prague as a teen and throwing stones at German tanks with his friends. We visited the Jewish cemetery and stood at the graves of distant relatives who had been killed in the Holocaust. We encountered a Czech bureaucrat who complained because we'd parked in front of his house, to which my grandpa returned some choice Czech curse words. After all he'd survived, my granddad wasn't about to be intimidated by some random jerk.

In a weird way, his deep commitment to his past kept my grandpa looking forward. No matter what happened, he stayed optimistic. My grandpa's pursuit of his American dream is something I consider when I represent the United States. I love when I get to meet the Czech swimmers at meets. They always recognize my last name is Czech. I know my grandpa would've really loved that I was making an effort to connect with them and bond over my family history.

Mostly, when I think of Grandpa Jerry these days, I think about how he pushed through every obstacle and tragedy. His intellect never dimmed. And he never lost his sense of humor. I loved it when he laughed. He was a serious person, but sometimes he would give me a knowing smirk and chuckle. We shared these small, private glimmers of connection.

Grandpa Jerry didn't live long enough to watch me swim in the

Olympics. He passed away about a year before the London Games. One of the last things he asked my dad was when my next swim meet was. As it happened, it was in Orlando, the site where I won my first Junior National race. That meet put me on the path for the gold; it was the start of my own American dream. I recall thinking of Grandpa Jerry on that day. Feeling his spirit and hearing his laugh.

Chapter Nine

BRUCE

The first time I met Bruce Gemmell was at the 2012 Olympic training camp in Tennessee. The Team USA domestic training was in Knoxville that year, and Bruce was there for a couple of days because his son, Andrew, was competing on the Olympic team in the 1500 free. Andrew and I were in the same group during the camps before London, coached by Jon Urbanchek, the legendary veteran who served on the staff of six separate Olympic teams over a fifty-year career.

Bruce had been a distinguished swimmer in the eighties. He qualified for the Olympic Trials in 1980 and 1984 but didn't make either final cut. During Bruce's senior year at the University of Michigan, the Wolverines hired Urbanchek to lead the men's team. After graduation, and while also earning his master's degree in mechanical engineering, Bruce served as Jon's graduate assistant. At the time, he considered becoming a full-time coach himself, but was dissuaded by Jon, who warned him that spending long hours at a job with little financial upside—not to mention, a lot of stress—might not be the happy career he imagined.

Bruce heeded Jon's warning and became a successful engineer instead. Yet as successful as he was, he couldn't shake the swim bug. He resumed coaching in 1992, when he took Andrew, then a toddler, for swim lessons and was asked by the folks running the program if he'd like to volunteer. Inevitably, Bruce took on more and more, until he found himself largely in charge of the Delaware Swim Team, then later, a USA Swimming junior team. By 2010, Bruce had quit his engineering job and committed to coaching full-time.

The day Bruce came to see Andrew's London Olympic training, we said a brief hello, but I didn't have any sustained conversation with him. It was more of a drive-by meeting. As Bruce recalls, he witnessed a teenage girl nipping at the heels of the male distance swimmers in the pool. Even at the level of the U.S. Trials, some swimmers find themselves pushing it at the end of the men's 1500 free to swim the final 100 in under a minute. In Knoxville, I was turning out one 59-second 100 after another.

All this meant was when Bruce came on the Nation's Capital Swim Club deck in the fall of 2012 to replace Yuri as my new coach, I knew who he *was,* but I didn't know much *about* him. At home, we had a bunch of dinner-table conversations. What might Bruce be like? What was his coaching style? What would he propose to do with my future training? On the heels of London, it felt like I was at a crossroads, and we were unsure what would be best for me.

Bruce had his hands full taking me on, as I'd already won an Olympic medal. The risks were twofold. I think the jury was still out on me when he moved to D.C., whether I would be able to replicate my strong Olympic debut. Bruce was also trying to break into a tight-knit circle, taking over from a beloved and long-term coach. There was pressure on him from all sides not to derail a good thing. At the same time, he was tasked with continuing to make me—and every member of the growing team, including eight-and-under swimmers—better.

Any worry I might have had evaporated after I'd met and spent time with Bruce. He was poised, unflappable. I understood right away that with Bruce, my career would be in the best possible hands. It helped that he approached swimming from an engineer's point of view. He had a meticulous plan. He concentrated on the technical, employing charts religiously in training, trying to get me to hit set times based on the heart-rate and color system that his mentor and former coach Jon Urbanchek had established.

Without diving too far into the swim-nerd weeds, the program matches colors to a variety of heart-rate zones, correlating lap times and training effort. Some of the laps are easier, others are harder, still others are designed to make your lungs feel like they are on fire. That's the entire point of those reps. To know you can push through the fire. This was the same high-intensity threshold-training method that, after a month of use at a pre-2012 Olympics camp, shaved 5.15 seconds off my 800 time in London. Bruce emphasized building yardage in the early part of the season. Then threshold training, pushing a high-volume workload. The idea is to produce a lot of stress on the body over a long period of time. Like months-long. Bruce was a big believer in sustained progression for swim development. The regimen is not for the faint of heart. But it works so well, it has become the universal standard.

I remember Bruce's first meeting with our swim group. He gave a little bit of background on his coaching history, his swimming history. He told a story about how, when he was a swimmer, he set out to swim 50,000 yards in a day, plotting out his course. Just a fully crazy thing to do. He was using that example to illustrate that he thinks outside of the box. I don't believe I really knew what that meant or what kind of coach he was going to be, but Coach Urbanchek, knowing both me and Bruce well, had expressed to me that he was convinced Bruce and I would be a great fit. His instinct was correct. We clicked right away.

Bruce brought a new perspective to my training. I found that I really liked his style. When we paired up, there was no feeling of having to slow down. We shared compatible personalities, philosophies, and work ethics, which made the ideal alchemy for what I wanted to do. I still missed Yuri. His departure for a new job right after I won my first gold—it was a bummer. But having a coach who brought a new and different mindset felt like a fresh start. And I had this intuition that Bruce would be able to take me to an unmatched level.

When Bruce took over that autumn, he had each of us write down on a postcard a little bit about ourselves and our goals. Short-term goals, long-term goals, basically a snapshot of where we wanted to go. I remember writing on that postcard, "Break the 800 free world record." Bruce took this goal seriously and helped me achieve it; the following year, I was able to break the record in Barcelona at the World Championships.

One of the first things Bruce switched in my stroke was breathing exclusively to my good side, my right side, when I swim. I breathe every two strokes to my right, when my left arm enters the water. It was the identical advice Yuri gave before my London race, and Bruce cut straight to it as well. No more left-side breathing, ever.

He also introduced a larger load of dryland training. With Yuri, I would do core work like sit-ups and working with med balls, passing them overhead, slamming them down, very basic things, two to three times a week. When I started working with Bruce, I also started working with a trainer named Lee Sommers, adding more complex exercises and weights to my dryland workouts. I was fifteen years old, and it reassured me to know that even though I had been to an Olympics, there was still so much that I could do to grow stronger and more resilient.

Much has been said about how sorry my fitness was even after I won my first gold. Bruce gave the media a lot of quotes about my physical capabilities on land, going so far as to label my overall athleticism "borderline poor." And it is true. I couldn't do many unassisted pull-ups. I was an average to slow runner. When the U.S. Olympic Training Center in Colorado Springs ran me through their battery of tests, the summary opened with a pronouncement that I was "remarkably unremarkable."

Maybe. Then again, I wasn't focused on pull-ups or running. I was focused on swimming. When I focus on something, I improve. And in the water, my pulling was a skill that needed work. The only time I'd done pulling drills had been for technical focus. In the past, Yuri had me use a pull buoy and paddles to encourage me to think about my catch—the front part of the stroke where the hand is entering the water and pulling the water under. Bruce noticed right away that my pulling speed was subpar. Especially for a distance swimmer, a group traditionally recognized as strong pullers. Bruce added more pulling sets to my workouts, and my pulling speed improved greatly, to the point where it became one of my biggest strengths.

Overall, with Bruce, I learned more. We got into the nitty-gritty of technique, workouts, and recovery. I was getting older, so I was more capable of focusing on the tiny details of training. This led me to take more ownership of my program. As I started seeing improvement, I got—I guess the best word is *obsessed,* with training and seeing my times improve. My starts, my turns, my underwater kicking off the wall all upgraded with Bruce. This was a boon to my shorter events. My underwater kicks specifically set me apart from some of my competitors. I was taking three to five kicks off some walls. I had more power, more strength in my legs. I had a breakout 200 freestyle in the spring of 2013, and I swam on the 4x200 freestyle relay for the first time that summer at the World Championships.

What Bruce came to understand about me is I don't quit. Once I decided to learn a new skill, I'd practice off on the side, usually during my warm-down laps, until I could do it. Which resonated with his prevailing coaching mantra, "Just do the damn work." Bruce totally got me. He knew my biggest internal motivator, deep down, was not Olympic gold or breaking world records. It was setting goals and going after them.

One goal Bruce focused in on was recalibrating my tempo. Tempo is measured by timing between when one hand enters the water to when that hand reenters the water after a rotation. Mine was 1.3 seconds. That's the tempo Bruce, and other technical advisors within USA Swimming who were collecting data, found to be my sweet spot. It was the tempo that I needed to lock into my stroke for the 400 and 800 free. For the 200 free, my tempo needed to be a little faster, just under 1.3 seconds. Dubbed "race pace," the target rate varied depending on the distance.

It helped me that Bruce wasn't the only Gemmell I trained with. Andrew was also on the team, and an exceptional puller. Trying to keep up with him was a huge motivator in improving and maintaining my tempo. I always kept an eye on him in his lane. Mentally, that was the most potent accelerant to my growth. Pushing myself to keep up with him.

Andrew and I both liked to get to the pool early. If practice started at 3:30, we'd be on the deck by 3:00. Bruce would generally come early as well, which meant we had time to sit around, stretch, and chat. More often than not, we'd talk about the upcoming workout, and Andrew would give Bruce a hard time about some set, or joke about Bruce's unrealistic expectations. Andrew and Bruce had a coach/swimmer relationship but also a dad/kid relationship that they were balancing or, at times, not balancing. There was a lot of bickering before practice. And during practice. And after practice.

I knew it was all in good fun. Their dynamic provided a welcome diversion to the monotony of training. It was like they were doing a comedy bit for the rest of us. I, for one, was delighted to be in the audience.

The biggest thing Bruce did was help me to think bigger. For Rio, we set lofty goals. Very specifically, the goals were to win the 200 free; to go 3:56 or faster in the 400 free; and to go 8:05 or faster in the 800 free. My world records at the time we set those goals in 2014 were 3:58 for the 400 free and 8:11 for the 800 free. We didn't even have to say the goal was to win a gold medal in those events, because I knew and Bruce knew that there was no way anyone else in the world was shooting for those insane times. I mean, these targets were *out there*. Bruce liked to call them "big fat hairy goals." We weren't approaching my swimming like "Let's shave off a teeny bit of time." It was full-out,

Back to the Future "Where we're going, we don't need roads," pie-in-the-sky stuff. The objective was to take me to the next level in the sport and see what I could do.

Back then my psychology was still at a place where I felt like I needed confirmation from my coaches that these outsize ambitions were possible. I don't think I necessarily came up with 3:56 or 8:05. I backed into it, asking Bruce, "What do you think? What time is feasible? What do you believe I can do in Rio?" Bruce volunteered the range of numbers. Of course, I certainly could have pushed back, offered alternative times. But I wanted to hear what he thought was *possible*.

When Bruce and I made our Rio plan, it shared echoes of the goal meeting I'd had with Yuri back in 2011, where I timidly admitted I wanted to make the Olympic team. I needed to hear Yuri say it first, just as I need to hear Bruce offer far-out times before I could really allow myself to commit to those objectives. I kind of relied on him to put those numbers out there. To crystalize our intentions. Again, knowing that he believed I could meet those times gave me the confidence and ability to rise to that level. Once he did, I was all in.

Let me back up and tell you about Beilke the pull buoy. The story begins in March 2011. I was swimming a Junior National meet in Orlando, my first at that level. I was fourteen years old and racing against eighteen-year-olds. Yuri was my coach at the time, and he'd brought a pull buoy that he'd retrieved from the lost and found at Georgetown Prep, where I trained at the time. Yuri told me to use the pull buoy to warm up.

The pull buoy had somebody's last name on it, "Beilke," written across the foam. I had no idea who that was. No matter. I used it as Yuri instructed. When you train with pull buoys, you hold them between your upper legs, near your thighs. You squeeze them so you can't kick. That hoists your legs a little higher in the water, so you can pull fast as you swim even without a kick. Distance swimmers really love pulling. It's a thing. Occasionally, I put a band around my ankles, which *really* prevents kicking. The most important part of this aside: after warming up with this random buoy, I unexpectedly won the mile at the meet.

After that Junior National victory, Beilke the pull buoy became a talisman for me. I took Beilke everywhere. Even to London. When Yuri left for California, I got custody of Beilke. In the fall of 2013, after I sat down with Bruce to set my Rio goals, I took a Sharpie and wrote on Beilke the numbers "565," to indicate 3:56 or faster in the 400 free, and 8:05 or faster in the 800 free. The "56" referred to the final seconds of the 400 free, and the second "5" referred to the final seconds of the 800 free. I was entirely focused on those final seconds in each race. I didn't have anything on there to signify the goal of winning the 200 free, but I had that in my head, too. Only Bruce and I knew what the figures meant. Every practice, I'd take out Beilke and stare at those numbers: 565. Every single day for at least two years, 565, 565, 565 . . .

I'm discreet about my goals. I don't share them publicly. Not prior to a competition. Not even with my teammates or my family. Is it superstitious? Possibly. A lot of Olympians share their goals in advance. I don't like to advertise my objectives, because then the media hypes them up and adds unnecessary pressure. Then, if you fall flat, well. That's disappointing. And sometimes if you put time goals out there, it can motivate competitors or be used as locker-room bulletin board material.

I learned discretion from that initial meeting I had with Yuri about making the Olympic team, where he told me, "Katie, you don't have to share this with anyone else." My "want times" when I was a kid were private, too. The more you're in the public eye, the safer it is to keep your goals to yourself.

Fast-forward to Rio, and I go 3:56 in the 400, I log 8:04 in the 800 free, and I win the 200 free. Exactly on the money. Of course, afterward I couldn't resist posing the question to myself: *What if I'd written 553 or something faster? Could I have gone 3:55 or 8:03?* Hitting those exact numbers cemented for me the power of goal setting and visualizing your aims every day. Keeping them top of mind. Or, in this case, top of my pull buoy. After my last race in Rio, Andrew texted me, "I had guessed on the meaning of Beilke—we have a lot of time to think sometimes! But knew you liked keeping that to yourself." Lol.

With all those years and hours in the water, Beilke eventually grew old and gross. He had to be retired. I got a new pull buoy, Beilke II, and I rewrote the numbers on it. That Christmas after Rio, when I came home for the holidays, I gave the OG Beilke to Bruce as a Christmas gift. He was touched. Only a true, down-to-the-bones swim coach could be touched by a cracked, mildewy pull buoy.

Over time, I got very good at rising to the level that Bruce required. Meeting his lofty expectations had the additive effect of instilling confidence in me before my races. Knowing that I had improved as much as I had in practices made each big meet feel less intimidating. I knew the training program was working. And because of that, I felt certain I could put up some great performances. Bruce used to say when I was swimming well, he could hear it. The long distances created a metronomic sound. Even in a noisy, crowded practice setting, he could isolate my cadence and know when I was swimming the way I should be and when I wasn't.

I broke my first world record at the 2013 World Championships. I broke more under tough outdoor weather conditions (rain and cold) at the 2014 Pan Pacific Championships in Australia. My training had improved too. Bruce and Jon Urbanchek studied Jon's color charts, filled with target practice times based on test-set swims and heart-rate zones, and observed that no female swimmer they had seen had ever hit the times I was hitting in training.

Sometimes Bruce grew weary of being questioned about my exceptionalism. He'd joke that I don't have webbed feet, that I'm not genetically advantaged. He told people I embraced the challenge. Not just the challenge during meets, but the challenge of the training grind. He'd tell folks I had the nerves of an assassin.

Bruce traveled with me for all the big international meets from 2013 through 2016 as part of the USA coaching staff. I was lucky in that regard, that my coach could be there to share those major moments with me. He also made a point of working in concert with my Stone Ridge high school coach, Bob Walker. Bruce felt it was important, even with all the noise around my swimming, that I continue to have a conventional high school experience. He insisted that I keep up my school swimming, explaining that it was beneficial to me to have the social time with my classmates and teammates.

These were big years in my life. I was coming off an Olympic gold medal. I was adjusting to life in the spotlight, not quite at the level it would become, but nonetheless learning what it was like to have that under my belt, a newfound sort of notoriety in the public but also in the swimming community.

Bruce handled that public relations component well, making sure that expectations were managed both within me and in the media. He did little meaningful things like making sure I didn't travel too much. He kept me focused on my training. He fostered my staying levelheaded and grounded enough to finish out my education like a normal kid, not to become isolated and singularly obsessed, as can happen with some young athletes when their career takes off. Bruce was all about maintaining balance—for both our sakes.

Bruce was shy about the spotlight. Even as a coach, he preferred to stay behind the scenes, helping others. The closer we got to Rio, the more we understood that level of limelight and media scrutiny was going to be a unique test for him. With London, I didn't get my Olympic Trials qualifying time until 2011, so Rio was my first full Olympic cycle where I was working toward it for four whole years. Coming out of London, I wanted to prove not just to other people but to myself that I wasn't a one-hit wonder. We both had something to prove.

At the 2016 Olympic Trials, we arrived in Omaha to find a huge multi-story photograph of me posted by USA Swimming on the large wall outside the center of the arena. In case we didn't already know, the stakes for Bruce and me were now billboard-high.

We needn't have worried. I nearly broke my own record in the 400 free. And I swept my other freestyle events. For the second straight Olympics, I (at age nineteen) became the youngest member of the U.S. swim team.

They say training is science, but coaching is art. Bruce trained me like no one else. But the art came in how he did it. We spent so many hours together, during such formative years for me. At some point I realized that he knew me better than I knew myself. Bruce possessed this sixth sense for my well-being. He could tell when I was about to get sick. He could tell when I was tired. He could tell when I was struggling with my self-esteem. He could deduce these things before I could admit them even in my own head, and that ability and the care he took with me bonded us.

Bruce made me stronger, faster, and more versatile. I dropped more than eight seconds from my 800 freestyle. I shed six seconds from my personal best in the 400 free. I lowered the world record five times in the 1500-meter free. I expanded my range, netting major gains in the 100 and 200 freestyle, races in which no one expected I would be competitive, given that I was seen as a distance swimmer.

Like Yuri, Bruce knew our aspirations were super-sized, but that wasn't the same as believing them to be far-fetched. He knew I could tick those boxes through diligent work and understanding the steps that led to excellence. He told me there was something different about me. Something that compelled me to be better every day. To outdo the competition, but really, to outdo myself.

When I go back home to Bethesda to see family or to spend the holidays there, I ask Bruce to train me for old times' sake. I love being able to swim for him again for a few days. To seek his guidance, about swimming, about life. He's always willing to listen. He never oversteps.

For the four-plus years that we worked together, prior to every race he said the same thing to me. Not a technical point or a strategy tidbit. No. Right before I walked to the ready room, he would grab my attention, look me in the eye, and say, "Have fun."

As dedicated as he is as a coach, he understands life is short. That in the blink of an eye, everything can change. So, while you're here, while you're healthy and happy and honing your craft, you may as well, even on the hardest day, have fun. With Bruce, I always did.

Chapter Ten

RIO

You really get to know your teammates at Olympic training camps. By the time you're there, the hard work is done. You're resting and tapering. And you have nowhere else to be, so you linger and you talk more. One hour turns into two or three. You eat three meals a day together. You swim, hang out, play games, and try to keep each other's minds off the upcoming competition.

Prior to the 2016 Rio Olympics, we had a week of training camp in San Antonio, Texas, then a second week in Atlanta, Georgia. Traditionally, the second week is international, held close to wherever we're competing, but that plan got ditched and or training was moved to Atlanta because of the threat of the mosquito-borne virus Zika, which was being reported in Brazil at the time.

Rio saw us preparing for an unorthodox schedule. The swimming prelims were going to commence at one p.m. and the finals at ten p.m. A traditional meet schedule is nine a.m. for prelims and six or seven p.m. for finals. The Rio timetable meant some of us could be racing at midnight. And then post-race, we'd have media, drug testing, medal ceremonies. We had to train with the knowledge that we might be getting back to the Olympic Village some nights as late as three a.m. and then need to squeeze in eight hours of sleep, so we focused on getting adjusted to that run of show. I remember progressively staying up later and later at camp, going to bed around two in the morning.

In 2012, USA Swimming made the "Call Me Maybe" lip-synch video during the training camps. (I still can't believe it got eighteen million views.) For 2016, we thought it would be fun to do our version of "Carpool Karaoke." The captains assigned us to cars, a mix of men and women. We filmed in Atlanta, and in my car was Anthony Ervin, who was over thirty-five years old and swimming in what was his last Olympics. He had made the team again after nine years away from the sport and was looking for his first medal since winning the 50 freestyle in 2000 (he'd win again in 2016). We also had David Plummer, a backstroker dad over thirty; Kelsi Worrell, who swam the 100 butterfly; and Molly Hannis, a breaststroker.

We recorded two versions of Queen's "Bohemian Rhapsody," a playful choice which gave everyone an opportunity to shine. I still didn't have my driver's license—I only had my permit—but at some point, everyone in the car convinced me to take the wheel. I was like, "Guys, I'm not comfortable driving four Olympians when I am not a seasoned driver!" To say I was stressed would be an understatement. This was a week before the Olympics. I didn't want to be responsible for crashing the car that carried America's gold-medal dreams. Ultimately, we decided that I would drive around a parking lot, a few feet, nothing major. And I still think I almost avoided a major collision. I couldn't get out of the driver's seat fast enough.

For the remainder of the song, we rode around Atlanta near our hotel, cameras set up in the front and the back of the car to film us belting out Queen's pop hit. We didn't have much time to practice, a conclusion any viewer can likely reach. But it was a lark, and when we released the video, fans of USA Swimming seemed to enjoy watching our team blow off a little pre-competition steam. Videos like "Call Me Maybe" and "Carpool Karaoke" made it clear we were appreciating the time we got to spend together. Especially me.

In the ramp-up to Rio, I remember feeling happy and solid about where I was at. I was adjusting well to the time change, getting ready for the late nights. It was kind of fun, honestly, staying up past nine p.m. instead of retiring to bed at my regular senior hour.

Another perk was that we had a deluxe team room at the Atlanta camp. Typically, a team room is the go-to place for athletes to spend time together. It's stocked with snacks—peanut butter, bread, yogurt, water bottles—whatever we need. They have massage therapists available. There are also games and puzzles to pass the time. Athletes will spend hours in the team room playing poker or Dutch Blitz. At the Atlanta training camp, the team room was an over-the-top, glitzy presidential suite. There was even a piano in there!

I'd played piano when I was growing up, so I was stoked to be able to bang out a few tunes. Our team manager rented a violin for Elizabeth Beisel, and the two of us played together while a bunch of our teammates sang along. Even the massage therapist chimed in. One of Team USA's coaches, Bob Bowman, is a virtuoso pianist. He and Elizabeth performed incredible classical pieces in that team room. And then breaststroker Lilly King had this lobster suit—I don't know why—that she would put on and dance around in while the music played.

The whole scene was warm and lighthearted and a contrast to the demands of Rio that we all knew were just around the corner. The vibes were, as the kids say, immaculate. And then, before I knew it, camp ended, and it was go time.

I remember walking into the Rio Olympic Village and having the thought: *Wow, I forgot how cool this was.* I love being immersed in that atmosphere, where I'm mingling with the international best of the best, living in these apartment-style dorms next to competitors from every other country, and eating in the mess hall with athletes who care as deeply as I do about their chosen sport. I even met a future Stanford classmate and friend, Albane Valenzuela, a member of the Swiss golf team. The unity and small-world aura of the Village has such potential as an example of how humans can come together. It may sound corny, but you really do feel hopeful and optimistic when you're hip to hip with the world, fostering these amazing relationships, and absorbing on a granular level that people are people, and we're all on this merry-go-round of life together.

We had some profound team meetings in the Rio Village. Two days before competition, our national team director at the time, Frank Busch, had us assemble in a circle, seventy of us, if you include all the coaches and staff members. In that giant loop on the ground floor of the Village lodging, we put our arms around each other and sang "America the Beautiful." We sang loud enough that the whole Village could hear. It gave me goose bumps.

Moments like that get you hyped up. I remember thinking: *Oh, we are raring to go. Let's get this thing started already!* It was that kind of energy.

In Rio, because I had so many events, Coach Bruce and I strategized that as soon as a race concluded, before I even got out of the water, I should begin contemplating the next one. I wouldn't have time to celebrate or rest on any laurels. All I had time do was execute exactly how I'd drilled for the past four years.

Psychologically, Rio was a massive improvement from London in that I had one Olympics under my belt. Additionally, between these two events, I'd been to two World Championships and broken a bunch of world records. I was still young, but I was far less green than I had been in my previous Games.

My first race was the 4x100 free relay. (A fun fact I love to pull out when I get put in the "distance swimmer" box. I'll just randomly be like, "Did you know I swam the 100 free at the Olympics?" Ahem.)

I actually swam the 100 free *twice* at the Olympics, in the prelims and the finals, and I managed to log a pretty fast split. I was in the top four in the U.S. in the 100 free the whole year before Rio. Then I swam the 100 free at Trials and earned seventh place. For the relays, they take the top six, which of course was no big disappointment. I was already on the team in the events that I'd trained for. But coming in seventh meant I was dangling out there as somebody the coaches could call up if they felt like I could throw down a time that was faster than what I did at Trials.

They put me on the prelim relay the first day because Dana Vollmer had the 100 butterfly, and the coaches were concerned about the turn-around time between her two events. They decided to use me instead, get the data of who put up the fastest splits, then take those swimmers to finals. I anchored the relay, swimming the fastest split of our team in the morning. Which locked me in for the finals.

When substitutions occur at the Olympics, feathers unavoidably get ruffled. Sometimes people know they didn't put up a good show-ing. That they shouldn't be included in the finals. Sometimes it's comparing two times that are almost identical, and then the coaches and statisticians review everyone's history in those events. When it's a really close call, they'll take other factors into consideration: Are you good as an anchor? Are you good at leading off? Things like that. I've witnessed people massively disheartened by substitutions that have been made. But it's part of the sport and part of being a team. We rec-ognize that the decisions are tough, but the decision-makers have to use the "hot hands," as they say. In other words, Team USA needs to use the people who are swimming the fastest on the day of the event to put us in the most competitive position overall.

Getting added to that race was slightly unanticipated, as I was already swimming the 200, 400, 800, and 4x200 relay. To be in the mix with the sprinters was amazing. Between London and Rio, I found more and more speed. I was focusing on things that other distance swimmers weren't focusing on, like my starts and turns. There's little room for error in the shorter events. By working on those details, I not only improved in the shorter events, but set myself apart in dis-tance too.

I've always prided myself on having range. It's not easy to train for the 100 and the 1500, or even the 100 and the 800. To be chosen for that relay, alongside Team USA's best sprinters, was an honor.

Short races are pure energy. For that Rio 4x100 relay, we were right next to Australia. I remember diving in, flipping at the 50, and coming off that wall thinking: *Whoa, this is a feeling I've never felt before.* The sensation of the waves, the level of speed going in and out of the turn. It's just more force. It sent a surge of adrenaline through my whole body. I swam a full second faster than my individual 100 free best time. In the end, we took silver, losing to Australia with a time of 3:31.89, a new national record for the U.S.

Participating in that race turned out to be an unexpected blessing in many ways. Kicking off with a team event where I had nothing to lose eased me into Rio. I also suspected that turning out a killer split would give me a lot of confidence going into my individual events. And that's exactly what happened.

By the time of my prelim 400 free the next day, I was fully relaxed. The nerves had been purged with the relay. I logged my fastest prelims ever up to that point, but it felt easy. I had a lot more in the tank for finals. Enough to make my 3:56. *All right,* I thought, *one goal* checked off.

I had the 200 free prelim the next morning and the semifinal in the evening. I was in a semifinal heat next to Sarah Sjöström of Sweden, who was more of a sprinter. She had come to the U.S. in January for one of the in-season meets, where we raced the 200 free. During that race, she had driven me to swim my best time to date.

The day of the 200 in Rio, I wrote in my journal: "Woke up really tired coming off 400 free the day before, felt horrible in warm-up. But I got through prelims with a 1:55 for top seed. Caught up to me at semis, heat included Sjöström and Federica Pellegrini. I went 1:54, but Sjöström out-touched me. She beat me on the last 50."

I reviewed the race video and saw that Sarah beat me on the third turn, when she got her feet over faster than I did. I never got into a good stroke after that. Losing to her in the semifinal race bummed me out and made me doubt whether I could win the next day. It was hard to fall asleep that night. Eventually, I convinced myself that I only needed to put up a good fight.

I recall when I got off the bus the day of my 200 free final, everybody in the team area was excited, chattering that "the basketball players are going to be here tonight!" That news flipped the switch in my head from nervous to: *It's meant to be.*

In London, the NBA players were in the audience when I won the 800 free. I took their return as a sign that this was going to be my night. I told myself: *If the basketball players are back again, I've got this, I can do this, I can win this gold.* As I later recorded in my diary, "The NBA players came to watch and cheer in the ready room. I felt confident and like a badass about to crush. I wasn't going to let anyone scare me. I know how to race."

I proved as much as soon as the 200 began. I found myself ahead of Sarah at the 50, then the 100. At that point, I knew I wasn't going to lose. Even as I felt her creeping up, going into the third turn—the very spot where I lost ground in the semifinal—I wasn't about to let that happen again. I was swimming blind for the final 50. I only breathed to one side, as Bruce mandated, and it was away from Sarah, so I couldn't see anything. I swam so hard I almost threw up.

If you watch the finals video, you can see there was a stretch where Sarah caught me, and we were dead even. At one point she was even slightly ahead. That's right when I felt like I was going to puke, halfway through that last lap. But then I dug deep. The last seven meters of that race, I put my head down and I didn't breathe for the final seven strokes of that race. Sarah breathed every two strokes right into the finish. And that did it. I got my hand on the wall first. I won by three tenths of a second.

In my journal that night I wrote, "I won, and it felt so satisfying/relieving." Touching the wall was something that I had practiced every day in training. Bruce made sure ending strong was something that I was devoted to—putting my head down into the finish. I'd rehearsed that kind of end to my swim, and it paid off when I needed it most.

As far as the part about being relieved, it was because I knew that 200 was going to be my toughest swim in Rio, my least comfortable race. I was swimming in tight competition. No room for error. It felt like an enormous exhale to have it done and dusted, to be heading into my favorite races, the 800 free relay and the individual 800 free.

That next night I had the 800 free relay with Allison Schmitt, Leah Smith, and Maya DiRado. It was the first time I got to be on a relay with Allison, which was special because she thought that would be her last swim ever (spoiler, it wasn't actually her last race, and we swam a relay together at the 2021 Olympics too!). She was super-pumped up going into that race. I anchored, and we were behind Australia going into my leg, but I always know who I'm going up against, and I knew that I had a few seconds on the standard times of the Australian swimmer. I caught her with more than 100 meters to go, and we won.

It was emotional seeing Schmitty hug her family afterward. They were front row for the medal ceremony. She was able to run up and embrace them, and everyone was weeping. It was also satisfying to see Maya bask in the win. She went to Stanford a few years ahead of me. I'd gotten to know her between London and Rio, and we'd become close friends. Rio was her one Olympics. She went in knowing that she was retiring. Being part of her first gold win meant the world to me.

My last race in Rio was the 800 free. The morning of the final I woke up with a brutal sore throat. I went to Sports Med to make sure I was okay. They checked me out, and I said, "I've got one event left, so I'm going to push through no matter what." I wasn't going to let a sore *anything* stop me from having an epic swim. What I realized later in the day was that my throat was sore not from any nascent illness but from screaming the night prior. My roommate in Rio, Simone Manuel, had won the 100 free. I was in the Village watching her alongside some of my teammates. It was an incredible race, and we were yelling our faces off.

For the 800, I warmed up in the competition pool. Normally, I warm up in the separate warm-up pool, but on this occasion, I wanted to savor the last event, soak it all in. As the Olympics progressed, I'd grown more and more comfortable in Rio. I kind of felt, not in a cocky way, like I owned the pool. I remember walking out of the ready room to the starting deck for the 800 final, bursting with confidence that I was going to hit my goal time, that 8:05 or faster. I just knew in my gut that it was going to happen. The Beilke pull-buoy prophecy would come true.

The buzzer sounded. I dove in and felt smooth and controlled. Quickly, I found myself far ahead of everyone. I can tell early on in a swim when I'm having a good one, based on how I'm riding in the water. If I can control my breathing to the halfway point of a mile or an 800, I'm going to have a killer swim.

The pain generally kicks in somewhere on that back half. The pain can be anything. My arms or legs giving out. Depletion. Cramps. Muscle spasms. Lungs scorched. The overall sense that I'm stuffed with glue. Mercifully, by that point, there's not too much of the race left. I'm able to gut it out. In Rio, I kept up my stroke and pushed through the hurt without changing much. When I touched the wall in 8:04, my heart flooded with happiness. I'd done it. I'd hit every single one of my goals.

I had to rush to the medal ceremony, where I wept on the podium after spotting my family right under the American flag. I was crying in gratitude. Every race had gone well. From one swim to the next, the domino pieces Bruce and I laid out had fallen right into place. I was the most decorated woman athlete in Rio, netting four golds and one silver, and the second most decorated Olympian at the 2016 Games behind my friend and teammate Michael Phelps, who took home five golds. I was also the first swimmer to win the 200, 400, and 800 free at the same Olympics since Debbie Meyer had in 1968.

There was a boatload of media waiting for me post-ceremony in the pool press area. Some reporters asked about Bruce, and I started crying again. It dawned on me that this was the end of my chapter with him.

The tears only fell more freely as the evening wore on. I was heading off to college in a month. We'd had an incredible stretch from 2012 to 2016: an undefeated record in individual international finals, world records in three distances, the 2015 "Ledecky Slam," and now Rio.

Walking out of the press conference, I saw Bruce being interviewed off to the side. He was teary-eyed too. I rushed over and gave him a big hug. He told me he was so happy and proud of me. We pulled ourselves together, then I went and did a sit-down with Bob Costas. I barely remember any of it. I only remember how I felt. Satisfied and content and deeply sad that Bruce wouldn't be my coach anymore.

It was two in the morning when I got back to my room in the Village. I was on my phone getting caught up on well wishes, responding to text messages. I had to wake up early for an appearance on the *Today* show, but I was so wired and emotional, I was like, *Who needs sleep?* I crashed for a total of ninety minutes. I woke up and did interviews all day before getting to sit in the stands and cheer for my teammates on the final day of competition.

The next month, every member of the U.S. Olympic team was invited to the White House for an address from the Obamas. It was September 29, 2016. The president gave me another special shout-out, which is as cool as it gets. After a funny and heartfelt introduction, he said, in part: "The story of this year's Team USA is all about firsts. Our Olympians came in first so many times, more than anybody else. It wasn't even close: forty-six golds. Not to brag, but *forty-six golds*. You made the U.S. the first country in forty years to top the medal chart in every category. And it was a feat built one unprecedented accomplishment at a time." He went on to name-check a list of brilliant women athletes: Simone Biles, Michelle Carter, Simone Manuel, Claressa Shields, Kristin Armstrong, Kim Rhode, Allyson Felix. Then he got to me.

"And then there's this young woman named Katie Ledecky. Katie's back there somewhere—there she is. I was nervous that she was going to ask me to, like, hold all her medals while I was speaking or something because—[*laughter*]. So she obliterates her own records in the 400 and the 800 freestyle, lapped the field in the 800—you all see it on TV? Like there's nobody else in the pool? Crazy."

He ended that part of the speech talking about how 2016 belonged to America's women Olympians. Team USA's women won more golds than most countries, sixty-one medals, the most ever by any women's team. There had been outstanding performances from women's teams as varied as gymnastics, basketball, track and field, water polo, and, of course, swimming.

You don't know where you will end up when you're swimming laps in the pool at four a.m. Pushing yourself to the brink when no one else can see it. Sitting there hearing how proud we'd made the president and first lady, hearing him marvel at my individual achievements, was a moment I will never forget.

Chapter Eleven

GRANDMA HAGAN

I was named after my grandma Kathleen Hagan. Though I've always gone by Katie, Grandma Hagan calls me Katie Gen in a soft midwestern way that makes me feel like I'm hers alone.

Grandma Hagan is ninety-eight years old. She was born Kathleen O'Connor in rural Sioux Pass, Montana, and grew up as part of a big family, with five siblings and even more cousins. A total of seventeen kids raised together like brothers and sisters. Enough children that they hired a teacher and created their own elementary school, which Grandma cleaned on Saturdays as part of her weekly chores.

Grandma Hagan came from tough stock. Her father and three O'Connor uncles ran a sprawling, active cattle ranch. Life on the ranch was no picnic, but complaining was as useful as a broom without a handle. She learned early to work hard, serve the greater good, and keep on the sunny side of life. In 1946 my grandma left the ranch to attend the College of St. Catherine in St. Paul, Minnesota, along with a couple of her cousins. At the time, nursing and teaching were the only careers available to women, and my grandma always said the last thing she wanted to do was be a teacher, so nursing it was.

After graduation, she moved to Philadelphia and went into public health. When one of her relatives back home fell ill, she returned to take a job as a floor nurse at Mercy Hospital in Williston, North Dakota, which was about forty-five minutes from her Montana home. It was there that she met my grandpa.

Grandpa was a doctor and had recently returned from serving in the war. The two met cute over the medical chart desk. Grandpa Hagan asked where she lived, and my grandma described the ranch. Grandpa said he was a fan of horses. Grandma suggested he come out to visit her family. That visit changed everything. Not long after, my grandma scrapped her plan to return to Philadelphia. A year later, the couple married on June 29, 1949, at St. Anthony's Catholic Church in Culbertson, Montana. Grandma Hagan was twenty-three years old.

My grandparents would end up raising seven kids of their own. Grandma Hagan retired from health care to manage the growing family, but she still acted as a de facto nurse when medical calls came to the house. She and my grandpa made a great pair professionally and romantically. Their marriage was one of mutual respect, and it was obvious to me even as a child that they cherished their life together. They especially loved sharing it with family. Christmas was an *event*.

When I was growing up, they lived on a farm in Williston a few miles outside of town. My grandma would decorate the house top to bottom. I remember how cold it was outside—there would be several feet of snow on the ground—but the house nevertheless felt so warm.

The basement had six or seven beds, enough for me, my brother, all our cousins. We'd set up camp down there and have the best time goofing around. When we visited, Grandma made sure the house was cozy, food was prepared, and the cookie jar was full to the brim. She was an incredible cook and an exceptional baker. She has a huge collection of recipes, many of which I make now. Her sugar cookie recipe is legendary. She calls them "Deedles." She also makes a mean gingersnap. When anyone tells me cookies aren't healthy, I say, "Well, my grandma's ninety-eight, and she eats one or two of these cookies every day, so I think it's fine." And, of course, there's her homemade chicken noodle soup. It makes the whole house smell delicious. Because there wasn't an airport in Williston when I was a kid, when we went to Grandma's, we had to fly into Minot and then drive another two hours to town. The whole car ride, I would obsess about that chicken soup.

Grandma made it a point to make every visit to Williston special. She liked to take me to this convenience store in Stanley, North Dakota, halfway between Minot and Williston, where you could get a milkshake called a Whirl-A-Whip. One of the photographs I cherish most is from when I was around ten. I'm standing with my brother and my grandma, and I have my Whirl-A-Whip in my hand. I'm grinning wide, and my grandma is looking at my face, also smiling. There's just something about the photo that captures our relationship perfectly.

She and my grandpa always had at least one dog, often more. There was an Airedale named Digger. Heidi the Rottweiler. The last three years of my grandpa's life, they had a cockapoo named Danny Boy. Danny Boy was wild. He'd race circles around the house, and my grandma would delight in his antics. Her most recent dog was Barney, a King Charles spaniel. Barney was, let's call it, *chunky*. Barney would eat Danny Boy's food. My grandma would also feed Barney under the table. We'd tell her to stop, but that was a nonstarter. Her generosity and kindness toward her dogs mirrored her generosity and kindness toward everyone.

Grandma Hagan was a role model for me. She had this immensely upbeat attitude and perspective on life, despite the sacrifices she made raising her family. When she was more mobile, we'd attend Mass together. I remember watching her dote on her church friends at breakfast after Mass. How much camaraderie they shared. My grandma doesn't leave her house as frequently now. She hasn't really been able to return to Mass in person. But those church friends come out to the farm and visit. And they laugh together like old times.

I make sure that we FaceTime often. When we do, Grandma never fails to inquire about my swimming. "When is your next swim meet? Is that one going to be on TV? Make sure you send us the schedule so that we can watch. I need someone to come turn the TV on and get it all set up." Sometimes she asks, "Now, who's your competition? Are you going to have any competition?" And yeah, naturally, I have tough competition. But I tell her, "Don't worry, I've got it, Grandma." And she'll smile and answer, "Of course you do."

I've been lucky to have my grandmother be a part of my swimming since I was a child. The memories of my swims intertwine with her support, like vines encircling a trellis. When I was younger, we would call after races to tell her and my grandpa what place I got. When she came to my Olympic Trials in 2012, she couldn't get over how far I'd come in the sport. In some ways, it was more mind-blowing for her than for me. She had such a fun time in 2012 that she insisted on returning for the 2016 Trials, even though she was already in her nineties. There would be no stopping her.

My grandma gets a kick out of articles written about me, that I'm on television talk shows or joking with late-night hosts. She's buoyed when people call her and ask about my swimming. She prints copies of any press and has my aunt Peg send them to people she knows. When I'm in Williston, she shows me off like a bouquet of flowers. It comes from a place of pride. That unique bond between a grandmother and granddaughter. I'm her namesake, after all.

In 2021, Grandma was glued to the TV during the Tokyo Olympics. My cousins, aunts, and uncles all congregated with her at one of my aunt's houses for a watch party. The photos of them clustered on couches, cheering me on, make me tear up. I'm delighted by my swimming record, but what makes me even happier is how my career has been able to bring my family together in moments like that.

In 2014, when the new pool named after Grandpa Hagan opened at the rec center in Williston, I traveled to North Dakota to swim the first lap. That was a particularly special moment with my grandma. I did interviews where I got to talk about how unique and influential my grandpa was in the community. I also did a mini press conference with my grandma by my side. She was dressed up in a dotted button-down shirt and blazer, a stick pin piercing her lapel. Unsurprisingly, Grandma Hagan handled the media questions like a pro. She was effortlessly charming, as always. In an interview with a sports radio station after the Rio Olympics, she joked with the hosts that she just wanted "to live long enough to see [me] do it all."

It's kind of always freezing in North Dakota during the winter. There's ice and wind and snow. Because of that, my grandma spends most hours indoors these days. We don't want to risk her falling, getting injured on the farm. She's strong as an ox, but I know I have limited time left with her. When I get to visit her, I do everything in my power to make the most of our days together. We hang out at her farm, sit and talk. I ask about her childhood. We catch up on my swimming. We cook delicious meals. We take naps.

Getting my grandma—this formidable, never-resting force of a woman—to consent to a nap was a struggle in the beginning. Even in her late nineties, she feels like she must entertain anyone who's visiting. She takes her role of matriarch to heart. The doctor says she needs to relax to stay well, so I go to her bedroom and encourage her to join me. I nap when I'm training, so it's very easy for me to say, "Hey, Grandma, I'm going to lie down for a bit. Come with me." After a bit of cajoling, she'll relent, follow me to her room, climb into bed, and snuggle up next to me. Still, the Hagan family mulishness remains strong. When she wakes, Grandma always insists she only slept five or ten minutes (not the actual hour). That she was only "resting her eyes."

Other than the perpetual nap resistance, my grandma seldom grouses. She claims that she never gets sick, and honestly, she rarely does. Even when she feels terrible, she doesn't bellyache or whine. She goes about her life. No matter what happens, she finds a way to ride it out without self-pity. She's the center of the family, the linchpin who holds everyone together. For me, probably for all of us, Grandma Hagan has always been our soft place to land.

She has no doubt forgone a ton. Being a woman in the eras she lived through wasn't always easy: raising seven children, giving up a nursing career to tend the family, and living in a small town. Yet she carved out a purposeful life. Grandma Hagan made the decision to mean as much as she could to those in her family and community. It's amazing how much impact that can make.

I remember noticing when I was younger how genuinely thoughtful she was to people. When we'd eat at a neighbor's house, she'd compliment the meal. Declare that it was the greatest meal she'd ever had. If a woman at church wore a new sweater, she'd notice and commend her taste. Every time I swam, she gushed about my abilities to me and anyone who would listen. Grandma Hagan made it a point to lift others up. She did this from a place of authentic esteem. She found reasons to appreciate even those who may not have warranted her admiration. When I think about what she's taught me about life, that example ranks as one of the most indispensable.

Simply put, my grandma showed me how to love the beauty of each day. To be thankful for the people who cross your path. To distinguish and amplify the good.

For many, living on a farm in North Dakota may seem difficult. But my grandma adores her surroundings. She loves her home. She loves the animals she's around, whether that's the dogs or the horses or the birds that frequent the feeder she's set up outside her window. She still takes joy in observing the deer that roam in her front yard, the pheasants that peck at the grass. She gazes outside upon the same land she's seen for seventy-five years and finds renewed wonder every day. It may appear simple and small, but I'd be lucky to live half the life that she's lived.

Chapter Twelve

STANFORD AND GREG

A t Stanford, a lot of us had nicknames. I was Dex. We had two Katies on our swim team, so Dex made sense, though my coach spelled it D-E-C-K-S, like a pool deck. No one else did. I was fine either way. I can always tell when someone from Stanford is around because they break out the "Dex!" Hearing it, I'm plopped right back in college—which feels like it was a thousand years ago, even though it's been less than a decade.

Stanford was always at the top of my list of preferred schools. I went through the recruiting process for swimming with a handful of other universities, but Stanford was the only place I seriously considered, and Greg Meehan was the only coach I spoke with. Greg immediately impressed me as a confident and determined coach. He had been named the head women's swimming coach at Stanford in late summer 2012, after previous coaching stints at the University of Pacific, Princeton, UCLA, and Cal. I started receiving communications from him the fall of my junior year in high school. We exchanged several emails and phone calls and had an instant rapport. Greg invited me for an unofficial visit to the college in April. I went, got an early application, and committed by May 2014, enrolling at Stanford in 2017.

As you can tell by my enthusiasm, when it came to Stanford, I did not play hard to get. This was in large part because, for as long as I could remember, I'd been hearing about the wonders of the school and swim coaches from my USA teammates. Maya DiRado was a senior when I met her in the summer of 2013. She was on the World Championship team and couldn't say enough about how much she loved Stanford. She spoke so highly of Greg and the coaching staff. Lia Neal, whom I roomed with during our training camp before London when we were the two young guns on the team, ultimately chose Stanford too. Add my club teammate Janet Hu, whom I had been friends with since I was seven years old. When Janet and I were rooming together at Junior Nationals in 2011, she was about to go through the selection process. She confided on that trip that she wanted to go to Stanford, and she committed as early as she could. And, of course, my friend and national team roommate Simone Manuel attended Stanford as well. When you see all your swimming peers gravitating toward the same location like sharks to a bait ball, you give it a serious look.

Stanford is an undeniably stellar school. But beyond that, boy, is it a great place to swim. The facilities are glorious. The pools—it's just kind of like swimming nirvana. They have two 50-meter pools and a 25-yard pool where the swim meets are held. There's even a diving well. Basically, a real abundance of water on campus. Paradise for me.

I entered Stanford without a major. I had some ideas. I took AP psychology in high school my senior year and was intrigued. My dad had majored in psychology at Harvard, and he ended up going to Yale Law School. I was curious about both fields and knew that with psychology, I could explore many different routes in the future. Plus, I found psychology fascinating. I like any subject that explains interactions with people or prompts you to think about your life in a novel way. We think we know why we do what we do, why we act the way we act. Any good Psych 101 lecture will disabuse you of those notions in ten minutes flat.

I decided to major in psychology with a minor in political science. I supplemented with a wide range of classes in human biology, communications, computer science, and art history. I hopped around the course list like a bullfrog. I wanted to soak up all the knowledge I could in as many fields as were open to me.

Once enmeshed on campus, I got to know my professors and classmates on a deep level. I hadn't realized when I'd enrolled that I would form those types of bonds. I was excited about the relationships that I knew I would build with my swim teammates and coaches, but the friendships I made beyond swimming took me by surprise. I think I thought that being part of a swim team would narrow my friend group, or I would constantly be doing everything with the team. When I was able to broaden my social sphere and click with other professors and students alike, I felt like I was living my best collegiate life.

In short order, I was bicycling across campus, leaves crunching beneath my wheels, backpack jostling on my shoulders, a poster child for the admissions office. As in high school, I enjoyed being around ambitious classmates. I remember there was one guy who was emailing a professor about research that he'd done on cancer replication. I was like: *This dude sitting next to me is basically trying to cure cancer.* Another student across from me spoke five different languages. And so on. Everyone was striving for greatness at Stanford in whatever their chosen field. And everyone had something extraordinary going on in their life, whether that was academically, athletically, socially, or all of the above.

I respond well to pressure. But Stanford didn't feel so much like pressure as it did opportunity. Being there a chance to expand my horizons around an electrifying student body. Living in the churn of all that ambition created this environment that made you want to be the very best version of yourself. It was almost like being in the Olympic Village every day.

One struggle I had was being that far from home. I missed my family. I missed the hustle and bustle of D.C. I even missed the traffic. But, like every college freshman, I learned to be independent. How to take care of myself. I had to look after my own nutrition, do my own laundry, and no longer had parent-chauffeurs to get me to practice.

While at Stanford, I trained in the water about ten times a week. On top of that, I'd do dryland and weight training. My schedule was morning practice from about six-fifteen to eight a.m., then breakfast and go to class around nine-thirty. Dryland training in the afternoon, then another two hours or so in the water. I'd usually try to sneak in a nap during the day. But I also had to get my homework done. I'd often be in bed by nine p.m. Party time it was not.

What I believed, and still think, is that college is for unearthing what you're passionate about so you have a path to follow post-graduation. I planned to connect my Stanford degree with my swimming in some way and use both skill sets to do good in the world. In my theory of the case, the better a swimmer I became, the bigger the impact I could make over a period of time and, hopefully, throughout my life. So, naturally, I would never do anything to throw a wrench into the works of that life plan. Keg parties and all-night raves would have to wait.

I entered Stanford at my peak level of media attention. I was transitioning into a public figure. I was familiar to most, if not known to everyone. Because of that, I carried an added burden of never wanting to let my teammates down.

During my freshman season, I set twelve NCAA records and nine American records. Stanford won its first national team title since 1998. The next year I set three more NCAA records, two additional American records, and was part of the Cardinal winning a second crown. At the end of my sophomore year, I was recognized with the Al Masters Award, given to Stanford's top student athlete, and named CoSIDA Academic All-America Team Member of the Year.

At the 2017 World Championships in Budapest, coming off my freshman year, I won five gold medals (three individual and two relay) and one individual silver medal. Despite that, my meet was termed a "let-down" and "disappointment" by a reporter at the Associated Press (presumably because I didn't win every race or set a world record). Naturally, I didn't view it that way, but it was enlightening to see how far the bar had moved in terms of what the swim world expected from my performance. I did what I could to keep that kind of external judgment at bay. To stop myself from thinking that I could or should be doing more. Thankfully, my awesome Stanford suitemates helped keep me levelheaded.

At Stanford, they don't tell you who your freshman roommates are until move-in day. I strolled into my dorm room to encounter three students I'd never met before. I was fresh from the Olympics, but I saw right away that my freshman roomies didn't know much about swimming. My roommate Tessa was told a rumor on a pre-orientation trip that I was in the same dorm. "Maybe you'll get to be roomies with Katie Ledecky!" this person speculated. To which Tessa responded, "Who's that?" Awesome. Tessa told that story on day one, and we shared a laugh.

It was a relief to live with people who didn't think of me solely as "Katie the swimmer." It meant we got to know each other as roommates and classmates first, eager young people entering an exhilarating stage of life at the same time. My Stanford roommates were also homebodies, like me. We liked being in our dorm room together, hanging out. None of us were big partiers. The RA for our hall lived right across from us. That kept things real quiet on our floor.

Being treated like any other student fostered my growth as a person. It was a handy reminder that, as central as it was to me, swimming didn't need to be *everything*. Being seen through my roommates' eyes as a peer kept me down-to-earth, which, ironically, helped make me a better swimmer.

My initial quarter at Stanford I could apply to a series of small introductory freshman seminars, with a class size of just twelve to fifteen students. The one I chose was a psychology class called "How Beliefs Create Reality," taught by Alia Crum, the principal investigator of the Stanford Mind and Body Lab. I wrote in my application about the goals

I'd set for myself in Rio three years ago, explaining, "I've seen firsthand how beliefs create reality because they did for me." Needless to say, I brought a significant amount of energy to that seminar, perhaps an unusual amount for a freshman in a nine a.m. class.

Professor Crum was a former athlete, having played hockey at Harvard. She'd done fascinating research on the placebo effect. Her Ph.D. study focused on hotel maids. She told one group of maids that the work they were doing daily, like changing the sheets, vacuuming, and dusting, is equivalent to exercise and good for them. She then compared that group to a control group of maids to whom she said nothing. Through blood tests and other measurements, Professor Crum discovered that the maids who were told that their work was good for them saw appreciable health improvements.

In our class, we examined my case and my swim times. We discussed whether faster goal times set by me would have led to even quicker results. I'd nailed my goals right on the money in 2016. What if I had set my goals one second faster? Could I have achieved those? The class knocked the theory around. I mean, the goals that I had set for myself were already so high, it was hard to know. Monday-morning quarterbacking is rarely useful. And yet, obviously, there was some power to me setting these goals for myself, because they came true almost exactly.

Professor Crum ended up becoming my major advisor. I decided to focus on social psychology, but I also registered for a couple of neuroscience classes where I learned more about the anatomy of the brain. I took additional classes in linguistics and cognitive development. Halfway through my junior year, I went on hiatus to prep for the Tokyo Olympic Year. For nine months, I worked with Professor Crum's research team in order to stay mentally engaged. Then the pandemic hit, the Olympics got postponed, school went virtual, and I was stuck in my apartment, doing weight training in my living room and swimming in a backyard pool.

When all that expectation abruptly halted because of the pandemic, I was devastated. I finished my degree virtually. I never walked in my graduation ceremonies. There's typically a dinner for the senior class that's held on the quad, which is a really meaningful tradition at Stanford. That was a no-go. I never got to celebrate with my family in the traditional sense. I got my diploma in the mail. Yet the people at Stanford and in the local community really looked out for me. We rallied the best we could.

Mercifully, it feels so long ago to me now. My memories of Stanford center less on Covid and more on the little things. Like how Coach Greg put together Pandora playlists for practices. The songs ranged from seventies music to pop to whatever he was vibing with that day. Wednesday mornings were *always* country. Frequently, Greg would turn the decision over to one of us, and we would revisit the music of our adolescence as we swam lap after lap.

On the Stanford swimming team, women are part of a separate program. There were around twenty-five of us. The dynamic fostered by Greg was 1) to have a lot of fun, and 2) to work as hard as hammers. Greg had assembled an elite group, and he and Associate Coach Tracy Slusser always brought out the best in us. Greg and Tracy were extremely well-organized and had detailed plans for each swimmer and the team as a whole. After we won our second NCAA championship, I spoke with the press and told them about my mom being one of the first women to benefit from Title IX. I talked about how grateful I was for the opportunity to compete, and how women had the power to push the boundaries of the sport even further. I knew the value of having the right to swim in college. I'd met swimmers and Olympians who'd competed in the 1960s and had to retire at age fifteen because there was no college swimming for girls. Those facts were never far from my mind while I was at Stanford.

On my twenty-first birthday, I won the 1650-yard freestyle at the 2018 NCAA championships. Not long after, I announced my decision

129

to go pro. I rented a condo in Menlo Park; selected an agent, Dan Levy; and, after the NCAA swimming season wrapped, waived the remaining two years of my collegiate eligibility and signed a swimwear deal with TYR Sport.

Coach Greg understood completely. I'd had two incredible years winning two consecutive national titles with my teammates. In fact, Greg was the person who recommended I turn professional when I did, so I could have the time before 2020 to focus on putting all the pieces in place for Tokyo. Two months into my professional career and in my very first race as a pro, I broke my own 1500 free world record by five seconds at a meet in Indianapolis. I hadn't even rested or shaved for the meet, so Greg and I were ecstatic about how my training was progressing in this new phase of my career.

Greg was also the person who supported me through the pandemic when Tokyo got pushed and everybody's dreams began circling the drain. Like my freshman suitemates, Greg helped me keep my eyes on the prize. It's one of the many reasons I still feel so tightly connected to him and the Stanford team.

I recently returned to campus for alumni weekend. I practiced a couple of times with the current swim team. Then I attended the alumni meet, which is all in good fun, stacked with silly relays, 25 and 50 frees, for the team and any alums who are in town for the reunion and want to get their feet wet. The meet attracted a wide range of ages and abilities. Summer Sanders, class of '94, was there. As were a bunch of my college teammates and a handful of older alums.

During the meet, all us swimmers chatted between events, using the opportunity to catch up on where we were and what we were up to. It felt natural to be back in the Stanford pool, bobbing around with old pals. I saw women from different graduation years mixing on the pool deck, brought together by the passion they had in common. I felt grateful for this lineage that I'd been able to be a part of, and I knew every woman in that room was rooting for my continued success.

As fate would have it, the competition took place right after an 8,000-yard practice I'd just completed. I wasn't pushing myself to do anything spectacular at the meet, that's for sure. But winning wasn't the point anyway. (The men's team always takes the meet more seriously. Make of that what you will.)

Instead, as I swam, I remembered all the good times I'd had in that pool with my teammates and coached by Greg. How, when I was on the Stanford team, I'd participated in the alumni meet. I was younger then. Naive about so much to come. Not quite an adult. But making my way. And in what feels like a blink of an eye, here I was, back swimming in familiar waters. Only now I was on the other side.

Chapter Thirteen

RULES

I 've always been extra-vigilant when it comes to following the rules. Are you surprised? I'm just that girl. I believe in holding myself accountable and staying within mandated restrictions. A wild child or boundary pusher I am not.

Swimming is all about rules. You have to start at a certain time, swim in a certain way, and, quite literally, stay within the lines. This applies to moral and ethical lines as well. Athletes are not allowed to take any type of drugs that would enhance performance. You're meant to swim on your own merits. To see what can happen between you and the water. The awe of seeing what you can do through practice and hard work is so profound—it's the best feeling in the world. Which is why I find it so surprising that some swimmers, and some athletes in general, rob themselves of this feeling by using performance-enhancing drugs.

One of my favorite swimming mantras is "no shortcuts." The "no shortcuts" part happens every day. All the hours of challenging work, alone in the pool, pushing myself. Those times I want to quit early or take a day off or give less than 100 percent, I tell myself, *No shortcuts,* and I press on, knowing the end goal won't happen without the incremental gains only I can control. Basically, I refuse to cheat myself.

I recognize I can do things in training that other people can't. I can go longer distances than most people. I have an engine that rarely conks out. Training with the guys is part of what pushes me. As I told a reporter at a meet a few months before the Rio Olympics when I was questioned about racing against men, "I'm not afraid to beat them." Which doesn't mean I can beat them, necessarily. More that my psychological game doesn't limit what my physical game can accomplish. The mind-body connection is essential to breaking through self-imposed barriers. I find that if you dream it, very often you can, in fact, do it.

I experienced this phenomenon in a major way after London, when I started getting into harder training. A lot of my newfound physical prowess was mental. I had Andrew Gemmell (Coach Bruce's son) swimming in the lane next to me. As I was grinding away to keep up with him, I would ask myself, *Why not?*

Why not? became another mantra circling my brain.

Keeping pace with the male swimmers? Why not? Shaving time off my records? Why not? Doing something significant every time I swim? Why not?

I knew if I visualized those goals, if I created an expectation for myself that I would improve, the odds of my doing so rose considerably. I applied this mentality whether the swim was a practice, a stop on the domestic Pro Swim Series tour, or a World Championship. I trusted that every time I stepped onto the blocks, there was zero reason why I couldn't make magic happen. Of course, you can't break a record every swim. But having the mindset that you can do something memorable will produce results—if you've done the work. And I always do the work.

I believe this tweak in my attitude, along with the acceleration of my training, is part of what led to the "Ledecky Slam" at the 2015 World Championships. When you are ramping up for an Olympics, there are usually signs along the way of what's to come. Some milestones are expected, trained for. Others take you completely by surprise.

For example, in June 2014, Coach Bruce took twenty of us swimmers to the Olympic Training Center in Colorado Springs to practice eighteen days at altitude. The idea behind this block of workouts was to prepare us for events later in the summer, like the United States National

Championship and the Pan Pacific Championship, which that year was in Australia. On the way home from Colorado, Bruce had us stop for a low-key meet outside Houston, in Shenandoah, Texas, at the Conroe ISD Natatorium.

Largely for high schoolers, the annual meet is hosted by the Woodlands Swim Team. Most of our peers (world-class American swimmers) were in California that weekend at a top-tier Grand Prix meet. But Bruce had us go to Texas, explaining it was an easy flight from Colorado Springs.

The event that year drew teams from all over the country. California, Colorado, Louisiana, Michigan, Oklahoma, Texas, Washington, Wisconsin, the District of Columbia. As I was only seventeen at the time, headed into my senior year, the environment felt entirely normal to me. I'd be swimming against other high schoolers instead of at a high-stakes international meet. I liked that the setup was relaxed and positive. All the swimmers were rooting for each other on the deck. There was zero pressure in Shenandoah, Texas, that weekend.

In my warm-ups for the mile, my split times were uneven. I figured I was recovering from the high-altitude training we'd just finished. I didn't let it bother me. Then the race started, and I thought: *Why not?*

As I entered the water, something about my swim felt organic. I found myself in a flow state and cruised along, carefree. After 400 meters, someone sidled up to Bruce and asked what the world record was. I had set it the year before, at the World Championships in Barcelona. Bruce shrugged off the question. This meet wasn't meant to be about setting records. It was a quick dip on the way home to work the kinks out.

But my mind and body had other ideas. *Why not?*

Thirty laps later, I'd broken my own world record, touching in a full 2.3 seconds better than my swim eleven months before in Barcelona.

To ratify a world record, a swimmer must be drug-tested within twenty-four hours. Needless to say, there were no United States Anti-Doping Agency (USADA) officials at the Woodlands. No one was expecting a gaggle of high schoolers or a club team coming down from altitude to be shattering world records and requiring urgent confirmation that the race was clean. USA Swimming sent my dad a text message. They'd be sending the USADA reps to my hotel to test me as soon as they could.

Three days later, I was back in the Conroe pool for the finals of the 800 free. I felt as loose as I had for the mile. Firing on all cylinders, smooth as butter. This time I touched in almost three seconds ahead of my record from Barcelona. I swam the final 400 meters three tenths of a second faster than the first 400, a thing that almost never happens.

During the back half of the race, I could hear the crowd roaring, so I knew I was at least close to the record. Also, I could see Bruce waving his arms. He only does that when he is excited. Immediately after the race ended, Bruce leaped into action. He fired off a text message to USA Swimming: "Send USADA again."

The point—beyond the fact that world records can be set in the humblest of environments (and that you should never underestimate the motivational power of a pack of cheering high schoolers)—is that American swimmers are tested constantly and consistently. Even in small-town Texas. The results are a matter of public record. Anyone can look up how many times I've been tested by USADA annually and see what the findings were. (I wish other countries and international testing agencies would similarly publish their data and results.)

The international swimming federation, aka World Aquatics, also tests us. I'm probably tested two times a month. I've been tested for more than twelve years, about twenty-five times a year. Just within the U.S. Anti-Doping Agency, I've been tested over 150 times. All to say, I've been tested *a lot*.

To comply, I provide my daily schedule to USADA so I can be found at any time for spur-of-the-moment samplings of both blood and urine. If I'm going to get groceries or run errands, I go to the app and let them know. That's something a lot of people don't realize, but

I'm happy to do it. I probably update more than I have to, but I want the agency to know where I am if they need to find me.

During 2020, there was a period when there wasn't consistent testing worldwide. Doping monitoring was being restricted by Covid, and getting staff to administer the tests was reported to be a health risk. The anti-doping agencies of certain countries ceased monitoring altogether, while a lot of countries apparently pulled back on frequency. I was part of a group of maybe fifteen to twenty American athletes who did a virtual testing program during the pandemic. I didn't want there to be any doubt in anyone's mind that I was staying compliant.

For the virtual tests, I would get a phone call that said, "Okay, we're going to do a test tonight." They sent me boxes of the kits to use, and I would do a Zoom call with the drug tester. We would basically go through the same process as in person. They wouldn't watch me pee, like we'd normally do, but I'd show them my bathroom over Zoom, prove there was nothing in there that could alter the sample. Then I'd box it up and mail it off. I even did the blood tests on my own. There's a technology where you put a device on your arm, and it draws a bit of blood.

For the entire pandemic, I was able to give urine and blood at random times so I could keep my record open and clear. I have no idea what other countries were doing during that time, or if certain countries took advantage of the period when there wasn't testing. And honestly, they could be seeing the benefits of that today. Which is maddening to consider but out of my hands. All I can do is guarantee that my rigor around transparency and testing is next-level.

I entered eligibility for drug testing when I was fourteen. After I cracked the top twenty world ranking, it made sense for me to be tested regularly. Since I was in high school at the time, this presented a particular set of challenges. My parents and the school coordinated to make sure I could be pulled out of class whenever USADA came knocking. This meant unfamiliar cars idling in our neighborhood, trying to find

"Katie's" house. The process opened my eyes to a different side of this sport I loved. Swimming wasn't just going to be swimming anymore. Swimming, from that point on, was also making sure that I could be accessed wherever and whenever. Swimming meant giving up some privacy and autonomy. Swimming meant the curtailing of some freedoms and ease of movement. But those were all trade-offs that I was and am happy to make.

Because I've been very committed to clean sport, I get irritated when I see athletes test positive and then weasel their way out of suspensions. Some athletes skirt the rules by getting therapeutic-use exemptions, which is basically a doctor's note allowing them to use certain drugs. There's a process where you get approval, and at times these exemptions are necessary and reasonable. But you don't know how much that's being abused worldwide, and there's no solid way to check how athletes are dodging the regulations.

I've been on relays competing against other teams that have one or two people on them who have already served a suspension or gone on to be suspended after the relay. I've seen the look of disappointment on a competitor's face when they lose, only to learn later on that they lost to someone who was cheating.

I've heard athletes say "I made a mistake" when they do test positive. Some are more sincere than others. They find an excuse, and some of those excuses may be more legitimate than others. Then they serve their small suspension and hop back in the pool.

It never feels good when you're competing against somebody who has been cited and penalized. It doesn't feel fair. Also, as a student of the sport who loves the history of swimming, I get really peeved when I read stories of the athletes who were robbed of medals back when the East Germans were cheating, and especially when there was state-sponsored doping. My heart breaks for those swimmers who didn't get the honors that they earned.

Sports are big business, so I understand the pressure athletes face, especially in other countries with less opportunity. Money is hard to resist. And winners make money, for themselves and for others. Perhaps they have no control over what they're taking, and they're doing what their coaches or their government is telling them to do. Or maybe they're obsessed with trying to achieve this singular moment, setting themselves up to suffer the physical consequences of putting their body through something that it shouldn't have been put through. I don't know. But it's sad that it happens. And it's sad that it persists.

When I'm competing, I try not to let my concerns about fairness bother me and I focus on my swim. As for the larger picture, I keep my fingers crossed that the anti-doping agencies are on top of things, and I try to trust the systems that are in place, hoping they investigate anything that raises a red flag. I like to think that even the people who aren't caught today might be later. That down the road, karma will catch up to them. And until then, they must reckon with the knowledge that they'll never know what they could have achieved on their own.

Cheating flies in the face of the fundamental principles of sportsmanship. And it makes anything you do achieve meaningless. That's one reason I admit I get frustrated when I see athletes complaining on social media or elsewhere about being tested at inopportune times or too frequently. If they wanted to test me every day, I would comply. It's part of the sport.

The NCAA rules are another set of restrictions that many athletes chafe against. This I understand a bit more. Though things have improved somewhat at the NCAA level with the adoption of the new name-image-likeness rules, the NCAA constraints could seem nitpicky and over the top when I was in college. But again, at the end of the day, following the rules is the cost of doing business. At least it is for me.

I remember right before I went off to Stanford, I went on *The Ellen Show*. I arrived at the greenroom, where they briefed me about the interview and asked if I would be willing to play a game called Foot Flickers. The producers had time to fill, and the call was to fill it with

Foot Flickers. The game consisted of kicking soccer balls at a bull's-eye on a huge Velcro target. I was told that Ellen had tried the game earlier but hadn't really liked it, so she wouldn't be playing. My competitor would be Grant McCartney, an American ninja warrior. I laughed. "Why not?"

The producers explained that the winner was going to receive a waffle maker. And then I was like, whoa, whoa—I can't take a waffle maker because of NCAA rules. I emphatically told them that if I win, whatever you do, do not present me with a waffle maker, because I can't accept free gifts.

So, I did the interview, and it was great. Lots of banter and fun back-and-forth with Ellen. Now it was time to play the game. Grant and I each had three soccer balls to kick at the target, alternating turns. Each ball that we kicked, we were getting better and better. Closer to the target. On my third ball, I hit the bull's-eye straight on, and Grant just fell to the ground. He basically gave up. It was hilarious, and social media went wild, flagging my soccer skills.

While I was kicking the ball, Ellen was off to the side, cheering us on while wearing my medals. After I won, I remember going over and hugging her. She was ecstatic that the game had turned out fun, not the dud she'd feared. In the excitement of the moment, some producers came out, and they presented me with the verboten waffle maker.

I was stuck. I tried to be as gracious as I could, but I had to refuse the prize. I thanked the show but explained, "I can't accept this because of NCAA rules."

Cue a media frenzy. Headlines everywhere bashing the NCAA because: *Katie Ledecky should be able to accept a fricking waffle maker.* Twitter and Instagram posts were railing, "It's just a waffle maker! She could have it in her dorm room, for Pete's sake!"

The thing is, I was erring on the side of extreme caution. I didn't want to jeopardize my NCAA career. I think some of my extreme compliance was because I felt I was more in the spotlight from the Olympics. I was on talk shows like *Ellen*. It would be easier for me to get called out if I broke the rules.

Oh, who am I kidding? I would have complied no matter what. I'm a rule follower. As I said, for better or worse, it's how I'm built. I mean, sure, there may have been certain gifts I could have accepted. Maybe even the waffle maker. But no prize was worth getting me in hot water with the organization I'd devoted years of my life aching to be a part of. Swimming is just too important to me. Besides, I'm more of a pancake gal.

Chapter Fourteen

KOREA

The sickest I've ever been was when I was twenty-two, during the 2019 World Championships in Korea. Our training camp was in Singapore the week before. Right as we were traveling to Korea, four days before the meet started, I began losing my appetite. Then my stomach started acting up. I chalked it up to normal nerves, even though that wasn't something I tended to suffer from. In retrospect, I was in complete denial.

Arriving in Korea, I noticed I'd lost a little bit of weight. Three or four pounds, which is significant for an athlete in peak form. Separately from that, I was getting all these bug bites. I'm somebody who gets bitten up anywhere, but it was unfathomably humid and hot in Korea. We were staying in the Worlds Village with all the championship athletes. I remember when we checked in, I was wearing shorts. I hadn't applied bug spray, and by the time I got to my room, I was covered in these huge insect bites. Probably ten on my leg, five on each of my arms. Huge swollen red circles all over my exposed skin. Add that to my stomach distress and overall discomfort, and I was painting a real pretty picture. Yet I did what I normally do when focused on competing: I ignored it.

I raced my first event. The 400 free. It started fine. But as the race wore on, I flagged. I gritted my way to the third 100 of the 400 only for my last laps to be one of my worst finishes ever. I tried to brush it off, but I felt horrible. Like trash on toast. My body was shutting down. But my brain kept trying to push the reality of my illness aside.

I'd worked long and hard to get to the Worlds. I couldn't let the opportunity slip through my fingers. I left the pool and told myself I'd be fine. That maybe my race was substandard because I'd split it wrong.

The next morning, I had the 1500 free prelim, which should have been an easy cruise of a swim for me. I got out far enough ahead in my heat that I could comfortably make the final. But around the 800 mark, I started to tank again. So much so that I considered getting out of the pool. A choice I'd never once considered in all my years of swimming. The reality was—gutting it out wasn't working. I couldn't deny it anymore. Something was very, very wrong.

I managed to swim a time that placed me first going into the final, but my subpar performance was obvious to anybody who'd witnessed the race. As I explained to the press as I exited the pool, "I just kind of blanked out and tried to finish it." Then I hightailed it over to the coaches and medical staff and announced, "I'm not myself."

I was immediately taken to the head of sports medicine for USA Swimming, where I was given water and an electrolyte drink. I was sweating rivulets at this point. I'd spiked a fever. My heart rate wouldn't come down. They got me one of those things you put on your finger, a pulsometer, but my heart rate stayed elevated for an alarming amount of time. Eventually, I felt able to stand up.

The team doctor decided I should return to the Worlds Village, try and eat something, and grab a nap. I did as prescribed. When I woke up, I visited the Village clinic to take general tests for flu, cold, etc. When I got there, the medical team was like, "All right, Katie, just keep resting, push your fluids, try to eat," that kind of baseline advice.

As I went back to my room to wait for the test results, I tried to sleep but couldn't. Those pesky bug bites were aggravating me. I was still feverish. I started imagining I'd contracted a mosquito-borne illness. Some mysterious, ill-fated disease. I began to get a little scared.

The next morning, I was supposed to swim the 200 free. The 1500 final would've been that night. I texted Coach Greg that the 200 was going to be a no-go, I'd definitely be scratching out of that. My symptoms weren't improving over time. In fact, they were falling off a cliff.

He texted back that I needed to go the emergency room STAT. Everyone was uneasy and anxious to discover what was wrong with me. Me most of all.

The emergency room visit to Chonnam National University Hospital in Gwangju became a whole-day affair. I was checked in and directed to a seat. The hospital was jam-packed. They barely had space for the patients who were coming in that day. I was probably the youngest person there by ten years, at least. For most of the afternoon, I was seated in an office chair next to the team doctor, who had come in with me. I was the only American patient, so we called in a translator, who sat nearby. We were all lined up along a wall maybe two feet from patients who seemed to be at death's door.

The whole scene was uncanny. Going to the ER is stressful in the best-case scenario. Add the language barrier, the remote location, and my mystery ailment, and my thoughts began to spiral. I doubled down on my half-baked mosquito-bite theories. I convinced myself I'd come down with an exotic, incurable disease they'd write about in physicians' journals someday. The heat in Gwangju wasn't enhancing my lucidity. I may have been stuck in that waiting room, but my usual optimism and chill had 100 percent left the building.

My brain began to dissect everything that had occurred since I'd arrived in Korea. There were very few hotels in the city, so our hosts had built this village just for the championships. There was a cafeteria for the athletes. A serve-yourself thing where everyone was using the same ladles and spoons to dish out their food. There were a lot of illnesses flying around at the meet. And after people started getting sick, rumors spread in the village that some athletes were taste-testing the soup using the communal spoon. Or touching the food and putting it back. People said the cooks were using the same utensils to handle the raw meat as they were using in the cooked dishes. I considered all of this as I waited to discover if I'd been food-poisoned or infected by a bug or who the heck knew what. Eventually, the doctors did a blood draw. An EKG. Then more waiting. At some point, I scratched out of the 1500 scheduled for that night.

When my blood results came back, they were accompanied by a giant red flag—my troponin level was high. The Korean doctor reviewing the tests was concerned. High troponin usually indicates a heart attack has occurred. If not that, it can portend sepsis, atrial fibrillation, congestive heart failure, pulmonary embolism, myocarditis, myocardial contusion, or renal failure. All way worse than cafeteria food poisoning. The Korean doctor immediately tried to admit me to the hospital.

Instead, we ordered a chest X-ray and heart ultrasound. To release me from the hospital, we needed to rule out the worst.

The ultrasound found that I had some fluid around my heart, which was basically consistent with having a virus. After a battery of tests, all parties felt certain I hadn't had a cardiac episode. The virus was shutting my body down. But I wasn't going to keel over.

I left the ER with the admonition to rest. The Korean doctor felt like I should not compete, but a Korean cardiac specialist who had reviewed the ultrasound and the team doctor believed if I could get some good recovery time over the next two days, we could then see how I felt in the water when I got my heart rate up. Maybe I could eke out my last two events, which were the relay and the 800 free. It was up to me to decide.

I went back to my room at the village, contemplating whether I wanted to keep going. I tried googling my diagnosis (never smart), but the Wi-Fi wasn't great. I was scared. Frustrated and scared. Exhausted, frustrated, and scared. Honestly, the Korean doctor freaking out had kind of freaked me out.

On the other hand, our team doctor had been calm and thorough. He explained the nitty-gritty to me and gave me his perspective. He said a lot of times certain data points send up flares for doctors who don't treat professional athletes. For example, I have a super-low heart rate, and my EKGs always come back noted as "abnormal," but they're actually typical of athletes at a certain level. Our team doctor felt like my results in the ER were akin to those anomalies.

I texted my parents to loop them in. I rarely see my family during big meets because of scheduling and other logistics. My mom and brother had traveled to Korea. I was due to compete that day, so I needed to update them before they showed up to watch me swim and discovered I was MIA. When my mom heard what was happening, she was concerned. She started emailing me my medical records so the team docs could compare that data to the ER's.

The whole experience was distressing. Getting all these tests that I'd never had before, in another country, unable to speak for myself or understand what was being said about my diagnosis. It was . . . a lot.

I took the next day completely off. The press was making a meal of my disappearance. I'd gone missing, and there was a lot of scuttlebutt about why. The official statement about my absence said something along the lines of "under the weather." I laid low, trying my best to recover.

After my rest day, it was time for the 4x200-meter freestyle relay. I was meant to swim along with Simone Manuel, Melanie Margalis, and Katie McLaughlin. I woke up wanting to support my teammates. I traveled to the pool in the morning to do a practice swim. I kept it easy, controlled. We tested my heart rate after. Everything felt mostly okay. I was medically cleared to swim the finals relay. And I felt comfortable enough to give it a shot.

My team was confident that even though I was nowhere near top form, I only needed to put up a single good split. And that's what I did. I swam decently. Swimming the second leg, I clocked a 1:54.61, which was the third-fastest split in the final, behind Ariarne Titmus's leadoff for Australia and Penny Oleksiak's anchor leg for Canada. With a time of 7:41.87, we surpassed the existing world record, set in 2009 by

China, but we lost to Australia, who came in at 7:41.50. We took home silver. I think if I had been at my best, we would've taken gold. But it was a small miracle I was able to compete at all, given my symptoms that week.

The 800 free prelim was the next day. When I got up that morning, I felt horrible, like I'd been punched in every organ. Coming off the relay, I'd convinced myself I was on the mend. Clearly, I wasn't. I forced myself to swim the 800 and touched the wall in 8:17.42 seconds, almost thirteen seconds slower than my world record. It was good enough for the second seed, but it was far from my best work.

Afterward I was sapped. I hightailed it to the warm-down pool without stopping to talk to reporters. I knew I had thirty-six hours to recover before the final. I rested like it was my job. I tried to eat bland food. Hummus and pita. Chicken and rice. I pushed fluids. Every second between, I psyched myself up to swim the 800 final.

Before I knew it, race day was upon me. I remember telling myself going in to try and forget that I was unwell. I hyped myself up: *You know how to swim an 800 free. You can do this. Just go in, take the lead, keep the lead. Just get out there and swim it.*

I dove in. I went out fast. I managed maybe a body-length lead through the 200. Then, at the 300 mark, I hit a wall. The swimmer next to me, Simona Quadarella from Italy, had won the 1500 free earlier in the week, after I had pulled out. By the 400 mark, she swam up even with me. I was hurting, but after sensing Simona there, I forced myself to stick with her, not let her get too far ahead.

Here's the odd thing. Having Simona so close helped calm me down. I could focus on her. Not on how cruddy I felt. It made the race go by more quickly. I knew at that point I was only swimming for gold. I wasn't swimming for a record or a ridiculous time or to do anything spectacular. I was swimming to keep up with her.

I did a good job of that. As the race wore on, I began thinking about if and when I could make a move. I was suffering. But I shut out the agony. I narrowed my attention to the last laps. With a bit more than 150 meters left, I told myself, *I'm going to blast off.* But when I got to that point, I reconsidered. It was too early. I didn't think I could sustain it. Then I got to 100 left and I was like, *Okay, I'm going to make my move.* But again, no. It was too soon. I ended up waiting until the final 50.

My plan was to push off the last wall, hit some forceful underwater kicks, and nail that final 50. I'm a student of the sport. I had confidence in my finishing speed compared to Simona's. I used that as motivation. I was confident if I kicked hard enough, I could get my hand to the wall first.

I may not have blown by her, but I got my hand on the wall first. It wasn't my fastest 800, that's for sure. But it's a race that I look back on now with so much pride. (Especially after the summer of 2023, because winning that day in Korea kept my streak alive in the 800 free, enabling me to log golds in six straight World Championships.)

The concluding night of the meet, I relaxed and watched the races with my teammates, then went back to the village and packed my stuff. The next afternoon I was scheduled to go to Seoul with my mom and my brother. I was attending a reception at the ambassador's house, as part of the sports diplomacy program through the Department of State.

We took a train, and as I watched the views of Korea tick by from my window, I felt myself exhale. It was like I had been holding my breath for days. There was another reason I had been worried about my health—a nagging fear in the back of my mind, something I'd discovered during my gap year in the lead-up to the Rio Olympics. It was something I hadn't shared with anyone publicly.

I WAS JUST COMING off Worlds in Kazan, Russia. My summer had been awesome. I felt strong and on track. The final evening in Kazan, after my last race, there was a team dinner with the families and friends of Team USA. I was sitting there, so happy to be among all these amazing people, when suddenly, I grew extremely hot and lightheaded, like I couldn't find my bearings. I'd never felt that way before. I waited to see if it would resolve, but I was uneasy enough that I left the party and went back to my room.

I told myself not to fret about it. I'd just finished a long, arduous meet, after all. I probably needed to rest and recover. No biggie.

I went home and got back into training for Rio. And it was . . . weird. I was swimming okay. But I was super inconsistent. I would have a couple of good practices, and then I would have a day or two when I had absolutely no energy. Some days I couldn't walk around without dizziness. I remember wrapping practice and struggling to get back to the locker room. Every swimmer has peaks and valleys in training, but to be so strung out? My desire to work hard was there. I just had no juice. I kept wondering, *Am I sick? And if so, with what?*

Bruce Gemmell, my coach at the time, began to worry. He suggested I see a specialist at Johns Hopkins. The doctor ran tests where he measured my heart rate and blood pressure lying down, at rest. Then he checked the same when I was standing for ten minutes. It turned out my heart rate was thirty beats per minute higher when I was upright compared to when I was lying down. After the entire work-up was done, he diagnosed me with what he believed was a mild form of POTS.

Postural orthostatic tachycardia syndrome (POTS) is a type of orthostatic intolerance that causes your heart rate to go up when you go from reclining or sitting to rising and standing. Around three million people in the U.S. suffer from POTS, with varying levels of severity. Normally, your body's autonomic nervous system makes sure your heart rate and blood pressure remain synced, regardless of whether you're up, down, or sideways. But if you have POTS, your body can't automatically coordinate blood-vessel constriction and heart rate. And it makes you and your blood pressure unsteady.

Because I have POTS, I pool blood in the vessels below my heart when I stand. My body then releases extra norepinephrine or epinephrine, which adds additional stressors on my heart, making it beat faster. Which, in turn, brings on dizziness, fainting, and exhaustion.

The good news was that I could treat my POTS nutritionally. I needed to up my sodium intake and increase my hydration. Studies also show that reclined aerobic exercise, such as swimming, and strengthening your core can provide relief. Which is kind of funny. What are the odds that the prescriptive exercise for my particular disease would be . . . more swimming?

I was relieved to get a clear diagnosis, even if having POTS wasn't the best news. After I was diagnosed, I decided to keep that revelation to myself. I didn't want something quote/unquote "wrong" with me to become the narrative around Rio or Team USA. I wasn't eager to become a distraction or to be distracted myself. I simply wanted to treat my condition as best I could and get back to going hard in the pool. Gradually, following doctor's orders, I started feeling better.

The thing about having an additional challenge like POTS is that I can't ever ignore the problem. Whenever I get sick or feel off, I have to check in with my health protocol. Am I being good about my hydration? Am I staying on the salt? How can I stay cool? I have to factor in a whole host of new concerns in order to perform at the level that I want to. And yeah, almost any time I'm feeling like I'm a little low on energy, it's the first thing that springs to mind.

Doctors reported that POTS cases spiked during Covid; other viruses can activate the condition or make it less manageable. POTS is also heavily amplified in hot environments. In Korea, it was an additional concern that I'd become so dehydrated the POTS would worsen and make it impossible for me to function, let alone compete.

When I experienced it in 2015, it was probably inflamed by a virus I'd had that spring. That last day in Kazan was probably the first time I noticed something was amiss in a way I couldn't mentally will myself out of.

I'm happy to report I have a solid handle on my POTS these days. It isn't too much of a burden, and it keeps me even more tuned in to my health, which as I age in the sport is only a positive thing. I'm sure new physical challenges will arise as the years go by. I've been unnaturally lucky so far. No injuries. No slumps. I have every intention of continuing to compete as long as my body allows. Just like I did in Korea.

Chapter Fifteen

GRANDPA HAGAN

Christmas was one of the few times a year when my brother, Michael, and I got to experience being part of a sprawling, boisterous family. All the relatives would come from Montana and Utah to stay at Grandpa Hagan's farm in Williston, North Dakota. I remember my grandpa got a special kick out of how I was the only girl among the cousins my age, but that I somehow still managed to rule the roost. He respected the fact that I could hold my own with a gaggle of rowdy boys.

We are a family who embraces the holidays, but nobody loved Christmas the way Grandpa Hagan did. He and my grandma went all out making it special for me, my brother, and our fifteen cousins when we were growing up. On Christmas Eve, we would go to Mass together as a group. Then we would come back to the farm and have a party with the cousins, aunts, uncles, usually the priest, and a couple of close friends and neighbors. As a tradition, my grandpa always made sure that Santa came to the door with an overstuffed bag of gifts that night. All the kids would get one present from the bag before we went to bed. A designated cousin would play elf and help Santa pass out the presents. When it was your turn, you would pose for a photo with Santa and open up the present. It was a full Norman Rockwell–esque production.

When Santa left, all us kids would rush to the window to try and spy Rudolph and the other reindeer flying off into the sky. Miraculously,

153

we always did. (One of my uncles would be waiting in the backyard for his cue to shoot off a red firework.) For me, it was extra pixie dust on the magic of the night.

Grandpa reveled in our energy. There were always heaps of kids running around the farm. We'd play pickup football or kick a soccer ball around. We had traditions like the gingerbread-house competition between the cousins. (I won't lie: my brother and I lived to win.) Sometimes we'd perform skits or sing songs. If there was snow on the ground, we'd go sledding and drink hot chocolate. It was important to Grandpa Hagan to give us an enchanted holiday. To spark memories and nurture our innocent excitement. To create a sheltered, joyful candy-cane snow globe around us all.

Even as a kid, I knew that Grandpa Hagan had survived some devastating events in his past. He'd fought in four of the bloodiest battles in World War II, seen things no human should. My mom revered our grandpa like he was a living saint, which in many ways he was.

Edward "Bud" Jordan Hagan II was born on October 13, 1916, in Williston, the third of four kids and the only boy. His father, E.J., a doctor, delivered him at home. E.J. was a physician ahead of his time. He was instrumental in the founding of Williston's Mercy Hospital in 1920, believing the town deserved a state-of-the-art facility after the 1918 influenza pandemic caught everyone off guard. When my grandpa was eleven years old, his father died unexpectedly from pneumonia, leaving a hole in the family that my grandpa always felt the urge to fill. Even as a boy, he was predisposed to taking care of people, to stepping in and offering any help he could.

After his father passed, Grandpa decided to become a doctor too. He grew up in Williston, attended Williston High, the University of North Dakota, and then Rush Medical College, a part of the University of Chicago, where he received his medical degree. He worked nights to afford school, living on a dollar a day. He was interning at a hospital in St. Paul in 1943 when World War II cut the final piece of his education short. Grandpa Hagan enlisted as a combat surgeon for the 1st Marine Division in the Pacific. He was twenty-six years old, barely younger than I am now.

His family was apprehensive about his decision to enlist. Letters from the time show them brooding about how their "peaceful, kindhearted" brother would fare in the fog of war. Their unease was not misplaced. The battles of the 1st Marine Division would become legendary, renowned for their high death tolls and unmitigated misery.

In 1944, my grandfather was in Peleliu, an island in Palau where ten thousand U.S. servicemen would eventually be reported dead or missing. More than ten thousand Japanese soldiers were also killed. The prediction when they arrived was that the fighting would be over within three days. Yet it would be a month before my grandpa's division was given any relief. The first week alone cost the 1st Marine Division nearly four thousand soldiers.

It was Grandpa Hagan's responsibility to tend to the wounded and suffering. He spent countless nights struggling to survive in foxholes, preventing men from bleeding out, doing anything he could to lessen their anguish. It was baptism by fire, and it was unrelenting.

Putrefaction starts immediately in hot, wet climates. "That smell of death in the tropics is unlike anything, and it never leaves you," my grandpa recalled. There was rot, there were rats. Disease on top of casualties. Bottle flies swarming bodies. Grandpa Hagan was a young man in the prime of life, dodging bullets and grenades. He witnessed dozens of men perish. He saw others lose their minds amid the horrors of battle, wandering the combat wreckage with "that thousand-yard stare." Of that period, my grandfather would say, "All I could do was what I was supposed to do, bury the rest of it as deep as I could and leave it there."

Grandpa Hagan was awarded a Silver Star and a Bronze Star for his service. Given the opportunity to leave the war and return home, he chose to do another campaign. It would end up being the Battle of

Okinawa, the bloodiest battle of the Pacific War, with 241,686 dead, more than 14,000 of them Americans.

Ceaseless bombardment during monsoon season made already gruesome conditions horrific. "The casualties were horrible," Grandpa said. Bodies couldn't be buried. Thousands of corpses lay decomposing on the ground, creating a macabre Hieronymus Bosch–like landscape from which there was no relief. Just looking around was a torment. Everywhere the eye could land was a fresh nightmare. There were thousands of reported cases of mental breakdown in Okinawa, far more than from any other World War II battle.

While there, my grandpa was injured. "I was late diving into a shell hole," he recalled. The force of a mortar barrage threw him fifteen feet down an embankment. He shattered eight ribs. A fellow doctor wanted him pulled from battle, but my grandpa asked to be taped up so he could go back in. He refused to leave combat, so he could remain tending to the wounded.

For his efforts on the battlefield, he was awarded a second Bronze Star and a Purple Heart. The citation on his Bronze Star says in part, "Though he was forced to enter extremely precarious fighting areas, constantly harassed by enemy fire, he immediately and repeatedly went forward to the action . . . disregarding all personal risks and dangers, he administered skillful medical aid to dying and wounded Marines. By his courageous and unselfish devotion to duty, he was responsible for the saving of lives and many wounded."

The war officially ended in 1945, but the fighting raged on in the Pacific where isolated pockets of Japanese troops refused to surrender. The day before Grandpa Hagan was to be evacuated from Okinawa, he spied a young girl running toward his sick bay. A shell landed at her feet, and she slid into a mortar hole. Grandpa could tell even from a distance that she was pregnant. He ran to help her and realized she was in the late stages of labor. He delivered her baby right then and there.

The next day, my grandfather left Okinawa with nothing but the uniform he had on.

My grandpa was just shy of twenty-nine when the war ended. "Those years of medical school and after are supposed to be the time when a man makes and keeps good friends that will remain close throughout life," he'd say. "When World War II ended, I looked around me, and all my friends were dead."

Grandpa Hagan returned to Williston and rebuilt his world, doing his best to leave behind the terror of what he'd survived. In 1949, he married my grandmother, Kathleen. He would go on to become the patriarch of his own large family. He and my grandma had seven children: E.J. III, Mary Kathleen, Mike, Mary Gen, Mary Anne, Mary Margaret, and Mary Colleen. (As a traditional Irish Catholic couple, they were very fond of the name "Mary.")

Like his father before him, Grandpa Hagan started a medical practice in Williston, the Craven-Hagan Clinic. He threw himself into his family and his practice, making himself an essential part of the community. As he had in the marines, he continued being of service. He had a burning desire to make a difference. To utilize fully the life he was grateful to be living.

Grandpa Hagan ran a general practice, but he could perform surgeries, which was a boon to a small town like Williston. Everybody knew him, and if you went anywhere in town with him, locals would rush up to chat or thank him for treating them or saving the life of a family member. My grandpa gave aid and comfort to those who otherwise might not have received either. The same was true at church. Members of the congregation would drop by the house, and I'd hear their stories. Everyone was always so appreciative of him for one thing or another. My grandpa truly lived his life for others. It impressed upon me how huge a difference a single person can make in a community if they choose to.

Unless pressed, Grandpa Hagan spoke little of his time in the war. He figured there wasn't much of a point in dwelling on the past. What was done was done. Instead, he leaned into the future. How could he make his world, the small world of Williston, the best it could be? My mom discovered letters he'd written to his mother amid the grisly battles. He'd never share the full truth, telling his relatives all was as well as could be expected: "We've been playing a lot of cards." He wanted to protect the people he loved from the pain he endured.

Surviving war can break a person. But my grandpa refused to succumb to cynicism, to give up on believing in the goodness of people. He kept moving forward, making his town better, tending to his neighbors. He saw no point in wallowing or wishing something had never happened. Instead, he grabbed the reins of his life and galloped ahead. My parents say I share my grandpa's optimism and tendency to live in the moment. I'm honored by the comparison.

In 1984 Grandpa Hagan retired from medicine. Ten years later he and my grandma moved permanently to their farm on the outskirts of Williston. Grandpa Hagan kept a huge library in his den, stuffed with books primarily about history and the military. The TV in his bedroom was tuned to the History Channel all day. He kept his Purple Heart, Silver Star, Bronze Stars, and other commendations in a display case on his desk in his den. I remember going in there and peering at them. Leaning in close to see the details.

The things my grandpa saw in the war put so much in perspective for him. He valued persistence. Devotion. He believed that his faith was central to his survival. He told my parents he wanted their kids to be raised Catholic. So we were. We went to Little Flower School from pre-K through eighth grade, and then Michael went to the Jesuit high school Gonzaga College, and I went to Stone Ridge School of the Sacred Heart. My grandpa hoped that Catholic schooling would reinforce in us the value of taking care of others.

When I was younger, I would tell people that I wanted to be a doctor when I grew up, like my Grandpa Hagan. Knowing he'd helped hundreds of people, I wanted to achieve that too. I deviated from the medical path once I recognized I wasn't going to be able to handle the gory requirements. Blood and fluids were not my bag. But many of my mom's siblings went into the medical field as either nurses or doctors. My cousins did the same. My mother was a hospital administrator. Other relatives are pharmacists and physical therapists. The shadow of Grandpa Hagan looms large.

Whenever we spent time together, my grandpa would tell me, "Always be kind to people and animals." It was sort of his life motto. No matter how old he was, he continued to make his way to the barn to feed the horses. I remember when I used to ride, he'd put on the saddle and the reins and gently guide the horse for me. He taught us what horses respond to. How to respect them. I was young, but I recognized how all the animals on the farm really trusted him. He had this benevolent command.

The last ten years of his life, Grandpa suffered from macular degeneration. He hated that he couldn't read anymore, so my mom and her siblings read to him. Usually history books. They'd pause sometimes and ask, "Did this really happen?" and he'd nod: "Yeah, yeah." He never betrayed much emotion. Another trait my mom says I inherited from him. Neither my grandpa nor I want to be a bother. We keep our lids on tight.

Grandpa Hagan loved that I swam. I remember when I was eleven, I showed him a swimsuit for a big meet. It was my first fast suit, super-cool-looking. Grandpa Hagan said something like, "Oh yeah, that's really sharp," even though he was nearly blind by then. He wanted to be involved, so he pretended he could see. He fought against being viewed as deficient in any way. Grandpa Hagan didn't believe in limitations for himself or for us. He encouraged his daughters to explore the world, to follow their passions. This was not typical for men of his generation. He resisted the notion that any human was fated to follow a particular path and pressed us all to discover what we were meant to be in life.

As a doctor, my grandpa saw a lot of patients who couldn't swim, some of whom barely escaped drowning in the nearby Missouri River. After a near miss when his own daughter, my aunt Katie, then four years old, fell off a dock, Grandpa Hagan made it a priority to push the school board to require swim lessons for every elementary student. The rule passed in the 1960s. The next step was building a pool the kids could use.

Williston isn't the first or fortieth town that comes to mind when one thinks of a swimming destination. Located sixty miles from the Canadian border with temperatures habitually hovering around zero, the place doesn't exactly scream "See you at the pool!" But my grandpa had a vision. In my family, there's this genetic through line of persistence. Once we get an idea, we execute it.

My grandfather ran for, then became, the president of the park board. From that perch, he advanced the construction of Williston's first indoor pool. Two years later, in 1969, the pool opened. My mom (his fourth child) was fourteen years old and excited to swim year-round along with her siblings. My grandpa would tell her, "Take the lead, keep the lead." Advice that would become a mantra for me decades later.

When my mother and her siblings swam, Grandpa Hagan rarely missed a meet. He had a busy medical practice, but he'd come running into the stands right before they dove into the pool. He passed away before he could attend any of my major events. That's one of the reasons Grandma Hagan moved heaven and earth to go to my 2012 Olympic Trials. She knew how much my grandpa would've enjoyed being there. She wanted to be there on his behalf.

Grandpa Hagan lived to be ninety-one. I was eleven when he passed away. My grandfather's legacy was not his valor in battle—though that was remarkable. It was what he did after that extraordinary test of character that ended up changing lives. Being there when people needed him most. Never shirking from a responsibility. He had seen the worst of humanity in the war. Instead of letting that destroy his faith, he doubled down. He made it his life's mission to give and be good, and in doing so, he helped heal countless people in his town. There wasn't a day he didn't give a part of himself to another person. The ripple effects of that choice are profound. And not lost on me.

In 2014 Williston reopened the E. J. Hagan, MD, Natatorium in the town's new state-of-the-art rec center. They named the pool after my grandpa. In his honor stood an eight-lane 50-meter competition pool with a diving bay and enough space for water polo and lifesaving classes.

That March, I flew to North Dakota during my Olympic training to be the first to take a swim. I was seventeen. All my extended family was there. Generations of Hagans, dozens of relatives, and cousins. All seventeen of Grandpa Hagan's grandchildren. In total, more than eight hundred people were packed in the natatorium, watching me as I climbed onto the block in lane five.

I felt a hush as I did. The crowd stood stock-still, waiting. It was 11:15. A voice over a loudspeaker intoned, "Take your mark." Then a horn blared. I dove in and swam back and forth across the water.

With every stroke, I thought about my grandpa. I recalled his care with the horses, his gentle manner, the war medals in their rectangular case, how much he loved my grandma. I remembered sitting beside him on our last Christmas Eve together, describing the scene he could no longer see.

All these memories flooded my brain as I made my way across the pool in the jubilant presence of hundreds of people whose lives he had made better.

That 100 was as meaningful as any swim I've ever done.

Chapter Sixteen

COVID

M y Tokyo Olympic–year journal is gold and embossed on the front with the words "Call Me Boss Lady." It spans the time from August 12, 2019, to June 11, 2020. Days when, let me tell you, I did not feel like a boss lady—not even a little. My Tokyo Olympic Year evolved into my pandemic year, and just as for everyone everywhere in the world, my life was upended in various ways.

The week before Covid began hitting the news, I had a swim meet in Des Moines where I put up some fast times. I felt optimistic and was tracking right on my training schedule to perform well in Tokyo. This was March 4, 2020, and there were maybe a couple of Covid cases in the U.S., a few more globally. I remember watching the coverage of the emerging virus, but it didn't seem serious. A few of my swim friends had heard some murmuring that Covid could affect the Olympics, since it's such an international event. But the general population simply hadn't really registered Covid as anything major. It seemed like a problem very far from home.

Then, barely a week after the Des Moines meet, the swimming NCAAs were canceled. Then basketball games started getting canceled too. Suddenly, the virus was everywhere. Famous people were contracting Covid, athletes were catching it, teams were starting to see the virus spread among their players. I wasn't participating in the NCAAs, but a lot of my teammates were. I wrote a journal entry that day that said:

"Coach canceled PM swim because he had to meet with the NCAA team. NCAAs got canceled today along with all sporting events nationwide because of coronavirus CRAZINESS! World looking really different and strange right now. Need to continue to stay positive, live in the moment and win each day no matter the circumstances."

The next afternoon, a Friday, we had a normal practice at Stanford. Then boom—by Saturday, the Stanford pool got shut down, and every student was asked to depart campus. A switch had been flipped. That Saturday, March 14, I noted in my journal: "What a week. Stanford students had to leave. Lots going on with finding a pool space and creating a plan moving forward."

I reminded myself to go with the flow, be flexible. "Find ways to stay entertained," I wrote. "Find ways to get better. Find ways to be motivated. Ask for help when needed."

Three days later, March 17, was my birthday. My diary entry logs my workout at the University of California, Berkeley pool, where my teammate and close friend Simone Manuel and I had relocated for one day after the Stanford pool closed. I deemed the workout "solid" and noted my tenuous mindset: "Everything around us is getting shut down. Take it one single day at a time. Only focus on today." I ended on a quote I'd read and adopted during this turbulent time: "The ability to embrace uncertainty leads to ultimate freedom."

I repeated those words to myself often as the weeks unfolded and the spread of Covid worsened. I did my best to embrace ambiguity and keep myself from projecting forward into a future that, on some days, felt very bleak. My life before had been so structured, filled with classes, swim practice, and other activities. To look into a future where I was isolated from my friends, teammates, and the pool—it felt a bit like being set adrift in open water.

After Stanford closed, a group of about six of us swimmers, including Simone, chose to stick around, hoping the shutdown might be a one- or two-week thing. The magnitude of what Covid was going to become still hadn't entirely landed. As the other five swimmers left one by one for their respective homes, Simone and I decided we were going to train together, come what may. I knew she would be a vital support to me, and me to her.

We had lots of people in and around USA Swimming trying to help us figure out if there were any pools in California where Olympic hopefuls could keep training. Staying in the pool is critical during Olympic training, or you risk what we call "losing your feel" for the water. So, while the Olympics were still officially on, we were doing everything we could to find a substitute pool. For a couple of days, courtesy of Ted Robinson, we were able to practice at a place called Menlo Circus Club, which was a country club pool about ten minutes from Stanford. A few days later, Menlo Circus Club closed. By then Simone and I were the last two hanging on.

We investigated our options. Could we travel to another city in the U.S. that still had pools open? We also reached out to swim-world connections to see if there were any private pools operating in the area. Since coming to Stanford, I had been training with Coach Greg Meehan. With him, we'd won NCAA championships in 2017 and 2018. Greg was talking to people in Naples, Florida, about a pool that was still open at the time. I even considered, could I go to Williston, North Dakota, stay with my grandma, and swim at the rec pool? Surely they would let me swim *there*.

All these options, once I thought them through, really didn't make sense. If we headed to Naples, what if that pool got shut down in two weeks? We'd have no place to live for who knows how long an amount of time. And if I went to North Dakota, I didn't want to get my grandma sick. Would I have to stay at a hotel? Would it even be safe to see my grandma in person?

Ultimately, Simone and I decided we were going to stay put and keep searching for a pool in the California area. The Olympics weren't canceled yet. We were trying to do everything we could to just stay in the water. The stress level was sky-high because we felt like people around the world were still training. Not having the same regulations we did in the U.S., other countries had facilities open. Some countries' teams are government-supported, and they prioritized allowing their athletes to train.

The Olympic Committee basically advised us to "do the best that you can." Which was frustrating. I remember feeling like, *We're elite athletes, we* always *do the best we can, but there's only so much we can do without support.*

USA Swimming wrote a letter to the USOPC, basically encouraging them to make their position clear and advising them if they intended to reschedule the Tokyo Olympics, they needed to do that as quickly as possible. I know a lot of other organizations were exerting the same pressure, trying to look out for the mental health of the athletes, knowing it wasn't sustainable for us to be in protracted limbo. We all needed a decision to be made ASAP. I understand now that there was no way to know how long or how severe the pandemic would become. But in those early weeks, for those of us who'd been training toward one goal, the not-knowing was paralyzing. Should we just keep swimming? And if we should, how could we when all public activity was on pause?

While we waited for news, I kept recentering myself on the present, the only thing I could control. Like many other people in the world, I turned to ordering stuff online. I bought free weights. A pull-up bar and some bands. An exercise bike. My objective was to remain in my apartment and do whatever I could to maintain my fitness. I did my dryland workouts. I did Pilates over Zoom.

I was living by myself in a two-bedroom apartment in Menlo Park. Whenever I ventured out, I barely saw other cars, let alone people. Nobody was about. As the days ticked on, I found myself writing lists of "Things I Did Today Besides Swim": *Talked to Mom and Dad. Watched news. Made oatmeal. Talked to Grandma Hagan. Watched an episode of*

Blue Bloods. *Watched Mass online. Talked to Mom again because I was a bit sad. Read a lot of Twitter.*

On March 19, 2020, California issued a statewide stay-at-home order. That afternoon I swam thirty minutes at a friend of a friend's local 15-yard pool. I worked on underwaters and breakouts. Did some kicking with drag socks. My legs were sore that night, so at least I knew it was better than no swim at all. Even so, it was a far cry from the distance training I'd been doing every day for more than a decade. Swimmers are attracted to consistency. We like routine. We strive to be as in control as possible. And yet here I was, like everyone else on the planet, surviving an unprecedented, alarming, disorienting time, scrounging for consistency wherever I could.

Shortly after California officially locked down, Coach Greg delivered Simone and me some amazing news. For days he'd called all over the country, looking for a suitable pool for us to use for training. A friend suggested he talk to Tod Spieker, an avid master swimmer and former UCLA All-American whose house was located mere miles from campus and just so happened to have a pristine two-lane 25-yard pool in the backyard.

To hear Tod tell it, he couldn't say no when Greg called. He said he would've felt guilty turning us away. Instead, he invited us to use his pool for as long as we needed. Back then we thought that might be a few weeks. It ended up being six days a week for more than three months.

When I tell you I swam in a backyard pool, I need to clarify—it was probably the finest backyard pool in the country. It had backstroke flags. It had a diving block for one of the lanes. It had a pace clock. Simone and I didn't even need to set anything up. We'd roll in, our suits already on, toting our snorkels, kickboards, and paddles. We settled into a rhythm as soon as we could.

Tod's daughter Lindy (who'd played water polo at Berkeley) often brought over her three kids, Ben, Delaney, and Beau—ages seven, six, and three—to watch us swim. Lindy's children were starved for diversion, and Simone and I provided an adequate one for a few hours a day. While we did laps, the kids played around the huge backyard, or raced up and down the pool deck, rooting us on from a safe distance. They had so much energy. The mornings when I was struggling to motivate myself to swim, their enthusiasm helped spur me on.

We were not "Simone" and "Katie" to them. We were "Simone Manuel!" and "Katie Ledecky!" They would scream our names and shout with glee, "Simone Manuel and Katie Ledecky are the best swimmers in the world!" They would keep repeating this, over and over, to the point where we would start giggling during our workouts, imagining that we were going to have these kids' voices ringing in our heads behind the blocks in Tokyo. If we ever got there.

For the next twelve weeks, the only people I saw were Coach Greg, Simone, and the Spieker family. I barely left my apartment, not even venturing to the grocery store. Because of those isolating circumstances, Simone and I became genuinely enmeshed in the Spiekers' lives. I gave the kids a giant Costco-sized bag of candy at Easter. (Sorry, Lindy!) For Beau's birthday, I brought him dinosaur books and a kit to make dinosaurs out of clay. It was honestly kind of sad when we had our last backyard-pool practice. I knew I was going to miss seeing those shining faces every day.

As far as the workouts went, Greg tried to come up with programming to keep Simone and me sharp mentally as well as physically. It was tricky because we were training for different events. Simone's a sprinter, I'm a distance swimmer. We meet in the middle for the 200 free, but for the most part, I would say 85 percent of the practices, we would have different main sets. Even so, Greg figured out over time how we could do a few of the same sets. He got pretty creative. There was one day when we did what the three of us decided to call "death by relay," where we weren't swimming against each other but as a team.

Simone and I raced in a mimicked relay format for a half hour. I'd start with a 500-yard swim and gradually decrease from there. Simone, a sprinter, swam shorter distances. Simone was basically doing 50's, 100's, and 200's. I think I did 200's, 300's, 400's. And our rest interval was the other's racing. Not for nothing, Simone was getting a lot of rest. And I . . . was not. I'm laughing now, but I actually remember that relay being really fun, because it was fresh. We were starved for variety and craved stimulation. Even "death by relay" stimulation.

There were times when I'd arrive at practice bummed and unmoored. There were some tough days when Simone and I would swim separate sets, or when my own sets were just bleeding my spirit. Doing distance on my own, it's a grind. Mentally, I get worn down. On those days, we'd finish practice, and I would linger in the pool to talk to Greg or Simone. I didn't want to go home and be alone. I think Simone felt the same way. When that happened, we'd sit together with our feet dangling in the water. Just being close. As close as we could be during Covid.

Sometimes before practice, we'd chat about the news. We were trying to remain hopeful. That was the biggest thing. We'd cling to any new research or study that was trending positive. Greg would give us updates on Stanford. He was part of the committee working on the plans for reopening. And, of course, any time the Spieker kids would come by, they would really lift our spirits.

Greg, Simone, and I were all doing the work, but it was a challenge not to wonder what for. We understood that anything we were doing in the Spieker pool was about maintaining our fitness, not making major strides. The coronavirus pandemic disrupted our Olympic preparation, first via lockdown, then because we were left unsure whether qualifying events would occur. And we still hadn't been informed if the Games would take place. That all changed on Tuesday, March 24, 2020.

I woke up to the news that the Olympics were officially postponed a year.

"The IOC president and the Prime Minister of Japan have concluded that the Games must be rescheduled to a date beyond 2020, but not later than summer 2021, to safeguard the health of the athletes, everybody involved in the Olympic Games and the international community," said a joint statement issued by the Tokyo 2020 organizing committee and the IOC.

USOPC CEO Sarah Hirshland wrote a letter to all of us athletes, saying, "Despite the feeling of eventuality that so many of us have felt in the lead up to this moment . . . my heart breaks for you, your fellow athletes around the world, our friends at Tokyo 2020, the people of Japan, and all who are impacted by this global pandemic and the decision to postpone the Tokyo Games 2020. We heard your concerns, and we shared them. I thank you for being so forthcoming with your perspectives, and also for allowing us the time to hear from your teammates across all sports before making a recommendation to the IOC."

The declaration was a gut punch. But I was relieved to finally have clarity. My task now became converting a four-year Olympic plan into a five-year one. For swimmers, we direct all we do toward peak points, which are few and far between. The ideal scenario is to peak during the eight-day Olympic period once every four years. Additionally, you have to hit mini peaks at Trials so that you make the Olympic team. As my coaches always explained, you miss that mark, and it's a long time to wait for the next chance.

So much of swimming success is about managing the stretches of time between the peaks. Believing that the effort you're putting in today will pay off in three, six, eight months. It's a mind game, and during Covid, it became even more grueling. I was already missing my family so much. My energy levels were low. I felt foolish continuing to push myself in the pool when every headline reported the spread of the pandemic and updated death counts. But what else was I to do? Sitting at home alone with no goals wasn't good for anybody either. Certainly not me.

The day of the postponement, I grabbed my suit and headed to the Spiekers' pool. Simone met me there, and we trained. The Olympics may have been delayed, but they hadn't been canceled. I intended to stay competition-ready.

During this period, there were ebbs and flows in my mental state. I appreciated how lucky I was to have a dream (albeit deferred), a place to train, a surrogate family. But when I'd leave the pool and go home to my quiet apartment, the loneliness crept back into my consciousness. I went from FaceTiming my parents once a day to three times a day. I needed to feel that connection.

I decided to make the most of my unexpected free time. I re-enrolled at Stanford and finished my undergraduate degree online, something I didn't think I could do when I was on my old, demanding, pre-Covid training regimen. I'd stopped taking classes in the spring of 2019 to gear up for the World Championships. I was planning on taking a leave of absence the whole year to devote myself to Tokyo. No need for that now.

I signed up to complete my major and minor. Then I added more classes to the mix to keep myself occupied. I took an infectious-disease course. It was unexpectedly reassuring, because I could turn off CNN, log onto Zoom, and get the benefit of a live Q&A with an infectious-disease expert. The class wasn't about Covid per se, but it was oddly soothing to get a scientific take on what was going on and learn some of the biology behind it.

While I waited, I had no clue how long it would be before I could see my family. How long our whole world was going to be living in this state of suspended animation. The holidays were tough. It was the first Thanksgiving and Christmas I'd spent completely away from my family. Zoom and FaceTime became my survival mechanisms. We did a Zoom Thanksgiving where my mom taught my brother and me how to make our family cranberry sauce. At Christmas, we revived our family tradition of a gingerbread-house competition, only we did it virtually. We each made our own house, sitting in front of the screen together, showing off our designs. We conducted multiple hours-long Zoom calls with extended family just to chat. I mean, I have fifteen cousins. Catching up with that many relatives will fill some time. Sometimes we would do a game night or trivia. It was almost like being together. Almost.

I found myself using the empty hours to Zoom with other folks who might be lonely. Before the pandemic, I would often visit the Children's National Hospital in D.C. to cheer up patients. The hospital broadcasts a show to the TVs in the kids' rooms. So I'd Zoom in to that and try to spread a bit of joy, or at least provide a distraction for the children there.

I also did outreach Zooms for swim clubs. A lot of teams were rudderless, out of the water. Their coaches were doing programming online, trying to motivate them. I'd log on, and they could ask me anything. I did what I could to offer encouragement. Talked to them about training and about racing, anything to get people's minds off the pandemic for a few hours.

I understood how they felt. I knew I needed to believe I was going to have a normal swimming career again. My life to that point had been about mitigating chance. Factoring in every possible scenario or outcome so that I would not be caught unaware. I researched my swimming competitors. I educated myself on pool conditions. I trained with an eye to detail that some might describe as obsessive. The frustration of the new unknown was difficult. The limbo I found myself in was intensely uncomfortable for me. I'd never been in a scenario where no amount of preparation mattered, where nothing I did made much of a difference.

At a certain point, I was just grateful that I had something to work toward with my training, as absurd as it sometimes felt to be doing it. The goal of a future Olympics gave me a light at the end of the tunnel. I was fortunate that none of my family got horribly sick. (I still haven't contracted Covid, as far as I know.) My teammates did a really good job of staying healthy in their bubbles. In the main, I was very fortunate.

I was lucky in unexpected ways as well. The pandemic gave me a greater appreciation for my health. It also put a lot of things in perspective. I've never felt like swimming was the be-all-end-all for anyone, including me. But there were definitely moments during the pandemic when I reminded myself that all of us are just fortunate to be alive. I was lucky that I got to swim every day, even in a backyard pool. I was so incredibly lucky, even if they canceled the Olympics and all of this training came to naught.

Once the vaccines finally arrived, I felt an indescribable wave of relief. I hadn't seen my family in over a year, which was unimaginable for a family unit as tight as ours. I reunited with my mom first. She flew out April 23, 2021; we waited until we'd both gotten our second doses. She took an Uber to my apartment, but I was already downstairs waiting for her. I wanted to see her as soon as I could. We hugged each other so hard.

She stayed with me a little over a week. I don't think she left the apartment. She cooked, and we hung out. She cleaned up my space, organized things. You know, Mom Stuff. Mom stuff that she couldn't do for a very long time.

We were relishing the fundamental joy of being in each other's company and not behind a screen. I wouldn't end up seeing my dad or brother in person until Olympic Trials in June. We were pretty careful there too. But each time I got to see my family again, it felt really, really good. I cried a lot of happy tears.

Around June 2020, we got word that Stanford was opening back up, the pool along with it. They had put additional protocols in place to make it work, including daily testing, limiting the number of people per lane, and temperature checks. Stanford was doing student testing three times a week or more. We swimmers were doing it every day some weeks—the full swab, all the way up the nose. I felt a lot of worry that I might test positive. It would mean a ten-day quarantine, ten days out of the water. I'd put in so much effort to be able to *stay* in the water during lockdown; I didn't want to test positive now. But that meant no socializing, no going out. I had conflicted feelings about it. Every day, it felt like an impossible choice. Swimming or everything else?

Looking back on those months now, I'm reminded that I am someone who learns to adapt pretty quickly. I remain steady. I generally don't get too high or too low. But there were certainly days when the seclusion hit me hard. When I broke down at practice, frustrated or crying. The fatigue set in differently than I'd felt before. I was way more emotional. I felt weary in my bones.

With the benefit of time and perspective, I can appreciate the upsides of the experience. I learned new things about myself. About what I can endure. And what remains once you endure it. What the pandemic did for me, as it did for many others, was recalibrate my relationship with the things I love. Those lonely days more strongly cemented my bond with my family. A thing I didn't know was even possible. Covid also gave me greater appreciation for swimming. A thing I *really* didn't know was possible.

During all those months on my own, swimming became more than a route to achieve goals. It became something that kept me happy, kept me healthy, kept me sane. Swimming gave me purpose. I've always been good at appreciating each day and enjoying the training. I love training more than racing, probably. I don't think too many swimmers say that. I think during that uncertain time, I had to lean even harder into enjoying the grind. I was training to train. Full stop. Nothing was guaranteed. Not the Olympics. Not a vaccine. Not a so-called normal life. The work I put in was in honor of the work itself. I came away with the knowledge that this was more than enough. In fact, it was kind of the whole point.

When my mom visited me that April, I took her to meet the Spiekers. She was ecstatic to be able to express gratitude to them in person. My mother had felt terrible she couldn't be with me all that time. She grew emotional thanking the Spiekers for stepping in to fill the family gap. I ran into the Spiekers recently when I visited Stanford for an event. I hadn't seen them since 2021. The kids were taller and more mature. When I hugged them hello, my eyes welled up. That time we had together was under terrible circumstances, but I came away with lifelong friends. The pandemic did that too. It turned strangers into family.

Chapter Seventeen

MOM

I was not the first Ledecky to make a splash in the pool. That would be my mother, Mary Gen. The word in the family is that my mom always swam full out. A mid-distance swimmer, she was known for starting fast and keeping a quick pace, no matter how much it hurt. Her old coaches have told me that her work ethic was akin to mine. She gasped for air after races. She gave it her all every practice.

My mother was a collegiate swimmer in the sprint and middle-distance freestyle events. One of the first recipients of a Title IX scholarship, she first swam at the College of Great Falls in Montana, coached by 1964 gold medalist Cathy Ferguson, then later went on to compete for the University of New Mexico, where she qualified for Nationals three times.

I was lucky to have my mom as a role model when I began swimming. As I've said, she didn't push me into the sport. Her first priority was making sure that I learned how to swim so I wouldn't drown. But the more I learned, the more attracted I became to the sport. I loved that my mom had been a freestyler too, and I could compare some of my times to hers. When I was young, I pored over the newspaper clippings that my mom saved from high school and college. Stories with headlines like "Lobo Gals in Nationals," above a headshot of my mom, smiling, looking off camera, hair cut into a bob not unlike my own.

Or another story titled "Congratulations Mary Gen!" The photo here shows my mom shaking hands with Coach Bob Miller at an award ceremony for the Lions Invitational Swim Meet. "After eight years of swimming, she has won approximately 50 trophies and 125 medals," the caption reads. Another article claimed she'd netted more than 200 medals and 60 trophies and had become "a household word around Williston and our neighboring states and Canada whenever swimming is discussed."

My mom would probably chuckle at that assessment, but I'm glad she kept all the press clips, including an opinion column that extolled not just her swimming bona fides but her character: "Really though, much more important than her swimming accomplishments has been the type of person she has grown up to be, an unselfish, humble girl with a strong faith and love in God."

Knowing my mom, that all tracks even to this day. It also sums up what the order of business has always been in our family. Try your best at what you hope to achieve. But be a good person first, last, and always. Be kind, be generous, and follow through. Those were the values my parents instilled in me, beyond the desire to swim and swim fast. My parents taught me that being successful at anything hardly matters in the long run if you can't look in the mirror and be proud of what you see looking back at you. I know for a fact that my parents are more thrilled by how I carry myself in the world than by any medal I've earned or world record I've broken.

When my swimming began pinging on the national radar, my mom made it a priority to keep me training but not overworked. To level set. She recalls being pressured to consider all kinds of major changes in my life and routine to capitalize on my nascent success. Well-intentioned people in the swim universe advised her which teams I should join, which coaches I *absolutely had* to train with. She watched as other families uprooted from their hometowns to swim in what were deemed the "right" clubs. She was told I should be homeschooled, to make more room for swimming.

That one got a big laugh. We were already devoting hours of our week to swimming. And homeschooling was a nonstarter chez Ledecky. My parents believed the social aspects of school were vital. I could have been swimming to the moon and back, and my mother wouldn't have taken me out of my school or shunted me into an even more high-profile situation. She and my father were determined that, outside of the pool, I remain a typical kid. They were always in perfect alignment when it came to parenting. It's part of what makes their marriage so great.

My parents met at a party in the Washington, D.C., area. My uncle Jon was living in the area, and he asked my dad to tag along with him to a gathering in Old Town, Alexandria. My mom was there, and she and my father both found themselves more interested in the World Series baseball game playing on the TV than anything going on at the get-together.

They found out they both enjoyed swimming. My dad covered swimming in high school as a sportswriter. He knew a lot of swimmers, so they bonded over that, among other things. It was not love at first sight. In fact, my mom says when my uncle asked for her card as she was exiting the party, and then my dad took it from his hand, she was relieved, because she figured my dad would be too shy to ever call.

He called the next week.

Their second date was a tennis match, which my mom says she won (and my dad agrees not to correct her).

My mom grew up in a wildly different environment than D.C. Raised in Williston, North Dakota, a modest town up in the northwest corner of the state, she was the fourth child of seven. My mom always said she was truly a middle child, in that she felt like either the youngest of the oldest group, or the oldest of the youngest group. She shared a bedroom with her three younger sisters, a single bathroom upstairs for all seven kids. Privacy and solitude were nonexistent. But in typical middle-child fashion, Mom got along with everybody, stayed even-keeled. (Even with one bathroom!)

My grandpa was born in Williston as well, and after World War II, he came back to set up his medical practice. The family owned a house in town, so my grandpa could travel to the hospital and around the area to call on his patients. There was also a family farm a few miles out, on which wheat was grown and cattle were raised. My uncles Mike and Ed helped with branding. It was nonstop hands-on labor. Farms and animals don't really allow for breaks. When she wasn't chipping in on farm chores or helping out at the house, my mom was content to do her own thing, which, soon enough, became racking up swimming medals.

She started swimming in the summer at the Harmon Park outdoor pool. There was no way to swim year-round until my mom was a freshman in high school, when the town, thanks to my grandpa's insistence, opened its first indoor pool. Before that pool opened, she still raced teams in the state that trained year-round, places like Minot or Fargo. During those winter months, she'd travel to the meets, not having practiced since summer, and swim the meet cold. That's amazing to me.

Back then, there weren't a whole lot of sports in which girls could compete. Guys at my mom's school could go out for basketball, baseball, football. The girls didn't have the same options. It would be another five years before Title IX kicked in and mandated sports access equality. Since there wasn't a high school team, my mom was a club swimmer. Once Williston opened an indoor pool, a swim coach was hired to coach the club team. Well, he was actually a former football player from the University of North Dakota who was helping with the high school football team, but hey, at least he was trying, and the swim club could now train all year.

My mom started breaking records right away. First meet records, then state, then regional. She was winning a lot. She told my grandpa she wanted to swim in college, but there weren't a lot of women's swimming programs in universities at the time. There was one small school in Montana she'd heard had a coach who had been an Olympian, the College of Great Falls. My mother decided that's where she should go. She stayed a year, managing to qualify for nationals. Because of a registration issue between what was then the Association for Intercollegiate Athletics for Women and the college, she ultimately couldn't compete at nationals.

My mom was crushed. All that hard work and she couldn't see it through because of paperwork. She decided she needed to find another college swim team and landed at the University of New Mexico. They had a combined women's and men's swim team. It felt like the big leagues. The practices were a lot harder than anything she'd ever done. One of the practices was so taxing she cried, but she kept at it, and then, midway through that first year in Albuquerque, Title IX went into effect.

All five or six women on the swim team got financial assistance overnight. My mother immediately got a scholarship. Her books were paid for. Same for her lab fees. The women had a meet schedule, and they traveled with the men. They went to nationals. Title IX, now a fundamental aspect of civil rights in the United States, changed my mother's life forever.

Because of my mother's experience, I grew up with a keen awareness of how limited the choices had been for female competitors not that long ago. Had I been born then, I likely wouldn't have been able to swim in college, much less carve any kind of career out of swimming. When my mom talks about those days in college, she tells me they were thrilling. She felt validated and supported in her swimming, and she found herself dreaming bigger and bigger with every passing year. She'd come from a small world (the University of New Mexico was twice the size of her hometown), in a state not exactly famous for swimmers, and had excelled despite every obstacle. She made a point to embrace every moment, including training. She could not believe her good fortune.

My mom's best race was the 200 freestyle. She could go up to the 500 and down to the 100. We're alike in that way too. Testing our limits in various distances. Never thinking we can't. Always giving it our all.

When I ask my mom why she stopped competing, she shrugs. She didn't see swimming as a career option. She knew once she graduated, she'd need a job, and that would require focus. She'd been working summers in the medical record department in Williston. She received her degree in health information sciences and worked in a hospital as the director of a medical record department for four years. She then went on to graduate school and received her master's in health care administration at the University of Minnesota. Swimming shifted from being a competition to a hobby.

There's a photo of my mom from February 20, 1973, where she is standing beside a wall covered from top to bottom with her medals, so many they look like wallpaper. Beside her are shelves lined with trophies. Below her, a display of swimming magazines. She's wearing a plaid shirt and jeans with a thick grommeted belt, smiling big, with the slightest hint of chagrin on her face. In an accompanying press clip, she describes being in the pool as being in her own world: "During workouts I may count laps, but sometimes I just rest," my mother says. "My mind is blank. I enjoy it."

This sentiment is uncannily familiar to me.

As was her telling the reporter how hard it was to explain to friends why she spent so much time in the pool. And why she wouldn't change the consuming demands of swimming for the world: "I don't think I could have found a replacement for swimming. It taught me to be competitive and how to set a goal and then work hard to reach it. I've learned a lot about myself . . . Swimming is so much a part of my life, it's like a blanket."

Swimming built my mom, just as it has built me. It gave her the assurance that she would always be able to take care of herself. It empowered her to build her career. To move all over the country. To be self-sufficient at a time when most women married before they graduated from college. I believe one reason we're so close is that my mom didn't have me until she was forty-two. She married later in life. By the time she had my brother and me, she was ready. There were no doubts. Nor would there be regrets. She was eager to be present. And she truly was. At every swim practice and meet. Always there when I needed a shoulder to lean on. My mom enjoyed her life, and that made it easy for her to enjoy being a parent. (Although she did sometimes complain while zipping around at a few of my birthday parties that her back hurt, joking, "I should have had you when I was twenty-five.")

I talk to my mom almost daily. We share an absurd sense of humor. There are times when we find something so funny we can't even get words out, we're laughing so hard. When I have a bad practice, I call my mom. She's great for getting my mind off my disappointments. She reminds me that it's all part of the process and that it's happened before. Sure enough, I'll have a really good practice the next day, or see a break-through on the horizon.

She's also a great cook. She makes a mean lasagna, these great chicken dishes. She borrows my grandma's recipes and makes them her own. There was a nutritionist who came and visited me once during high school, the year after the London Games, to introduce herself and share some tips with my mom about what kinds of food I should be eating now that I was an Olympic athlete. That was likely a waste of time. All through high school, other swimmers' parents would chase my mom down and ask, "What does Katie eat for breakfast? What does Katie eat for dinner?" And my mom would answer, "Well, strawberries are on sale right now. So, a lot of strawberries."

I remember one time when I was twelve, my mom saw something on USA Swimming's website about how you should eat low-fat yogurt before practice, but somehow she decided low-fat chocolate ice cream was close enough. There was maybe a whole year when I was having chocolate ice cream at four-thirty in the morning. It's one of those things that I look back on and laugh at, but I also wonder if that was part of what made it so easy for me to wake up that early. If so, genius move on Mom's part.

When it was my mom's turn to drive me and my brother to those crack-of-dawn weekday practices, we would literally wake up, pull on our suits, and shuffle out the door. Post-practice, Mom would be sleeping in the car, and we'd have to bang on the windows to wake her up. She would cart us to the pool while every normal person was still cozy in bed. But she did it without complaint for years. She knew how happy swimming made her kids.

I've kept a single stuffed animal from my childhood. A long-eared rabbit I named Baby Lulu. Her legs are half quilted—the result of patchwork to preserve her limbs—as are her ears. She has no eyes or mouth, just a stitched-up face sewn together from various soft fabrics.

My mom bought me Baby Lulu on a beautiful summer day. The same day she received troubling mammogram results. We went into the physician's office, and my mother was informed, "The doctor has to come talk to you." My mom, the daughter of a doctor, knew instantly that was a bad sign. She was taken into a back office and told that she would need a fine-needle biopsy.

I was only a year old, so I couldn't understand why my mom was crying. Why she was calling my dad. Why Grandma Berta would need to come take care of me and Michael. After booking an appointment with a surgeon, my mom took me from the radiology building to Treetop Toys. She plucked Baby Lulu from the shelf and said, as she handed me the floppy rabbit, "Whenever you're missing me, give Baby Lulu a hug."

Thankfully, my mom's biopsy was clear. We were fortunate. Life, brought to a halt by a frightening diagnosis, resumed anew. But that day has always stuck with me. I still have Baby Lulu. She's on my bed as a reminder of the selflessness my mom has always shown me. Even when she was scared, her first instinct was to comfort me. I'm lucky to have my mom—and, of course, Baby Lulu—by my side.

Baby Katie.

Grandma Berta with baby Katie.

Mom.

Laughing with Uncle Jon.

Grandpa Jerry on the boat that took him to America, circa 1947.

Taking a poolside call.

Playing soccer for my Little Flower School team.

With Grandma Hagan, holding a
Whirl-A-Whip in Stanley, ND.

With my brother, Michael, at a Palisades swim
meet.

With Palisades teammates.

With Dad on the day of my First Communion.

With Michael and Grandpa Hagan raising American flag on the farm in Williston, ND.

Swimming is a small world. Meeting Michael Phelps (Katie Ziegler seated next to him) with my club swimming and eventual Stanford teammate Janet Hu right behind me.

With Michael at Podolí Pool in Prague.

With my Potomac Valley Swimming Zones team.

The 2011 Junior Nationals was held at Stanford, my future alma mater. That year, I won the High Point award.

With Coach Yuri Suguiyama at a team luau party in the summer.

Riding my grandparents' horse in Williston, ND, with my aunt Colleen guiding.

Prior to the opening ceremonies in London, with Kate Ziegler, me, basketball player Kevin Love, and Kathleen Hersey.

Swimming in the women's 800m freestyle prelims at the London Olympics.

My open-air meeting with Yuri and Jon Urbanchek after the prelims at the London Olympics.

With Grandma Berta at the St. Patrick's Day parade in Washington, D.C. I was a parade division marshal in 2013.

The medal ceremony for my first gold medal, at the 2012 Olympics in London. You can tell how happy I am.

With Coach Bruce Gemmell following the 2015 world championships in Kazan, Russia.

STONE RIDGE SCHOOL SWIMMING & DIVING RECORDS							
GIRLS SCHOOL	TIME	YR	EVENTS	GIRLS POOL	SCH	TIME	YR
GARCIA, KRONFLI, HALEY			200 MEDLEY RELAY	CLEARY, HAASE, MILLER			
LEDECKY	1:49.13	13		MULQUIN	GC	1:53.44	11
LEDECKY	1:41.55	15	200 FREE	LEDECKY	SR	1:49.32	12
LEDECKY	1:57.88	15	200 IM	LEDECKY	SR	2:05.52	15
LEDECKY	23.19	15	50 FREE	MCTAGGART	HA	23.44	15
O'ROURKE	246.05	06	DIVING 6 DIVES	HOSTAGE	AHC	260.00	06
O'ROURKE	376.95	06	DIVING 11 DIVES	GRINKER	SID	407.35	11
LEDECKY	54.38	13	100 FLY	LEDECKY	SR	57.65	12
LEDECKY	49.45	15	100 FREE	LEDECKY	SR	49.93	15
LEDECKY	4:26.58	15	500 FREE	LEDECKY	SR	4:45.98	13
GASAWAY, HALEY, GARCIA			200 FREE RELAY	GASAWAY, GARCIA, KRONFLI			
LEDECKY	1:36.14	14		LEDECKY	SR	1:40.98	11
LEDECKY	59.06	14	100 BACK	LEDECKY	SR	59.06	15
ROGERS	1:05.68	04	100 BREAST	LEDECKY	SR	1:06.80	15
GASAWAY, HALEY, GARCIA			400 FREE RELAY	GASAWAY, HALEY, GARCIA			
LEDECKY	3:30.36	14		LEDECKY	SR	3:39.82	13

With my family at Stone Ridge pool following my high school graduation.

Meeting Bruce Springsteen and attending his concert with my family at Nationals Park was an experience I'll never forget.

A freshman on the Stanford campus.

My Stanford coaches and teammates celebrated my 1500m free world record with giant balloons (my new time was 15:20).

With Michael before USA Swimming's Golden Goggles Awards.

With Coach Greg Meehan at the end of the Tokyo Olympics.

With Florida coach, teammates, and friends at 2023 Golden Goggles Awards. *Back row, left to right*: Bobby Finke, Jake Mitchell, me, Coach Nesty, Brennan Gravley, Kieran Smith, and Emma Weyant. *Front row, left to right*: Ellie Zweifel, Bella Sims, Nina Kucheran, and Julia Restivo.

Medals from the 2021 Tokyo Olympics.

If you need me, I'm probably in the pool.

Chapter Eighteen

TOKYO

I was twenty-one years old when I turned professional. I had just competed and won the 500- and 1650-yard freestyle events at the 2018 NCAA championships and was deep into prep for the 2020 Tokyo Olympics. I made the announcement at an event with the National Press Club in my hometown, which meant a lot to me, because my family and local friends were in the audience to hear the big news.

My reasoning was I'd come off two incredible collegiate years, winning back-to-back national titles with my teammates. These experiences had made me inordinately happy. But the time had come to transition to the next level. Little did I know then that a pandemic would set fire to the training calendar, delaying Tokyo a year, and pushing me—and many other athletes—to our psychological limits.

The "will they, won't they?" of the decision to hold the Games was the hardest to manage. Public support for going forward, especially in Japan, was low. The prevalent opinion was that holding the Olympics at any time during the pandemic would be risky for Japan's health and security. In July 2021, on the cusp of the Games, polls showed more than half of the local citizens still wanted the Olympics canceled. There was widespread doubt that organizers could control the viral spread athletes might bring from their home countries. While the IOC recommended vaccinations, they weren't required. This created further alarm and depressed enthusiasm for the Games.

When the Games officially commenced, it felt like a minor miracle. None of us athletes had been certain they would happen, even as we prepared to compete. Covid taught everyone that you can't count on anything, so expecting to travel across the world and swim in an international event during a global emergency seemed as likely as my winning *Dancing with the Stars*. (Not very.)

Even with the ups and downs, I'd kept training and set myself an ambitious meet agenda, taking on a big load of races from the 200 up through the 1500. One might have thought that my program was too ambitious. It's a well-known fact that it's extraordinarily difficult to be a top 200 freestyler and a top 1500 freestyler simultaneously—they require different training, different skills, different everything. But I *love* the challenge of swimming all these events. In Tokyo, I was gunning for all the races, even if it would require a lot of juggling. I just couldn't resist.

It's in my blood to expect improvement, faster swims. But after Rio, I found it tough to match my own times. I was nineteen then. The media likes to emphasize age. How could an athlete possibly get better as they grew older? Unlike wine or cheese, which famously only get better with age, most athletes tend to peak early. Leading into Tokyo, I had to ignore the skeptical chatter, overcome self-doubt. I did everything I could to eliminate all that external noise from my head and trust myself.

The pre-Olympic training camp was in Honolulu, at a pool in President Obama's old high school. Camp was when we allowed ourselves to believe the Games were really happening. We got stuck in Hawaii for an extra day due to a logistics issue, then flew to Tokyo for another week of training camp before moving into the Olympic Village. By the time I landed, I was at peace with the work I'd put into my prep. I felt good, confident.

Once we arrived at the airport, we were cautioned that it might take anywhere from ninety minutes to a few hours to get from the terminal to our rooms. By the time we made it to the hotel, five hours and twenty-two minutes had elapsed.

What took so long? Covid testing. Customs. Pandemic protocols. Everyone on every team had to produce a negative test before we could exit. Officials parked roughly twenty people each in a series of waiting rooms while testing was carried out. This was the furthest thing from Covid-safe, but we wore our masks and waited.

After maybe an hour and a half, one of the workers at the airport entered our room and passed out a piece of paper. The first line said, "Somebody on your flight may have tested positive." A bit farther down the page it read, "We are going to take you to the quarantine hotel . . ."

My heart sank. I couldn't believe it. As the news made its way through the room, there was incredulity, despair, and a few curse words. How could this happen? Was our time at the Games over before it even started?

The managing director of the national team, Lindsay Mintenko, was pacing the hallway between the various waiting rooms. Lindsay swam in the 2000 and 2004 Games, earning three medals, two gold. She was the first female senior executive to lead the USA Swimming National Team. After reviewing the papers, she advised us to hand them back to her, take a deep breath, and hold tight. She surmised that they were handing out documents prematurely. That we should try and relax until we knew precisely what was going on. Maybe they were retesting? They had counseled us that the saliva test could be finicky. Thankfully, Jay Litherland, who swam the men's 400 individual medley, was in our waiting room.

Jay was born in Japan and lived there until he was three. He spoke Japanese fluently. He began communicating with the airport staff. Soon enough, we had our intel. There was an inconclusive test, Jay reported back. We waited another hour. Then another.

The whole time, I was texting with my mom. "I hope this is rock bottom for the entire trip," I wrote, fighting the urge to give up prematurely. The flight had been long and exhausting. Waiting hours in a sterile room packed with weary, frightened athletes was fraying our collective nerves. Finally, after nearly six hours, we were given the all-clear.

The Tokyo Olympic Village was a sealed bubble within a sealed bubble. Masks were always mandatory. When we arrived at the Village, we got a bunch of tubes we had to fill with our saliva each morning when we woke up, before we brushed our teeth. You had to provide a certain amount of spit, then give the tube to the team manager. Who knows how the testing was done or how they were able to collect and track all those samples from every single person in the Village. But they did. Ideally, you'd hear nothing. That meant you'd tested negative. Every day I prayed I wouldn't get notified.

There was also an app that tracked our every move. We had to constantly enter our data so there could be contact tracing. Team USA stuck close together, especially on bus rides. We were always fretful that if we sat next to a stranger who tested positive, then the app would ping that we'd been within a certain number of feet. If you got pinged in a contact trace, you were out of the competition. The randomness of disease and the high stakes of competition had everyone on edge.

In Rio five years before, I remember the thrill of going to meals, settling down at a table, waiting to see who would sit across from me. Athletes from other countries would strike up conversations. Same thing on bus rides to the venues. But no one could do that in Tokyo. You barely interacted with other athletes except for quick nods and hellos.

I was in a suite with five other swimmers—Allison Schmitt, Natalie Hinds, Hali Flickinger, Lilly King, and Simone Manuel. I had a single, which was awesome, because my competition schedule was so frenzied that it was beneficial to be able to come back, turn the lights off, and sleep whenever I needed to. My twin bed, like all the others, was constructed of stacked cardboard boxes and pushed flush against the wall. (The room itself wasn't much larger than a cardboard box, but that's typical in Olympic housing.) There was a tiny common area, which contained a modest circular table and maybe three chairs.

The cafeterias had plastic cubicles dividing the dining tables so you could eat comfortably without fear of spreading anything to the person across from or next to you. I sought out spaces that had fewer people around. Team USA brought a couple of chefs to Tokyo who lived outside the Village, and if you wanted, they'd prepare meals for delivery. If you were competing that day, you could get a meal right after your race, or when you wrapped your media spots. I ate a lot of Team USA dinners. It was like our own personalized Grubhub.

My lineup left scant time for me to relax. There was one day when I had the 400 free final in the morning and a single hour before I had to head back to the aquatic center for the 200 free prelim and the 1500 free prelim. Three races on the same day. Team USA had sent me spaghetti and meatballs with broccoli as a quick meal between the races. I remember getting back to my room in the Village, propping my legs on my cardboard bed to aid circulation, and eating as fast as I could as I tried to recover for my next race. I was able to close my eyes for maybe five minutes. I don't think I fell asleep, but I remember when I came back for prelims that afternoon, I could still taste the spaghetti and meatballs.

The Tokyo pool was stunning. My first reaction when I walked into the venue was "Wow!" Followed by: *This would be incredible filled with spectators.* There was seating on three sides. I knew it would've been electric if they could have packed that stadium. Fans were prohibited in the arena. Instead, on the left side of the pool, there would be dignitaries or certain invited team representatives, then, far enough away to be safe, a small media section.

Our teammates were permitted to sit in the stands on the right side. You could see and hear them from the pool deck, which was a welcome twist. One thing I loved was I could distinguish their cheers. I could discern who was shouting, "Let's go, Katie!" as I climbed behind the blocks. It felt intimate and personal in a way no other Olympics had before.

That said, I was still largely alone on the biggest international stage. My family was thousands of miles away. Without them there in Tokyo, I had no one I could turn to for connection. We would text and FaceTime, of course, but it wasn't the same as seeing their faces in the crowd or being able to hug them after a race. My teammates and I had each other's backs. We filled the void by joking about the overall bizarreness of this Olympics, lifting each other up when we were down, celebrating each other's successes with even more gusto since we were the only ones there to bring the cheer.

My first event, the 400 free, was one of the most anticipated showdowns of the Tokyo Games. It was described as "mouthwatering" (weird), "the duel of the century," and the "rivalry of the Games." Loads of coverage in that vein. Australia's Ariarne Titmus was being positioned as my rival in the press. (The press loooooves rivalries.) Coming into the Tokyo Games, Ariarne was the only swimmer who had beaten me in a distance race at a major meet. That was at the 2019 World Championships, when I was battling my mystery virus. But there was no denying we were in each other's sights.

The buzzer sounded, and the 400 began. For 300 meters, I was in the lead. But in the final lap, Ariarne pulled ahead to win by 0.67 seconds. I took silver. It was the first time in an Olympics individual event that I'd missed gold.

The finish was a showstopper. As I told Ariarne in the pool, "We delivered a great race."

I'd swum the second fastest time of my career at that distance, behind only my Rio swim. But in terms of the media, there was shock and awe that I'd come in second. Headlines latched on to the fact that it was my first silver at an Olympics in an individual event. When questioned about the race, I explained I'd fought tooth and nail, and that's all you can ask for. That it's never an easy journey to the podium. Ariarne just got her hand to the wall first.

"I don't want anyone to feel sorry for me or feel like silver or any other medal besides gold is a disappointment or anything," I told the press. "Just because I've won golds leading into this doesn't mean the silver doesn't mean something to me."

No matter how often I expressed those sentiments, I was repeatedly asked if I was upset or disappointed. It wasn't as if I had swum terribly. Anyone in the swimming community would've seen that I swam a great race. Coach Greg did his best to keep me balanced and positive. He reinforced in my mind that my 400 free was a good, solid swim. I minimized reading coverage of the event because I needed to stay focused and in my own head, rather than digesting the way other people were viewing my performance. I remember my Team USA pals and I would roll our eyes about how those headlines were silly, when reporters wrote that somebody "settled for silver" or "lost" a race when they won a silver medal. I mean, you're second best in the entire world for a single moment in time. That is not cause for an existential crisis.

In fact, I built a lot of momentum for myself after my 400 free. I'd gone faster than I had at Olympic Trials. My splits were good. I left the event excited about the rest of the week. Coming off that race, I rolled through the 200 free prelim, 1500 free prelim, and 200 free semifinal. All went well until the final of the 200 free.

I always knew the challenge for me in Tokyo would be that the 200 free final and the 1500 free final were on the very same day. In fact, they were only about seventy minutes apart. Greg and I figured there would be a medal ceremony for the 200 in between that would eat up rest and warm-down minutes, which would make my recovery time even shorter. We needn't have worried.

Maybe it was a cumulative weariness, maybe it simply wasn't my day, but I dove into the pool for the 200 and, like a wet match, I never quite ignited. My stroke felt off. My finishing kick didn't engage. It was as if I wasn't even in the race.

I came in a disappointing fifth, with a time of 1:55.21. That was slower than I had gone at Trials; slower than at a meet in April that Greg and I had used as a yardstick; slower, by about a second and a half, than what I'd swum in Rio to win the 200 five years earlier. This time Ariarne took the gold, beating my time by 1.71 seconds. It was the thirty-sixth final of

189

my international career, and it was the first time I didn't earn a medal. Now, *that* result was a blow.

I was mad at myself after the race. But the 1500 free final was happening in under an hour. I needed to get my head straight. I was fatigued, but I knew I'd have to dig deep and fight.

When I saw Greg, he told me the loss was something we could use as a positive. We had more time to warm down. To be honest, after all the racing I'd already done during the week, I needed that.

In the warm-down pool, I strained to find constructive self-talk. The 1500 has historically been my most dominant race. In 2013, when I was sixteen years old, I bested Kate Ziegler's world record by six seconds. Since then, I'd set the world record *six times.* I reminded myself of these stats. But my brain continued to cloud with doubt. I was keenly aware of the ticking clock. I knew I was running out of time to relax and reset. I desperately needed to find a way to get past the 200—to shake it off—and focus on the 1500 free. That's when I started thinking about my grandparents.

I envisioned both of my grandmothers watching me on television back at home. I thought about how invested they were in my swimming. How much they loved me. How much I wanted to fill them with pride. I imagined their faces. The tenderness I felt for them both. What they meant to me. If I was going to dwell on anything in those heightened moments, it was going to be on the toughness and fortitude and warmth of my grandmothers.

The cloud began to lift. I told myself, *If I use the race to channel my grandparents, there's no way I'm going to lose. If I get a cramp, it's not going to distract me. If my lungs burn, I'll push through.* And that's when I mentally turned the corner.

Usually, when I dive into the water in the 1500 free, I obsessively count my laps. I use the count to keep my mind occupied, away from the pain I know is around the corner. This time I didn't count. Instead, I repeated my grandmothers' names over and over again, like a song I was singing in my head. Grandma Hagan, Grandma Berta, Grandma Hagan, Grandma Berta. A genealogical mantra. Links on a chain that connected me to the women who had come before me—and to the task at hand.

I built their names into the rhythm of my swim. Grandma Hagan, Grandma Berta, Grandma Hagan, Grandma Berta. Every stroke, lap after lap, I kept them top of mind, swimming with me. The 1500 is nearly a mile. I led for the entire time, ahead by 10 meters and finishing in 15:37.34. I touched the wall first. The grit of my grandmothers had pulled me through.

After I won, the feelings rushed in. I hugged my teammate Erica Sullivan, who took second, over the lane rope. I let out an uncharacteristic victory roar. My eyes welled with tears.

This was in part because my victory wasn't mine alone. At every other Olympics since 1968, the longest women's race had been the 800. The second I won, it hit me that I was the first woman to compete in and claim the debut gold medal in the women's 1500-meter Olympic freestyle. That was genuinely historic.

In the media Q&A after the 1500, I acknowledged how much this specific gold meant to me. It was my sixth, but somehow it carried more weight because of the specifics of the event. I remember saying I hoped all the women who came before me and Erica, and who didn't have the opportunity we had, understood we were swimming for them as well. I also addressed the people who kept reminding me that I wasn't winning everything. I told them there's much more to life than swimming and the Olympics, like faith and family. That was a nod to my grandparents.

After that, the 4x200 relay was on deck. Team USA wasn't favored to win the relay. There were four teams in the medal mix, between Australia, China, Canada, and us. Everyone swimming was prepped for a dogfight. Australia was widely seen to have the edge.

From the start of the event, we were right there with Australia and China, which was a surprise. I was the anchor, so I could see the race was playing out differently than what everyone had expected. On the third leg, Katie McLaughlin, who is about my age and had been on a couple of Worlds teams with me, turned before she stepped up on the block, looked me in the eye, and said, "I got you." She wanted me to know she was about to go ham, setting me up in the best possible position she could. Watching her swim, I realized if I did my part, we could get a medal, challenging Australia for silver and potentially catching China for gold. I dove in and delivered one of my fastest splits ever. Faster than my individual 200 free.

In the end, we won silver. Far better than predicted. We nearly overtook China. It was an emotional high for the entire team. Allison Schmitt, a great veteran, brought so much heart to the pool that day. I remember going to breakfast with her leading up to the race, and she was telling me every ten minutes how excited she was for the relay and how stoked she was to be on the team with all of us. That kept a smile on my face all the way up to the blocks.

Another quirk of Covid was that when we received our medals, they were served to us on a literal platter, and we had to pick them up and drape them around our own necks. For the relay medals, we gave them to each other, which was unexpectedly touching. Katie gave me mine, and I returned the favor. We were allowed to take our masks off for one photo on the podium, so we did, and smiled big.

The 800 free was my last event of the Games. By that point, I was at peace with how my Olympics had gone. I'd swum some superb times. I'd had a legacy swim with the 1500; I'd overcome letdowns and subpar performances. Most importantly, I'd stayed healthy and eligible to compete. The 800 was an old friend. I'd swum it so many times. I was ready.

Ariarne was right there in the pool with me, lane seven. The buzzer sounded; I dove in. From the jump, I built a commanding lead and kept it the entire race. When I touched the wall, I became the first woman to win three consecutive Olympic golds in the same event.

All told, I raced 6200 meters in Tokyo. More than any woman in the pool in any prior Olympics. I left Japan the most decorated U.S. female athlete across all sports, just as I had in Rio. In nearly every other way, Tokyo contrasted with the looseness and freedom and promise of my Rio and London experiences. But I learned more about myself.

I surprised myself by staying so steady throughout the Games. Being part of an Olympics during Covid was indisputably abnormal. There was the potential for massive chaos, so many things that could have gone wrong. The whole meet was stress on stress, wrapped in a stress burrito. But amid all that insecurity, I remained calm. I handled everything that was thrown at me. And that was the biggest win in many ways. Because that carries past any competition. That carries into life.

I recall a post-Games headline proclaiming my Tokyo Olympics "less golden." I guess that's one way to describe it. But that's not how I felt. It had been a long slog for every athlete to continue training during Covid, to keep the faith throughout a global crisis. In Tokyo, I felt the honor of representing my country in a deeper way. Back in March 2020, when the IOC and Japan's government confirmed that the Olympics would be rescheduled, a press release labeled the Olympics as a "beacon of hope to the world during these troubled times" and a "light at the end of the tunnel." Given everything the world had been through, I was grateful just to be there. I felt uniquely present in the moment.

After I went home, I took some time out of the water. I visited North Dakota and my Grandma Hagan. I thanked her for being in the pool with me in spirit. Then I went to New York. I saw my Grandma Berta there, hugged her hard. I did an interview on the *Today* show, visited the Empire State Building. I kept my break low-key. I needed to decompress from the training, the travel, the competing.

After two weeks, the gears started turning in my head about what was next for me and swimming. My apartment lease was up in California. It was time to decide what my next step would be. With Tokyo under my belt, I felt ready to make a major move.

Chapter Nineteen

GRANDMA BERTA

M y Grandmother Berta was a woman before her time. Born in New York City in 1933, the daughter of Milton and Eleanor Greenwald, Grandma Berta attended Erasmus Hall High School in Brooklyn, where she excelled academically and discovered a passion for writing. Being a Jewish woman in the 1940s, my grandma knew nothing would be given to her. She had to be dexterous and resilient if she was going to live the life she desired. Which is precisely what she did.

Grandma Berta blazed through an elite education, a rare path for women then, attending Brooklyn College and the Columbia University writing program. Her efforts won her a New York University creative writing award and a New York State scholar award. While in college, she answered a cryptic job posting by a retired professor looking for someone who understood German to take dictation of his memoirs. That retired professor ended up being none other than Albert Einstein. She would work for him for more than a year, a twist of fate that seems bananas but, if you knew my Grandma Berta, would seem perfectly in keeping with her larger-than-life existence.

In 1956, Grandma Berta married Grandpa Jerry. They had two sons: my dad, David, and my uncle Jonathan. My grandma didn't let motherhood dim her professional or creative ambitions. She published fictional short stories in various national magazines like *Redbook, Good Housekeeping,* and *McCall's.* Her piece about an American medic in

Vietnam who adopted a Vietnamese child, written at the height of the Vietnam War, received wide acclaim. It was republished in more than fifty languages.

Her writing career led my grandma into the business world. She climbed the masthead at a medical publication called *Patient Care* to become a managing editor, after which she was recruited to work in medical advertising agencies. She excelled there too, eventually becoming chief operating officer of the health care advertising division of Bozell, Jacobs, Kenyon & Eckhardt. That she was able to rise through the corporate ranks as a woman in those days was extraordinarily uncommon. And a testament to her nerve and talent. She worked long hours to help put my dad and uncle through college.

Regardless of what she achieved, Grandma Berta never rested on her laurels. When she climbed one peak, she checked the horizon for another. That tendency is one I am grateful to have inherited.

When she turned sixty-four, Grandma Berta gave my family a packet of letters from her ancestors, including her parents. The correspondence is fascinating. Both of my great-grandparents' families immigrated to America in the 1890s. The letters track the six-year tumultuous courtship of Grandma Berta's parents, my great-grandfather Milton and my great-grandma Eleanor. Milton was routinely bullied on his way to and from Hebrew school, attacked by gangs of boys searching for easy targets. His father, Simon, was a bespoke tailor and was furious when Milton would arrive home at the stoop with his clothes soiled and ripped from fighting.

Eleanor's father was a baker specializing in elaborate and complex confectionaries. He suffered from asthma and was continually sick from inhaling the flour, but it was the only job he could secure. Hunger and poverty were the order of the day in the tenements. As one of my relatives wrote, "I had wanted so much and had so little." There was also mention in the letters of the women in our bloodline possessing "superhuman endurance." That caught my eye.

Maybe because she never forgot the hardscrabble beginnings of her family legacy, Grandma Berta took nothing for granted. She was wise to how cruel and cold the world could be, so she deliberately made herself a counterweight. She celebrated. She engaged. She stayed curious and open. All examples I longed to emulate, even as a kid.

Like my mom, Grandma Berta was very social. She gabbed with the doorman, with waiters and taxi drivers and bodega owners. A true New Yorker, she walked everywhere she could. There were no strangers in Grandma Berta's world. Just friends she hadn't met yet. She made an effort to become close to everyone, including my mother's family. She trekked to visit them in North Dakota. She and Grandma Hagan would phone each other after my swim meets: "Did you see that?" They were both tickled by my success.

Though, as a Brooklyn Dodgers fan, she spent a lot of time in her youth at Ebbets Field, Grandma Berta was never particularly into watching Olympic sports. I'd wager she'd have never watched a single swim meet if I wasn't a swimmer. She was a good swimmer and she did swim now and then in the community pool in Queens, but I know she preferred the beach. She went to Coney Island as a child, and took me to beaches a few times, but I was wary of the ocean. Even as a senior citizen, she was bolder than I was when it came to the open water.

The arts were what really mattered to Grandma Berta. *Culture.* She came from a very musical family. Her dad was a fantastic jazz pianist. Her uncle Bernie did radio, TV, and movie scores as a composer, arranger, and orchestra conductor. Her brother, Joel, was a keyboardist as well as a trumpet and saxophone player. Grandma Berta is why my brother and I learned to play piano. She even paid for the lessons. Whenever she would come to Bethesda, we'd perform for her, and she'd sing along. She had perfect pitch.

The first musical I saw was with her, *The Music Man.* Then she took me to *Chicago, Amazing Grace, Jersey Boys, School of Rock.* We'd catch a Broadway show every time I was in town. My grandma loved everything about New York City. She took us to the Statue of Liberty, all the delis and restaurants, the museums and parks. She made sure we experienced every neighborhood. She wanted us to absorb all the city had to offer.

When she was living in Queens, my grandmother stepped in when her adult Japanese neighbors were being harassed by some kids. She would not abide hatred of any kind. Over the years, we celebrated some of the Jewish holidays with Grandma Berta, including celebrating Hannukah and Sukkot with her. I was fortunate to have the experience of learning about Jewish history and tradition in conjunction with my Catholic upbringing. As a Jewish woman, Grandma Berta was accustomed to fighting prejudice and bigotry. I remember when we were in Prague in 2007, she took my brother and me to the Jewish quarter to educate us about the Holocaust and what some of our family had endured during the era. We were young, but she believed we were old enough to learn about basic freedoms—and how quickly they can be eroded or denied.

I've kept all my text exchanges with Grandma Berta. I have them from as far back as 2013. When I revisit them, my eyes well up. My grandma always called me "darling" or "precious darling." Just typing out those words brings her back to me in a small but concrete way.

In April 2015, she texted me about that trip to Prague. I'd just referenced my visit there in the press. Grandma Berta wrote, "Dear Katie, it was so sweet and dear of you to mention Grandpa Jerry and your family's trip for his birthday. I know what it meant to him to have you and Michael and your parents there with him. I spent hours looking for a good swimming pool there for you and Michael, never cognizant of the significance your swimming would ultimately have."

My grandma truly had devoted days to locating a pool for me to swim in, even though I was only ten years old at the time. She settled on the Podolí pool, but not before checking out the locker rooms to make sure everything was up to snuff. I've met Czech swimmers at the Olympics, and when I tell them that I swam at the Podolí pool, they're always happy and surprised. That pool was my first taste of swimming internationally. My first time ever leaving the country. (The second was to London for the Olympics.) My grandma's herculean efforts, though she didn't know it then, helped put me on the path to success.

In 2012, Grandma Berta was diagnosed with intestinal cancer and couldn't travel to attend my inaugural Olympic Trials. She and my uncle Jon watched the meet on television at her apartment. During the qualifications, my uncle recalls he was almost out of his mind with anticipation and worry that I wouldn't make the team. But Grandma Berta sat there calmly as I raced for a spot at the Olympics. My uncle asked, "Mom, weren't you nervous?" To which my grandmother shook her head and coolly replied, "I knew she had it all the way."

Despite a tough cancer surgery and her grim health prognosis, Grandma Berta lived another nine years. "Superhuman endurance," indeed. She and Uncle Jon were able to attend the Omaha Olympic Trials in 2016. All my cousins and relatives on the Hagan side of the family were there too. I have some great pictures of her sitting with Grandma Hagan, the pair of them cheering and smiling. You'd never suspect she was battling cancer at the time.

In the summer of 2018, we were visiting Grandma Berta in New York when we noticed that Leslie Jones, Dave Chappelle, Colin Jost, Pete Davidson, and Michael Che were doing a stand-up night at Radio City.

Leslie had, during the run of the Rio Olympics, tweeted fan videos of over-the-top commentary on the events. The clips were hilarious. All the athletes loved them. The bits went viral, and NBC decided to bring Leslie to the Games. I was dying to meet her while I was there but unfortunately didn't get the opportunity. Then, the day we were flying out of Brazil, my mom spontaneously ran into her on the airport moving walkway. My mom was going one way, and Leslie was going the opposite. My mom jumped, waved, and yelled across the terminal, "I'm Katie Ledecky's mother, and we love you!"

Leslie was super-cool about it, stopping to meet my mom. They sent me a video they made, Leslie riffing on my being a little swimmer, swimming in my mom's belly, all this stuff. My mom sent me the video and told me to come to Gate 34 ASAP. I hightailed it over there and finally got to meet Leslie in person, a fantastic cap to my Rio experience.

Thanks to Leslie's fervid Olympic fandom and that spontaneous airport meetup, we were able to procure tickets for me and Grandma Berta to the stand-up night at Radio City. Leslie even got us a backstage meet-and-greet afterward.

Leslie was the perfect hostess, introducing us around. We met Dave Chappelle and Pete Davidson. Dave went to school in D.C., and we discussed that commonality. Colin Jost was a swimmer growing up, so we geeked out on the sport with him. Leslie was Leslie, cracking jokes and poking fun and generally being the charismatic social butterfly that she is.

My grandma was in the mix of all of it. She was fully in her element, bantering and chatting with all the comics. My eighty-four-year-old grandma Berta gleefully soaking in a boisterous, smoke-filled showbiz room is an image I'll never forget. But that was who she was. A gutsy New York gal, not intimidated by much, always up for anything.

In July 2015, Grandma Berta texted me while I was at training camp in Croatia, right before the World Championships in Kazan. "My prayers and love will be there with you. If you ever want to talk with me, just ask the operator to reverse the charges and I'll have the joy of hearing your voice." That sweet text cracked me up. Grandma Berta may have understood how to operate an iPhone, but she continued to exist on a timeline where there were operators and reverse charges. Like it was the forties and I was on the lam from the law.

There's a text from 2014 where she said she was pleased I was liking psychology, since she loved it in her first year at Brooklyn College. She made mention of a stranger asking her whether we were related, and thrilling to the fact that she heard my name spoken "on the sidewalk" of the city. "So many emails from all over the country telling me how remarkable Katie is. I try not to be too boastful, but it takes a lot of self-control."

When I tossed the first pitch at the Nationals game, she texted about seeing the press coverage. "You're quite a pitcher darling Katie and quite a girl, and I love you so much. Speak to you soon. Grandma Berta."

She always signed her texts, like she was penning a letter.

In February 2015, she texted me about her love of short stories. She was writing them up till when she died. Whenever I would stumble on a story I'd enjoyed, I'd forward it to her, and she'd read it and then text her critique. It was like a book club of two.

My last text from Grandma Berta was January 21, 2020. It's a painful silence made more so by the warm, lively exchanges before it. When you lose someone who thinks of you every day, who keeps you alive in their heart, it's like a part of you dies also.

Grandma Berta passed away in November 2021 at age eighty-seven. She had done everything she'd set out to do in life, undertaken and achieved more than a dozen people her age.

Prior to her passing, my family and I visited Grandma Berta in New York after the Tokyo Olympics. I showed her my medals. It was the first time I'd ever seen her tired, frail. I remember we were sitting around her kitchen table finishing lunch when she began to sing. She had mild dementia by this point, but she knew every lyric to every song. We all joined in. We sang show tunes. The final song we sang with her was "The Star-Spangled Banner."

A few months ago, I purchased a piano keyboard for my home. I'm refamiliarizing myself with the instrument, calling on the lessons Grandma gave me. I've been playing one of my favorites, the Beatles' "Let It Be," and noodling around with some other classics from Tom Petty and Bruce Springsteen.

When I play, I imagine my grandmother perched beside me, singing along. I can hear the lilt of her voice in my head. My Grandma Berta, as always, perfectly in tune.

Chapter Twenty

GAINESVILLE AND NESTY

In July 2021, at the end of the Tokyo Olympics, I found myself at a professional crossroads. I'd won golds in the 800 and 1500 free, silvers in the 400 free and the 4x200 free relay. A terrific showing. And yet my times in the three individual finals were a combined ten seconds slower than what I had swum in Rio to win the 200. Finishing second to Ariarne Titmus in the 400 was the first time I'd been beaten in an individual Olympics final. I knew some folks in the media and the swim community viewed my performance as "Oh, Katie must've been so disappointed with how she did in Tokyo." Chatter like that. Which wasn't strictly true.

As a member of Team USA, you're always striving for gold. There are psychological studies that silver medalists are the winners who express the most disappointment with their facial expressions on the podium. (Bronze medalists are happy because, hey, at least they won a medal.) Perhaps that resonates with some silver medalists, but I'm proud of mine.

I think what continued to feed the "Katie is bummed" narrative is that after Tokyo, I left California and, in the fall of 2021, relocated to train in Florida with Coach Anthony Nesty and the Gator Swim Club. I understand people perceived my uprooting to Gainesville as some grand statement about moving on. But there were several rationales that played into my decision. Chief among them: I missed the East Coast.

I wanted to be closer to home and my family. Perhaps the biggest factor was the opportunity to train with world-class distance swimmers under Coach Nesty's guidance.

Anthony Nesty is no stranger to breaking barriers in the sport. But he's an incredibly humble person—you wouldn't know that he's the only Olympic gold medalist from his country, achieving this in 1988 when he competed for Suriname in the 100-meter butterfly. This also made him the first Black person to win an Olympic gold medal in swimming from any country. Back home, he was feted as a hero, and a coin was minted in his honor in Suriname.

Coach Nesty trained at the Bolles School in Jacksonville, Florida, and then at the University of Florida. Then he became an assistant coach at the University of Florida. In 2018 he was promoted to head coach of the men's team there. In 2021 he took over the women's program as well. He made history again when he was named the USA men's swimming head coach for the 2024 Paris Games, making him the first Black head coach of a U.S. Olympic swimming team.

At the University of Florida, Coach Nesty presides over one of the most stacked pools in the nation, overseeing more than eighty swimmers at the top of our respective games. I mean, Caeleb Dressel is there; he's the best male sprinter in the world. There's Bobby Finke, Olympic gold medalist in two distance events. There's Kieran Smith, Jake Mitchell. We have something like eight U.S. Olympians from the last Games, plus several foreign Olympians. We've got swimmers from Germany, Venezuela, Jordan, Canada, Brazil. The distance group is deep.

At Stanford I had great teammates to practice with, but I couldn't train with the men on a regular basis, and at the time, there wasn't anyone on the women's team who could really push me in the distance events. Now I'm part of a distance group with twenty men and women, the finest distance swimmers in the world. I get challenged to swim better every day.

Some sets I might be racing Bobby. Then other practices I might be racing a freshman guy who puts up similar times to mine. I like to compete with the guys. I revel in tough practices. The combined men's and women's swim program just gives a different energy. The guys, they talk a lot. Sports talk. Trash talk. Talk talk. Arguing about who would win in a 200 back-stroke between Bobby and Kieran. Spending a whole practice bickering about some random thing. They bring a lot of attitude and energy to the deck. As does swimming with a newbie college team. Whenever a group of freshmen comes in, there's renewed, palpable enthusiasm in the water.

I take care to ensure that the younger swimmers feel comfortable training with me, that they're not intimidated. Coach Nesty believes team chemistry creates a competitive edge. He emphasizes getting behind every teammate, having empathy for each other, being kind and patient. A bunch of us are currently training for Paris. Working toward the same goals, knowing we could be going up against each other during the Games. Coach Nesty urges us to keep the mood light during training, not to fixate on what we're all competing for.

Instead, we commiserate, we make sure we're laughing and joking at practice, we pump each other up. We make the pool a positive place to be. We're all extraordinarily driven, but nobody has too big an ego. Nobody's cocky. That outlook stems directly from Coach Nesty.

When I was considering making a move, Florida was the only place I visited and, as with Coach Greg at Stanford, Nesty was the only coach I called. He wasn't a stranger to me. We'd been around each other during the five weeks of training camp in Hawaii and the Tokyo Olympics. I'd observed the impressive way he ran things there.

Greg was supportive of my exiting California. As he viewed it, I wasn't leaving Stanford so much as I was looking for the best fit for what I needed over the next three years. It was obvious to me that I'd found that at Gator Swim Club. I've already seen the benefits of the move.

I won four gold medals at the 2022 World Championships in Buda-pest and continued improving into 2023. At the 2023 USA Swimming National Championships in Indianapolis, I won the 400, 800, and 1500 free. My time in the 800 (8:07.07) was my fastest at that distance since the Rio Games seven years earlier. I used a longer, more effective stroke, completing sixteen lengths in 644 strokes, thirteen fewer than in Rio and thirty-two fewer than in Tokyo.

Nesty sharpened my stroke, which he described as "choppy" and "inefficient." He also wanted me to get in better shape. "To become more athletic," he said. (I tried not to take that one personally.) To be fair, Nesty had warned me that he was going to tell me things I may not want to hear. "I know you're Katie Ledecky," he said, "but as good as you are, you're not perfect."

He was correct, of course. Not that I pushed back. Coach Nesty knows what it's like being an athlete and striving for the Olympics. He's literally been there. He also understands the individuality of each of us in the club and how we tick. Every swimmer on our team has a unique story. We race different events and have traveled our own paths to the pool. Coach Nesty absorbs all that disparate history and finds a way to create team harmony and synergy. That is an invaluable coaching skill in any scenario but a mandatory one when your field is as seasoned as ours. I have a big career behind me, but I'm continuing to try to get better. So is Caeleb, who has won seven gold medals. As are the younger pros like Bobby Finke or Kieran Smith, who recently finished their NCAA eligibility. Under Nesty's guidance, we're all identifying ways to improve and function as a collaborative unit.

Before the 2023 World Championships, Nesty, a thorough planner, gave me a months-long calendar outlining my main swim sets every day for the next *twelve weeks*. He has an eagle eye for my technique. He has a good sense for when it might be slightly off. When it looks good, he nods approvingly from the pool deck. Since I've been with him, he's recalibrated my stroke and rotation. He's refined my kick. These adjustments are making me faster at an age when most swimmers are looking to hang up their suits.

One of the biggest factors we identified early on was that all the tempo work I did leading into Tokyo was maxing me out to my detriment. My tempo is one of my strengths. I'm able to maintain a faster tempo for longer than most of my distance competitors. But what we found was

I was losing my efficiency in the water. I was thinking too much about how fast I was moving my arms, and I wasn't thinking enough about how much water I was holding and pulling while I was swimming.

Nesty took me back to stroke count. How many strokes I was taking each lap, and trying to reduce that number, rather than tempo. This shift has stretched out my stroke, so I can swim longer and taller and kick a bit more. I'm getting more bang for my buck, so to speak.

The other big technique modification since I've been at Florida has been a mental one. I'm thinking about swimming with perfect technique even when I'm swimming easy. What that means is that even on recovery days, my mind is fully engaged in my swimming style. I'm not thinking about swimming fast so much as I'm thinking about swimming "pretty."

That was something new for me. For years under Yuri, Bruce, and Greg, I didn't always focus so heavily on my technique when I was swimming easy. Now I use each lap to try to get better, as an opportunity to sharpen style. Each stroke is a chance to reinforce good habits mentally and physically.

One thing I appreciate about Nesty is how he makes sure that I, and we as his team, see him as more than a swim coach. He checks in. Fosters relationships with us away from the pool. He tends to the human parts of his swimmers.

Coach Nesty and I have developed a shorthand. He's quiet and guarded. We share a similar nature. He's pulled a lot out of me. Somehow he intuits how I'm feeling in the water. If I'm pleased with where I'm at. If I'm wracked with dissatisfaction. Like my other coaches, he senses the right questions to pose in the right moments, to lead me to the right answers. And it is this reason, way more than the improvements in my times or the growth in my technique, that Florida has felt like a great fit.

All my years in the pool have led me to training with this group and these coaches, and it's utterly satisfying. Even if I were going slower, I'd still be happy. That said, going faster heading into my fourth Olympic Year feels amazing. Cut to: the 2023 World Championships in Fukuoka, Japan.

I had what I believed were reasonable expectations for Japan. I was aware when I went into it that there was conversation about my having the chance to "make history" (should I beat Michael Phelps's individual World Championship gold-medal total). I did a couple of interviews prior to Worlds. At a virtual press conference from our training camp, I was asked about the medal tally. As early as a year before, at the World Championships in Budapest, the media had noted that there would be this possibility to surpass Phelps's record. So, yeah, it was out there in the ether, but it wasn't something I was heavily targeting. I only wanted to do the best that I could in each of my races and let history take care of itself.

I swam the 400 free the first day, which was next-level hyped because it featured the three fastest swimmers of all time in the race: Australia's Ariarne Titmus, Canada's Summer McIntosh, and me. An A-list lineup like that hadn't happened in years, where three people who had held the world record in the same event were swimming against each other. The 400—dubbed the "Race of the Century"—was as wildly anticipated as any race I'd swum.

Prior to the meet, I was asked tons of questions about that 400. Commentators wanted to know: Was I daunted? In point of fact, I was looking forward to it. I was in the rare underdog position in that I had the third fastest time among the three of us. And I hadn't logged that time in a few years. Nevertheless, I believed in myself.

I finished second to Ariarne, who en route broke Summer's world record. Summer placed fourth, and Erika Fairweather of New Zealand broke four minutes for the first time to take the bronze. Even though I placed second, I was gratified. It was one of the fastest 400 freestyle fields ever. It heightened my confidence heading into the 800 and 1500. I knew I was ready.

I swam the 1500 free and won, hitting my best time in I can't remember how many years. My third fastest time ever, just shy of my world record from 2018 and my final swim in Kazan. In winning the 1500, I'd officially tied Phelps's individual-gold record.

The following day I had off. The relay was the next race on my dance card. As I recuperated, I thought about an activity our head women's coach, Carol Capitani, had the team do early in training camp in Singapore. The staff made these poker chips that said "USA Swimming" on them. At a meeting, each team member was handed a chip and asked to write our name on one side and our "superpower" on the other. Then we all had to stand, explain why we wrote what we wrote, throw the chip onto a table, and forcefully declare, "I'm all in!"

On my chip I wrote: "on/off." I told the room that I feel like I have a switch. Once I get behind the blocks, I'm able to turn on racing mode and harness all the energy in the venue—just the way Coach Yuri taught me. My superpower is my ability to instantly channel every single molecule into what I need to do down a 2.5-meter lane of water. But, I clarified, don't let that scare you, because once the switch flips back, I become the biggest cheerleader for everyone else. "No one has a better time at the pool than I do," I told them.

Over the rest of training camp and throughout the meet, the coaches handed out more poker chips. The idea was we were supposed to give our chip to somebody we saw do something exceptional or significant as a way of showing that we were "all in" behind them. On my down day between the 1500 and the relay, I realized I still had one of my chips.

The relay finals ended up being me and three teenagers, which was unusual. My teammates were Erin Gemmell (Bruce Gemmell's daughter), who I've known since she was seven years old; Bella Sims, who'd swum on the relay with me the year before; and Alex Shackell, a sixteen-year-old from Indiana on her first World Championship team who'd been assigned the relay anchor post. I decided right before finals that I was going to give my chip to Alex.

To be the anchor at sixteen years old? I knew how it felt to shoulder that pressure. She was in a nerve-racking position and on a massive international stage. I wanted to remind her that we all have each other's backs—and that I believed in her. I put the chip in the pocket of my parka. Just as Erin was mounting the blocks to swim the first leg,

I passed the chip to Alex. She lit up as she read it. I'd written on the back, "You've got this."

We won silver in that relay. Alex killed her leg. We were only a half second off the American record from 2021 in Tokyo. After the event, Alex thanked me. She even talked about it in a couple of interviews later, how it meant a lot to her, which made me happy.

Time for the 800. I was in the zone. Physically and mentally, my game felt tight. Everything was locking into place. Snap, snap, like LEGOs. It was the first time in a while that I sensed I could get close to my world record, the 8:04 I had set in 2016. Nesty had even indicated to me that he believed I could do something epic. I was beyond keyed up going into that race.

There's an interesting thing that happens at certain meets, where record breaks occur in clusters. World Championships are likely candidates because athletes are peaking. But sometimes it's due to the pool or the energy of the competition or, who knows, something written in the stars. I've seen it time and again. For whatever reason, at particular events, swimmer after swimmer set personal and statistical bests.

In Fukuoka, several world records were broken in the 50-meter sprint events. Now, *that's* a cluster. Two world records happened before my race the night of my 800, set by swimmers who had been around as long as I had. When I saw those record-breaking numbers stack up, I was like: *Yeah, I want to add to this.* It reinforced my belief that I could swim my best time ever. Everyone else was, why not me?

The horn sounded and I dove in, brimming with conviction. I got out to a fast start. I took the lead and kept the lead. A tad more than halfway through, the pain came. I started hurting, then I began questioning myself. Maybe because of my bullishness about the 800, I went out too hard. Why did I always do that? I began flagging.

Because I was so far ahead, I managed to win the race, but when I touched the wall, I'd gone about a second slower than I had at Nationals, 8:08.

Outside the pool, the crowd went wild. I'd just become the first swimmer to win the same event at six straight Worlds. In doing so, I'd eclipsed Michael Phelps's record for the most individual world swimming titles. He had fifteen. I'd just earned number sixteen. The media was already covering the outcome, calling it a "stunning achievement." But as I exited the pool, my body roiled with a mix of emotions.

Mentally, I was dissecting my choices even after this incredible race, a swim I'd won by four seconds. It didn't matter. All I felt was stunned. I didn't even warm down after my race. It was the last meet of the season. Nothing to warm down for, right? I wasn't doing another race for months. That alone made me feel horrible. I knew I should be thrilled that I'd broken Phelps's record and swum as fast as I had instead of flogging myself for what I perceived to be mistakes. Yet all these wheels were turning in my head. How could I do better next time? Why did I fail to break a record? I felt a slight sense of disappointment. I at least wanted to be better than I had been at Nationals. And I wasn't.

I managed to field the media questions, reflect on my career, all the different World Championships that had led to this moment. I spoke of my longevity, how much I'd accomplished over the last eleven years, smiled, expressed gratitude. Internally, I was decidedly less composed. I retreated to the team area, where I sat down by myself and took a deep breath.

Though I was tucked in the corner, Coach Nesty saw me. Concern flooded his face. He'd never seen me like that. He rushed over.

"Don't worry. I'm just overwhelmed," I assured him.

I explained I sometimes feel depleted after end-of-season meets. I have so much tension built inside of me. When the meet ends, I take my first deep breath in months. There's this emotional release after being laser-focused and locked down for such a long period of time. I can't control it. I deflate like a balloon. I get in my feelings.

A similar thing happened after the Rio Olympics. The whole meet, I got gold, gold, gold, yet on the outside I looked composed. It wasn't until the last race that I felt like I could finally breathe regularly.

Nesty understood. This reminded me of his philosophy of empathy. How he'd taught us to be kind and patient with one another as a team and always bring our best attitude to practice. He suggested I do the same for myself, get some rest, and enjoy the time off before we got back to the hard work in a few weeks. So I tried.

By the day after Fukuoka, I'd reset and regained perspective. I didn't break my world-record time. So what? I mean, it's a really tough record. Besides, the 800 at Trials was my first race, whereas the 800 at Worlds was my last race. That alone could explain the one-second difference.

Sometimes I fail to put things in context, and in this instance, context was everything. I began to appreciate what I'd achieved, which was to win more individual world titles than any other swimmer and become the first swimmer ever to win six world titles in the same event. As a rule, I tend to focus on one race, one practice, and one season at a time, never really aiming for larger medal-count records. When I happen to break them, it takes me a beat to process the significance of what some might call my "legacy."

Recently, I received a text from Alex, the rising swimmer I'd competed with in the relay in Japan. It was a photo of her holding the poker chip I'd given her. She was on her way to Winter Junior Nationals. "Bringing this reminder," she wrote, the red chip perched between her painted nails, the mottled tile of the pool deck in the background. You can barely make out my ballpoint scribble of "You've got this!" But it's there. (I should have used a Sharpie!)

The fact that she continues to bring that chip with her to meets, that my words are her good-luck token, that they lift her up and make her believe in her capabilities—that's what legacy means to me.

Just as Coach Nesty's investment in the whole swimmer—beyond the medals, beyond any records we break—is his. The person before the pool. That's what counts.

As soon as I got her text, I wrote back, "Good luck Alex!!!" I'm not embarrassed to say I added a few watery-eyes emojis.

Chapter Twenty-One

FRIENDS AND NEIGHBORS

C asual fans who see me on a race day probably view me as a little intimidating. I have a pretty straight "game face" behind my dark goggles. I probably look a little intense, like someone with nerves of steel. I pretend the cameras aren't there; that I'm in my own world. Which I kind of am. I've never been one to pound my chest or stare down my opponents. I appreciate and respect my fellow competitors, but most of the time I'm not focusing on them at all. It's not a selfish or antisocial thing. I'm focusing on what needs to be done to put forth my best effort. On realizing the promise of all the training and hard work that led to that moment.

My baseline personality is quiet and happy. Once I get to know you, I can get a bit louder. I do feel somewhat self-conscious celebrating after a win. I might pump a fist or slap the water if I win a big race or set a record. The time I will really let loose is when I see a teammate do well in a race, whether I am in it or not. When I see them edge into the lead, or win a race they've been training hard for, then I might hoot or holler with the best of them. I suppose in some ways I find it easier to celebrate my friends and teammates than myself.

For a striving athlete, there is no substitute for relationships with people living and breathing the same experience. The dedication and deprivation. Few folks know what it means to get up before the sun, log lap after lap, monitor every meal, put so much of your life on hold in the pursuit of a singular goal. But ultimately, it's a blessing, right? It's a blessing to get to compete in this sport, and to do it with other people who love it as much as I do.

Though my occasionally quiet or reserved personality may have perplexed or frustrated my coaches a time or two, I really do like to laugh. Like everyone else, I have my favorite television shows. On the drama side for so many years, it has been the New York police show *Blue Bloods,* with its tremendous cast of actors (bummed that it's in its final season). On the comedy side, it's *Curb Your Enthusiasm* (again bummed, another final season). My family and I really like to laugh in the face of life's little absurdities and insults. If something funny happens to us, or if we mess something up ourselves, we try to brush it off by quietly humming or whistling the instrumental *Curb Your Enthusiasm* theme song. I owe Larry David a thank-you card for creating a show that's an instant mood lifter.

The flip side of the laughter is that I feel distressed when I hear or read about other swimmers or outstanding Olympic athletes (or other athletes) who have experienced anxiety, depression, or other mental or physical problems or who have suffered abuse as a result of sports participation. To me, in a perfect world, sports should be recreational and fun, bring happiness and joy. It shouldn't just be "the thrill of victory and the agony of defeat." In some ways, sports should provide momentary escape from a lot of the misery that exists in the world. And we need to work harder to end that misery. I'm proud to compete as part of my country's team, but I blanch sometimes at the nationalism and politics and corruption that seep into international sports and the Olympic movement. It would be great if the Olympics could be viewed more as an upbeat sports festival than as "a war between nations," as I was disgusted to hear it once called by a foreign swim coach.

The comradery between me and my fellow swimmers is a large

part of why I love swimming so much and has been true of every team, from clubs to high school, to Stanford, to the U.S. Olympic team. There's a lot of laughing and even more support. At practice, there's always some teasing. In many ways, the energy hasn't changed that much from when I was a Palisades Porpoise. For example, my Team USA teammate Lilly King brought beads and yarn for us to make friendship bracelets during training camp before World Championships in 2023. (She's a total Swiftie.) I made a couple of bracelets with "USA" spelled out. Lilly made one for me that says "Fearless."

When we have time, my teammates and I hang out on dry land. Several other women swimmers and I have a standing breakfast Saturday mornings after practice. We chitchat about all manner of things—dating, movies, our families. Admittedly, the conversation generally reverts back to swimming. I train with a wide range of ages, some college kids, some pros. We have a variety of interests and are at different stages of life. But what we all have in common is the sport. When I spend time with my fellow swimmers, I feel seen and appreciated in this very specific space we all share. We get to be mirrors for each other's efforts and triumphs. Simply put—we get each other.

I've also been lucky enough to cultivate meaningful relationships outside of the pool. I believe when you're an athlete, it's vital to nurture friendships in as many realms as possible. The wider your circle of friends, the deeper your well of support, your depth of knowledge, your range of experience. If all my friends were cut from the same cloth as me, my life wouldn't be half as rich. For example, I had the good fortune to have two wonderful godfathers growing up, my Uncle Jon and Jesuit priest Father Jim Shea. My mom met Father Shea in 1989 when they were both new employees at Georgetown University Hospital, where he was the head of Chaplain Services and my mother was hired as an associate administrator. Father Shea has guided my faith since childhood. He baptized my brother and me, and later administered my first communion and sponsored my confirmation. In 2016, he came to Omaha to cheer for me at the Olympic Trials. He gave me a special blessing at the end of the Olympic Trials as I prepared to travel to Rio.

Right now I often hang out with my new neighbor, a former swimmer named Kathy Slaton. Kathy swam for the University of Florida in the eighties. She lives on my street in Gainesville, Florida. Gainesville has a real college-town vibe. It's small and neighborly; everywhere you look are students, families, older couples—a nice mix of people. That appealed to me. So I bought a house. I wanted enough space that my relatives could visit and stay as long as they wanted. I host the Ledecky family Thanksgiving now. (Talk about all grown up.) After living out of suitcases during my college years, I finally feel settled. I do have a pool, but it's a typical Florida splash-around fun-time pool. I'm not in it that often.

Kathy and her husband, Bobby, frequently invite me over for dinner. They have a piano, so sometimes I'll play music for them. Bobby's really into karaoke, and there have been nights when we all belt out the tunes. I know it sounds odd, but hanging with Kathy feels familiar and comforting. She was a swimmer too. She gets my hours, my training. And I get to hear stories about her history in the pool. Or as the case may be—in the river.

When she was at the University of Florida, her coach made the swim team practice in the Ichetucknee Springs. This was at a time when the springs were showing signs of degradation, and swimmers were reporting strange skin rashes, possibly caused by algae. Oh, and there were occasionally alligators. And poisonous snakes. In the water.

Despite all that, the coach instructed Kathy and her teammates to swim upstream, against the current. They'd do this for a few hours, then turn around and coast back in a third of the time. Swimmers clocked a lot more yardage back then. Conditioning was less specific to your events and all about slogging it out. Kathy was a breaststroker. I joke that she's the fastest breaststroker on the street.

Chris Olmstead (better known to the swim world as Chris von

Saltza) is another former swimmer and friend I consider family. Chris reached out to me between the London and Rio Olympics after watching me compete. She knew that I was headed to Stanford and felt a kinship with me. Chris attended Stanford too, but she didn't swim there because there was no women's team at that time. She retired after competing in the 1960 Olympics, where she won gold in the 400 free, fifty-six years prior to my winning that same event.

After we grew close, I introduced Chris to Coach Greg and invited her to speak to the Stanford team. She stood on the pool deck and recounted what it was like to be a woman athlete in the sixties. I could see my teammates were moved by her story. I certainly was.

My peers and I have opportunities to continue our careers into college and beyond. I think a lot about the fact that this was simply not possible back in the day. The unfairness haunts me and is part of what drives me to make the compromises I feel I must to succeed in my sport. It's almost like we owe it to the women who came before us to seize the day now.

I won't lie, that impulse to seize the day can make it challenging to be my friend. My commitment to swimming and my goals in the sport come first. Which means I'm not available to be the life of the party. My training hours prohibit late nights. I eat at senior-citizen hour. When I have free time, I'm napping. Exciting stuff all around.

I've been fortunate that I haven't suffered much peer pressure. Athletic pressure, yes. Being prodded to smoke or drink, nope. I know from a physical and mental standpoint what's good for me, and I'm not going to do anything that messes that up. I'm not going to swim through a hangover. I'm not going to date a ton of people and get distracted. I'm not going to do any stuff that undermines what I'm good at. No shenanigans. No hookups. No keggers.

I *have* been to one school dance.

It was the winter ball my sophomore year in high school, right after I came home from the London Games. Honestly, I wasn't planning on going. Then I found out that the student body had held elections for the winter ball, much like picking a homecoming queen, electing one person from every grade to be, like, the snow princess or something. I heard I was on the short list, and I thought, *Well, it would be really embarrassing if I don't go to the dance and I get crowned.* Which made me feel I had no choice but to attend the winter ball. Which meant I had to find a date.

I wracked my brain but couldn't think of a single guy to ask. Eventually, I went to my brother, who attended an all-boys' school. "Is there *anybody* on the Gonzaga swim team that you could just ask for me?" I probed. "Maybe you could give me a couple of names or at least a recommendation?"

Michael came through, asking a teammate—a guy named Brennan who went on to swim at Harvard. Brennan was pleased to be invited, and so it was that he and I shuffled off to the winter ball.

My mom has photos of us in front of his family fireplace. Me in my black sequined knee-length dress and pearl bracelet, Brennan in khakis, a white shirt, and a navy blazer, with a matching blue tie. Both of us are smiling in that uniquely awkward way of every school dance photo taken by someone's parent. One photo captures me pinning on Brennan's boutonniere, Christmas wreaths hung in the background.

My mom and I picked my date up at his house because neither Brennan nor I could drive. She dropped us at the dance, where, sure enough, I was named snow princess (or whatever it was called). I had to go up onstage. I don't remember if they gave flowers or a little crown, some sort of tiara. I don't even have a picture of the moment. It literally was the quickest—well, I *made* it the quickest—thing ever because I was so mortified. I exited that stage as fast as humanly possible.

Brennan was a very nice guy, but we barely talked, at the ball or after. I did enjoy being with my classmates and dancing—though I'm using the word "dance" very loosely. It was more like jumping around and head bobbing to the spirited Christmas jams. A few hours later, my mom returned, picked me and Brennan up, and drove us home.

And that, in a nutshell, was my one high school dance experience. I did not go to homecoming. I did not go to prom. Even if I wanted to go to prom, it probably fell during the weekend of a swim meet. But to be transparent, proms and dances weren't really my thing. (I did like my sequined dress—I wore it to the Golden Goggles Awards a year later.)

That's the thing about swimming. To do it right takes commitment. I've never had an alcoholic drink in my life. Or a puff of a cigarette. I've cared so much about swimming my best that it's been easy for me to say no to parties and dances, even at Stanford, where I lived the life of a very sporty nun.

Needless to say, this rigorous devotion to training has not been awesome for my romantic life. I have a lot of deep friendships. I never lack for invitations to hang out or go to dinner. But dating, well. Simply put, I haven't done a lot of it.

There have been times when I've questioned: *Am I putting myself out there as someone who's hard to reach? Am I subconsciously shutting myself off to people?* I never want to come across that way.

While I'm still neck-deep in training and working toward being the best swimmer I can be, I'm mindful of what drains me versus what recharges me. There's a level of focus and attention I put into my sport that naturally limits my investment in other pursuits, even romantic ones. Maybe I've been a little one-sided on the balance of that scale, but I feel like I'll know when it's right for me to fall into a serious relationship. I'm still young.

At some point, I want to have a family. I want to have kids. But when I think about starting a family in terms of my career, well, I see myself swimming professionally to 2028, maybe longer. If I get to 2026 and I've found someone I love and want to have children with right then and there, maybe that shakes up the plan. At the same time, I'll be thirty-one in 2028. I could have kids well after that. My mom was a later-in-life parent. I can imagine myself following the same path.

When and how to start a family is such a complicated issue for women athletes. We are often racing more than one clock. Some of us choose to be a mother and stay in our sport. Others can't envision being pulled in both directions. It feels like an impossible choice. I'll confess to some mixed feelings, in that I'm at the age when I have peers who are getting married and having babies, but I also feel content with my life right now.

The great thing is my friends totally understand my values and never pressure me to feel like I need to do everything they are doing, be that getting engaged or staying out into the wee hours of the evening. I've gravitated toward people who are generous with me and my rigid schedule, folks who just want to go for a nice dinner or sit on a couch for hours and talk about random stuff. I appreciate that they're nonjudgmental when I have to say no or "I can't." Those are the friends I've stuck with because they forgive me when I can't be available. What makes them special is they keep inviting me.

Chris Olmstead emailed me recently. She never fails to check in about when my next meet is, how training is going, what events I'm racing. Her husband, Bob, told me he hadn't really seen Chris's excitement about swimming until she and I met. She avoided dwelling on her past, a career cut short. Our friendship reopened her to swimming and brought her back to a sport she loved.

Knowing that makes my heart sing. Because really, that's what swimming is about for me long-term. Making connections. Being part of a community. Swimming with friends.

Chapter Twenty-Two

SWIM LIKE A GIRL

In the summer of 2020, the marketing team behind chocolate milk asked if I would be willing to do a promotional TikTok. As a long-time chocolate milk lover, I agreed, and we met at the Soda Aquatic Center at Campolindo High School in Moraga, California, a few miles over the hill and east of Berkeley. The milk team sent a husband-and-wife production duo who planned to record the video on a phone with a tripod. The whole idea with TikTok is that it's pared down and authentic, so we set up the phone camera and got to work.

Marketing had provided a handful of thought starters for what I could do with a glass of chocolate milk, but none of them really popped out at me. I asked if I could get in the pool and play around with some ideas, test out a few things. I climbed in the water and was toying with balancing the drink when it hit me. I should swim the length of the pool with a glass of chocolate milk perched on top of my head. I explained to the production team that balancing items on your head is a common drill for backstrokers. It trains them to maintain head position. But I'd never seen anyone do that drill freestyle. They looked at me skeptically. It was very much the "Sure, Jan" meme energy.

I donned my fins and snorkel and did a couple of test runs with a glass of water. I knew I needed to make the whole fifty meters without a breath, hence the snorkel. After maybe two or three laps with water,

I felt ready to try with actual milk. The tripod was set up, the chocolate milk was poured, and off I went.

I made it on my first try! Typically, I take thirty-eight or -nine strokes to get across the pool; for this, I counted thirty-six. I had to lock my abs to keep my core rigid, so my head remained flat and still. I let my kick do most of the propulsion work. I tried to keep my arms as smooth as butter.

I swam with the milk cup a couple more times after that first 50. But the maiden lap was the most genuine and perfect, and that was the video I ended up posting. I had an inkling when we filmed that my stunt would be a big deal, because after I sent the clip to my parents, both of them lost their minds, like, "Are you kidding me? Did you actually do this?" If my parents were blown away, I suspected TikTok swim fans would be too. I don't know if the chocolate milk people realized how crazy the feat was, not being swimming experts. They liked it. But they had no sense of the difficulty. They wanted to shorten the clip. I pushed back. I emphasized to them that we needed to post the entire lap. They conceded. And what do you know? The clip went viral.

My chocolate milk swim was picked up by television stations every-where. People all over the world were reposting and sharing. It got millions of views. Other swimmers began to join in the fun, doing their own laps with drinks perched on their heads. Even champs like Mark Spitz, who won seven gold medals at the 1972 Munich Olympics, and Susie O'Neill, an eight-time Australian medalist, who, in true Aussie fashion, did her lap with a beer instead of milk. Matt Grevers, the American backstroke champion, did the same with a nonalcoholic beer. The video was unexpected and injected a jolt of levity into the sport. It was also a super-hard trick to pull off. Everything about it was surprising—the concept, the execution, the public reception.

Sometimes I think being a successful woman athlete is a lot like swimming across the pool balancing a glass of chocolate milk on your head: something many people can't believe is possible, something challenging to pull off, something we women make look easy even as we understand that one tiny slipup could bring the whole thing tumbling down. I've been fortunate to have had amazing women as role models, who were willing to steer me through my many years as a female competitor.

First and foremost on this list is my mom, who set the bar high for hard work and achievement as well as how to exhibit grace and good sportsmanship. When I was growing up, she showed me how to handle all the complex emotions and choices that go into being a woman athlete. Whether I knew it at the time or not, she taught me what would later become guideposts in my sporting life.

Catherine and Natalie Pitcher were two of my first summer-league swim coaches at Palisades. They were older teenagers on the team. These cool girls were awesome swimmers but also took the time to mentor me. My club swimming experience was similar. I was coached by Carolyn Kaucher, who was instrumental in lifting me to the next level. Carolyn was there when I started to fully embrace practicing daily. I give a lot of credit to her for teaching me how to manage my energy, how to warm up, how to warm down, how to take care of myself. She walked me through swim meets. What to expect. What to avoid. For example, thanks to Carolyn, I know that you don't have to stand behind the blocks twenty-five minutes before a race. Even if you're nervous, it's probably a better use of time to wait elsewhere.

At the time, a lot of my fastest teammates were girls. There weren't very many boys in our group who could keep up with us. Having other confident, outstanding female athletes around was formative. No one was apologizing for being great. And we *were* great. Swimming relays together was the ultimate power-bonding activity and made a huge impression on my younger self. I knew then that I never wanted those teamwork/dreamwork feelings to end.

As I moved up the ranks, women coaches became fewer and farther between. There's a lot of discussion in swimming about the leadership gender gap and the lack of female coaches at all levels. Improvement is being made, but the 2021 Tucker Center for Research on Girls & Women in Sport graded swimming an F in its equity evaluation, finding that only 20.5 percent of women's swimming programs were led by female coaches. Which is a bummer, of course, but it's also bad business.

A 2019 *Harvard Business Review* study found that women outscored men on seventeen of the nineteen itemized leadership capabilities. The *Journal of Applied Psychology* revealed that despite testimony that men are perceived as more effective than women in leadership positions, a meta-analysis across ninety-five studies rated women as significantly more effective than men. Basically, men excel at confidence, whereas women stand out for competence. And yet, even in the face of evidence like the above, bias persists, and women still often need to work twice as hard and have twice the success just to remain in the game.

For women, there's a whole set of contradictory and unnecessary opinions thrown our way the minute we enter the arena. About our bodies. About our looks. Social media adds fire to the flame. There's a reason so many female athletes suffer with eating disorders. It's not something that I've personally experienced, but I have observed it first-hand, and it concerns and saddens me.

There are spoken and unspoken rules for us too. So many things a female athlete isn't permitted to be. Even when we are the very best in the world at what we do. Women can win so long as we win with humility. Male athletes are celebrated for braggadocio. But women athletes are knocked for it. We're often told we're too masculine, too aggressive. Or that we're too sexy and don't deserve to be taken seriously. Or we're not sexy *enough* and still don't deserve to be taken seriously. Back and forth, like a game of ping-pong you can never win.

I firmly believe female athletes deserve recognition on the basis of their performance, and that should be enough. I don't think you should have to portray yourself in a certain way to get noticed, or conform to certain stereotypes to advance in your career. Men don't have to do that. Men break records, they win championships, and that's all they need to do to get validation (and a paycheck). You don't see male athletes pressured to "smile more." They also never have to wear a bikini or Facetune their Instagram posts or master the perfect red lip. Literally no one has ever told Michael Phelps he isn't "hot enough."

The upside is that we women athletes know we are part of a unique sorority. That we need each other. I felt this bond on the teams at my all-girls' high school and then again on the Stanford women's team. At the professional level, my female teammates *and* my competitors have been equally collegial. In 2012, for example, Rebecca Adlington was extremely gracious after I won gold. I was so green, I didn't know what to do at the medal ceremony, and Rebecca guided me through it all. She could have been devastated about her performance, but she treated me with such kindness. I wrote her a note thanking her after the Olympics, because her generosity made such an impact on me.

Since then I've gotten nothing but tremendous backing from other female athletes, especially the veterans. When I was fifteen years old and navigating my first Olympics, Rebecca Soni and Dana Vollmer from Team USA really looked out for me. They were the big sisters I needed in that moment.

I've tried to pay it forward. When Lotte Friis, the Danish swimmer, moved to the United States to train at the North Baltimore Aquatic Club, I invited her to D.C. to spend time with me. We went to a couple of museums. An IMAX show. Walked around Georgetown. I showed her the Danish embassy. We were fierce competitors at the World Championships—Lotte won gold in the 1500 free at the 2011 Worlds in Shanghai; in Barcelona in 2013, we dueled for nearly fifteen minutes in the 1500 before I won in what was my first world record—but at the local level, we were happy to bond over the shared experience of being female distance swimmers.

Truth be told, I can't think of a single woman athlete I have beef with. The media has a thing for pitting women against each other. Particularly female athletes. Ronda Rousey vs. Holly Holm. Tara Lipinski vs.

Michelle Kwan. Chris Evert vs. Martina Navratilova. Every basketball or soccer season, two female players are selected and reported to be at each other's throats or at least very much in each other's heads. The real story is almost always so far from all that manufactured drama.

In my experience, women athletes motivate each other. We know who is crushing their game, and we want to be as good as they are, if not better. I know that I must be at my best to beat the women in my sport. They push me to go further and faster. They help me dream bigger. Authentic, gut-deep animosity between us is exceedingly rare. Chris and Martina are one of the most storied rivalries in sports history, and they are literally best friends. (The exception that proves the rule is obviously Nancy Kerrigan and Tonya Harding, but that whole mess was about far more than figure skating.)

Over the course of my swimming career, the media has tried to place me into conflict with my fellow women athletes. Some of that comes with the territory; we are *competing*, after all. But overall, I find the hyped-up rivalries you see in the media to be totally counter to my experience on the ground. Women are amazing at lifting each other up, at giving a kind word when someone has a great race, providing feedback on a particular technique, or commiserating on the actual struggles that women in sports face—in general, less coverage, less money, and less respect. The truth is women athletes have way bigger fish to fry than each other.

In 2016 I won the 800 freestyle the same night that Michael Phelps tied for silver in one of his races. I remember scanning the news the next day and seeing an AP article with the headline "Michael Phelps ties for silver in 100 fly." And then the subhead, in tiny print, "Ledecky sets world record in women's 800 freestyle."

I don't often read press when I'm in the middle of competing, but this occurred at the end of my meet. And it came to my attention because it went viral on Twitter. People were dissecting what it represented in terms of the differences in coverage of female and male athletes. The chatter was fired up, most folks arguing that I had earned the main headline. I'd made the news. I'd broken the record. There was a bunch of hand-wringing about the persistent gender bias in our culture. I got a kick out of it—it led to a good conversation—but it did make me think about how the men, more often than not, receive top billing, whether they warrant it or not.

Media coverage of female athletes is improving. Slowly. We're getting more full-throated press, and female athletes do a great job of amplifying each other. But there remain instances where it could be better. What still needs fine-tuning is the prism through which the media views female athletes. Like, as long as I've been swimming, there's been a whole subgenre of reporting where male swimmers are interrogated about my abilities. It's bizarre. (Personally, I prefer it when my performances are placed in the context of other female athletes.) Here are examples culled from various interviews over the years:

Michael Phelps: "She'll literally beat all the guys in the workout, and it looks like it's nothing, like she is barely breathing."

Connor Jaeger: "Her stroke is like a man's stroke. I mean that in a positive way. She swims like a man."

Leading up to the Rio Games, Ryan Lochte told a writer for *Sports Illustrated,* "She swims like a guy. Her stroke. Her mentality. She's so strong in the water. I've never seen a female swimmer like that. She gets faster every time she gets in, and her times are becoming good for a guy. She's beating me now, and I'm, like, 'What is going on?'"

I like Ryan, I like all these guys, and I know they meant what they said as compliments. But it should be examined why "swimming like a man" is the yardstick for excellence. Just as it should be questioned why "getting beaten by a girl" is considered inherently demoralizing. Thank goodness for swim commentator Rowdy Gaines, who announced during my races, "She doesn't swim like a man. She swims like Katie Ledecky."

When I swim, I'm focused on my own time. I need to beat the clock. That's my endgame. Like Rowdy pointed out, I'm an individual, my own person, in the sport. I'm out there racing my own race: setting new bars and trying to raise women's swimming to a new level.

When Tokyo added the women's 1500 free to the Olympics, I was the first winner to benefit from that addition. For the whole meet, it was never far from my mind that there were countless female swimmers who didn't get the chance to swim that distance at the Games. Women who were phenomenal swimmers, who could easily crush that distance, but who hadn't been given the opportunity to show it on the biggest, baddest world stage. Fifty years of women who couldn't enjoy the opportunity that I had.

I'd wondered since I was young why only the men could swim the 1500 at the Olympics. What was the origin of that bias? Why wasn't it changed sooner? I've heard the powers that be didn't believe women *could* swim a 1500. Even though we'd been swimming that distance at the World Championships for eons. Realities like that are what keep me grounded, keep me motivated. They are also a good reminder to appreciate my time in the game, enjoy the fact that I get to continue to pursue what I love, set goals in the sport that I adore, and earn a living at the same time. Something that was unheard of for women not so long ago.

We still need parity across the board. Investment in women's teams, in salaries, in branding. The excitement women athletes generate deserves a larger slice of the media and sponsorship pie. Statistically, when women's sports are promoted and made more visible, they net more viewers and fans. Go figure.

I've discussed these issues with my family, my friends, and the rest of the swimming community. We're all aware of the dearth of support for many women athletes and the lack of representation in coaching and commentary. We're all doing our part, including the great female journalists I've met through swimming. I know the sports universe can be a boys' club, so when I intersect with a woman in media, I feel a kindred connection. I enjoy reading their coverage and watching them chase their passion.

I remember I shed a few tears after I swam in that inaugural Olympic

1500. When you cry in the pool, it's called "croggling" (crying in your goggles). I've only ever cried in the pool a dozen times. Well, maybe a few more than that. I cried after my last race in Rio. I've cried during hard training sets. Those tears I try to hide. When those cries happen, usually you're tired or frustrated and you just want to move on. I've had happy tears too. Happy croggling.

I'm also somebody who empathy-cries if I see somebody else tearing up. Or even getting emotional in a positive or negative way. Like, I've cried at team meetings when I'm inspired. If a coach gets me really pumped, I'll let the tears fall. There's a reason romcoms are my favorite films. I'm *going* to be crying at that happy ending.

In one of my first news spots after I returned from London, they filmed my seven-year-old neighbor sitting with me, recounting how she watched me swim at the Olympics. She is full of excitement, describing what she thought of my performance. As I sit beside her, tears stream down my face.

I realize now that I was reacting to how much it meant to her to see me succeed. I don't think I'd experienced that dynamic in real time before. I was overcome. I still am. Over the years, I've noticed girls in the stands at meets, hoisting signs bearing my name. That never fails to cause a flutter in my chest. That what I do means so much to another person is something I don't take for granted.

All I ever want is to be a good example for young athletes. When I give talks to groups, I stress that you can't be afraid to take the lead and, when you get it, stay there. Don't wait for other people to set the pace. Take the lead in your community, your activities, your faith, in the world. Be confident in your ideas and in yourself. Make no apologies for your greatness. This is a universal message. But I know that girls need to hear it more.

We need to be reminded to believe in ourselves. To trust in our abilities. To know that if we must, we can perch a glass on our head and coast across the pool, not spilling so much as a drop.

END

Two years after I graduated from middle school, I was asked to speak to the Class of 2013 at Little Flower. I was honored to be asked to deliver the address, even though I felt very much still a kid myself.

I came up with a top-ten list that I hoped would help prepare the students for the future. I advised them not to be intimidated because they were young. I told them I was the youngest of 530 people on Team USA in London, but because I was well prepared, age didn't matter. I told them to pay attention. To be a good teammate and classmate. To be gracious in both victory and defeat, and to keep a sense of humor. To not let setbacks get them down.

I emphasized that they should stick up for the less fortunate. To work in the community to help others. And I urged them to look for their role models and inspiration in places apart from sports. I'm sure this was unexpected. But I meant what I said. It wasn't to diminish my—or any other athlete's—accomplishments, more to widen the lens of what is seen as worthy of glory.

In sum, I advised the graduates to follow the rules but not necessarily a set plan. Life is full of surprises, so chart your own course. Swim without fear. Go out and do something special.

And it's precisely what I intend to keep doing myself.

I'm swimming faster now than I was two years ago, shaving several seconds off my race times. No one expected this to be the case. Maybe not even me. Nonetheless, it's dawning on me more and more that I've been doing this swimming thing for a while, and I won't be doing it forever.

As I've gotten older, the pool has meant different things to me. When I was much younger, swimming was simply having fun, being around friends, splashing in the water. When I joined a year-round swim team, the pool became a place I could retreat to after school to forget about class and commune with a new group of people. As I got better and better, the pool provided a space where I could stretch my limits physically and mentally. The challenge of water pushing me to push myself.

These days the pool still means all those same things to me. Even in the intensity of my Olympic Year, I'm careful to incorporate joy into my routine. I work like a beast. But I keep myself open to the playful moments, the goofiness, the *Curb Your Enthusiasm*–type farcicalities that flesh out a full life. I've learned that you can't control everything. No matter how much you might want to.

It's a noteworthy gift of swimming that it demands you stay mentally engaged in the present. As much as nagging thoughts can creep into your head, the water forces other concerns to the margins, letting you forget, go on, and, well, *immerse* yourself in the moment. You can listen to music or have music playing outside on the deck. You can have silence. You can have teammates around you, or you can swim on your own. Swim long enough, and you come to learn that swimming is a living, breathing thing that shows you a new piece of itself just when you think you know all there is to know. It's a sport that offers different seasons, a chameleon changing colors.

For me, swimming has also been a gateway to a higher purpose. As an Olympian, I am invited to visit schools, churches, clinics, and hospitals. Without that perk of being able to reach people and inspire them, the swimming on its own would be a bit meaningless. Sure, in some ways, it's a noble thing to reach the pinnacle of achievement in a given field. But it's way more satisfying when that achievement leads to a broader calling.

Walter Reed National Military Medical Center was one of the first places I went after the London Olympics. I met some of the wounded veterans. It was my very first time putting the gold medal around somebody else's neck. I remember one guy was hesitant, like, should you really do this?

Unlike in the military, there's no protocol for Olympic medals, so I draped it over his shoulders and watched his face light up. I call it the power of the gold medal. I've seen it time and again since then, how holding or wearing the medal excites people. They always say the same thing: "It's so heavy!"

When I visit the kids at Children's National Hospital, the power of the gold medal is even stronger. They see the awards like a superhero accessory and love posing for photos wearing them. The kids beam and model with these big medals bouncing around their tiny necks.

I am as grateful for those experiences as any I've had as a swimmer. They opened my eyes to the hurdles faced by so many. The resilience and determined spirit I observed in those children and veterans recalibrated what I knew to be heroic. And changed how I want to be remembered.

I'd like to be known as a noteworthy swimmer, naturally. But it is equally important to me to be seen as a kind, caring person who helped people, was nice to children, and was a good neighbor; someone who took my work seriously and was a reliable teammate throughout the years.

It matters to me that I live a balanced, well-rounded life despite being a pro athlete. Thanks to my family, coaches, friends, faith, and Bruce Springsteen, I've been able to do that. I'm precisely in the pocket of where I've always hoped to be.

If you're healthy, you can swim until you're ninety. I've watched videos of master swimmers who are nearing a hundred years old, crushing the 500 freestyle in a meet. To think about having that gift taken from me because of illness or injury rattles me. If I'm afraid of anything in this universe, it's of not being able to end my career on my terms. I want to know before my last race that it's my last race.

At this point, I have zero clue when that might be. I've told everyone who will listen that I'm not going to be done after Paris. I find it enticing that the 2028 Olympics will be held in Los Angeles. If I could dream of the perfect way to cap my career, it would be competing in the Olympic Games in my home country with tons of family and friends around. What an amazing ending that would be.

But! I can't even say that I would necessarily want that to be my last race. I may want to swim at one more meet after the 2028 Games. One more World Championship. You never know. I suppose what I'm admitting is that I love swimming too much. How could I ever stop?

I'm not delusional. I'm aware that elite athletic competition is the domain of the young. I'm only twenty-seven, and I've already witnessed heaps of teammates and peers retire. Many of them right out of college. I've also observed Olympic teammates in their early thirties bow out. But then you have Michael Phelps, who said 2012 was going to be the finale of his career, and he ended up taking a break and coming back to swim one more Olympic Games.

There are swimmers I talk to who swear they're never going to look at the water again after they retire. Others plan to compete in masters swimming, swim meets held for adult swimmers (some hundred-year-olds still compete!). Whenever I hear those kinds of things, it makes me reflect. What am I going to do when I stop swimming? Am I going to keep logging laps? Or am I going to pivot to running marathons or take up pickleball? And if I do swim, am I going to be capable of not looking at the clock? Am I going to be capable of not comparing myself to what I used to be?

I don't have all the answers, but I do know that I picture myself swimming my entire life. I need to touch water.

Which is why today I'm in the pool.

It's Sunday. I swim Sundays now. I started doing it because I had the Monday-morning blues. Our team in Florida practices Saturday morning, and then we have the remainder of Saturday and all of Sunday off to rest. By the time Monday morning practice rolls around, it's been nearly forty-eight hours of idle time. For me, that's too long on land.

What this means is I swim every day. No time off. It's already helped me. I've been practicing better on Monday. Sleeping better. Feeling better. More like myself.

That said, Sunday is my day. I don't do a whole practice. My coach doesn't even write me a practice. I go in and I do as much or as little as I want. Nothing for time. I keep it easy.

My Sunday swim helps me start my week at a better level. And it helps me keep my feel for the water. As nutty as it sounds, I genuinely believe I lose a little bit of my feel after as few as twenty-four hours dry. So I go in on Sunday.

Sometimes an assistant coach will be getting laps in, or one of the student managers. Now and again, a teammate joins me. But more often I'm on my own. I coast back and forth. I let my body tell me what it needs. Sometimes I focus on my technique and think about my stroke. Sometimes I turn my brain off, space out. I let whatever comes to mind come to mind. It's my "me time."

I remind myself: there are no rules. I don't need to do a certain amount. I don't need to go a certain speed. I can just be in the pool and play. No pressure. Just me and my connection to the water, exactly as it started when I was young, when I submerged my face beneath the surface for the first time and couldn't wait to do it again.

For me, the pool will always be a sanctuary, a place to quiet the mind, to return to the water we all come from. A place to dive in and feel transformed. And that, as much as anything else, is why I continue to swim.

In some ways, my Sunday practice is a preview of what I'll be doing in the future. Once I'm finally done competing. It's almost as if once a week I am teaching myself how not to look at the clock. How to be the future me.

I'm in the pool, with a smile on my face, and I just keep swimming.

POSTSCRIPT

When I was in second grade, I was given a childhood diary as a gift. It was part of the American Girl product line, a fill-in-the-blank journal for young girls called *Pages and Pockets: A Portfolio for Secrets and Stuff*.

It may have been called that, but inside mine, there were zero secrets. There was barely any "stuff." Instead, there were repeated entries revealing how much I loved swimming. Under the *Best thing about practicing is . . .* prompt, I answered, "Practice makes perfect." Under the fill-in-the-blank *Here's what I don't like about practicing . . .* I wrote, "Nothing."

It's crazy to look back over those scribbled pages and read my entries. My shaky handwriting in number two pencil. The newly learned cursive of my name on the cover. All the hallmarks of a girl who knew what she liked and was slowly trying to find her place within it.

When I recently moved to Florida, I transported all my training journals with me. Paging through them, I realized they included so many elements of my story, my accomplishments, and my feelings. That maybe these scribbles were the start of a story worth sharing. I also felt like it was a good opportunity to highlight the people who have impacted me along the way. For me, swimming has always been a team sport.

I think athletes can do a lot of good in this world. We have a platform and the ability to bring the world together. I hope there are some lessons in this book that each reader can take away.

POSTSCRIPT

I never imagined I would make it to the Olympics, or be at this level, or write a book about this unlikely career that I've had. But I've really enjoyed the ride, this improbable journey.

Swimming is a magical sport.

And I've been fortunate enough to make the most of it.

ACKNOWLEDGMENTS

Obviously, it was not a matter of *just* adding water. There are so many people who have helped me along the way and without whom my swimming career and this book would not have materialized.

Family is the most important thing in the world to me. I thank my parents, my brother, Michael (the reason I started swimming), my grandparents, and all of my aunts, uncles, and cousins for creating a strong support system. The Hagans, the Ledeckys, the O'Connors, the Manaras family, the Greenwalds, the Keoghs, the Letendres, the Nichols family, the Martinez family, the Blakes, the Nygaards, the Beddows, and my godfather, Jim Shea. Uncle Jon Ledecky deserves a special shout-out— he has provided so many fun family experiences and so much love and support over the years. Aunt Peg Hagan has enthusiastically functioned as a family historian and photographer to preserve memories for all of us. I'd also like to recognize Carla Kelly, who worked with my Grandpa Hagan to document his early life and World War II experience.

Thank you to Simon & Schuster. It has been such a pleasure working with Allison Glock on this project. She has been tireless in her efforts and always asks the right questions. Thank you to Simon & Schuster CEO Jonathan Karp for taking a personal interest, and editors Priscilla Painton and Emily Simonson for bringing it to publication. Thank you to all the other individuals at Simon & Schuster who worked on this project, including Jackie Seow, Jonathan Evans, Emily Beth Thomas,

Wendy Blum, Alicia Brancato, Julia Prosser, Margaret Southard, Irene Kheradi, Elizabeth Venere, and Amanda Mulholland.

Super book attorney Robert Barnett and his colleague Emily Alden at Williams & Connolly were stellar in every way.

Alan Abrahamson was invaluable in getting me launched into the book arena.

TYR Sport has a special place in my heart, and I could not do this without them. I appreciate Matt DiLorenzo, Joe and Rosemarie DiLorenzo, Steven Locke, and everyone at TYR for their commitment to me and to the sport of swimming.

Thank you to Casey Wasserman and the Wasserman agency for their astute guidance. Thank you to Dan Levy, Lindsay Kagawa-Colas, Mary Anthony, and all their colleagues.

Leading Authorities has worked to put me in front of audiences around the world. Thank you to Matt Jones and Lauren Wolf.

It was wonderful to grow up in Bethesda, Maryland, and the Washington, D.C., area. I received a great education at Little Flower School and Stone Ridge School of the Sacred Heart. Thank you to Little Flower's legendary principal, Sister Rosemaron Rynn, all my amazing teachers and all the IHM Sisters, Monsignor Peter Vaghi, pastoral and school staff, and all the great LFS families. Thank you to Stone Ridge's outstanding head of school, Catherine Karrels, and the following people who made/make SR such a special place: my high school coaches Bob Walker and Paul Boman; Malcolm McCluskey, Connie Mitchell, the RSCJ Sisters, all my teachers, and others who provided much support during my high school years and beyond; and, of course, all my friends from the Stone Ridge Class of 2015, high school swimming, and other activities at Stone Ridge.

My family and I are lucky to have many longtime friends in our Bethesda neighborhood and beyond. Kurt and Alison Newman have always been lifesavers and pointed the way for us to the Palisades pool. The Miller family and Dick and Diane Powers have always been such kind friends. Special thanks to Greg Rosenbaum, his wife, Marti, and their family; among other things, Greg was a hero in locating last-minute tickets at the London Olympics for some of my relatives, and he is a big supporter of Team USA. Thanks to all our other neighbors on our Bethesda street, I wish I could list all of you!

Swimming on the Palisades swim team as part of the Montgomery County Swim League (MCSL) was a formative experience for my brother and me. Thank you to my incredible coaches at Palisades and to the great parents who threw themselves wholeheartedly into volunteering at the pool every summer to help their kids, the coaches, and my great teammates.

Nation's Capital Swim Club (NCAP) provided a remarkable year-round swim program. I'm thankful to have had many great coaches at NCAP, including Carolyn Kaucher, Yuri Suguiyama, and Bruce Gemmell. I have so much appreciation for Tom Ugast, Lee Sommers, Tim Kelly, Nicole Gamard, John Flanagan, Pete Morgan, Jeremy Linn, Marilyn Mangels, and Sue Chen. Andrew Gemmell was one of many remarkable training partners in the years leading up to the Rio Olympics.

I also would like to thank the members of the DMV sports community who have been so supportive over the years. Ted and Lynn Leonsis and family have always been great friends. It was so much fun watching the Washington Capitals growing up, and Dick Patrick and family and George McPhee were always so welcoming. On the baseball front, the Lerners and the Washington Nationals have been so wonderful to me as well. Special thanks to Mark Lerner, Mike Rizzo, Dusty Baker, Davey Martinez, and Bryce Harper.

Of course, I remain a huge hockey fan. Let's go, Islanders! Thank you to Scott Malkin, the Malkin family, and the entire New York Islanders organization for allowing us to share in the fun.

Stanford University was a wonderful place for both school and pool. Coach Greg Meehan and Coach Tracy Slusser took our team to Pac-12 and NCAA Championships but also created a family-like culture. Thank you to Bernard Muir and the Stanford Department of Athletics. My extraordinary Stanford swim teammates and, in particular, my sophomore-year swim roommates—Ally, Ella, Leah, Kim, and Erin—will be lifelong friends, as will many other Stanford friends, such as my freshman roommates, Tessa, Karly, and Emily. Dr. Alia Crum was the perfect advisor for me as I pursued my undergraduate degree. Professor Jody Maxmin was the first professor I met at Stanford, and I am lucky to consider her a friend. Rafael Pelayo, Cheri Mah, Scott Kutscher, and the late William Dement have taught me much that I have been able to apply to my life, my training, and my travels.

I owe a deep debt of gratitude to the Spieker and Hopman families for opening up their backyard pool to me, Simone Manuel, and Coach Meehan during three months of the pandemic. They became like another family to me, and along with Simone and Greg, they brought joy into my life during the hard days away from home. Stanford men's coach Ted Knapp helped make that connection. Ted and Mary Robinson also were especially helpful in supporting me during this time.

I am appreciative of Anthony Nesty for allowing me to join his swim program at the University of Florida. In addition to Coach Nesty, Coaches Whitney Hite, Kristen Murslack, Jack Szaranek, Annie Lazor, Alex Dehner, and Tracy Zimmer all have been incredibly supportive and create a positive environment at the pool and in the weight room. Erva Gilliam, Mike Spiegler, Katherine Edenfield, Ricky Ray, Christina Garvin, Tariq Kelly, Blaire Wolski, and many others play instrumental roles in the success of the team, in and out of the pool. I am grateful to be surrounded by great swim teammates every day. Thank you to Scott Stricklin and the University of Florida Athletic Association. My Gainesville neighbors Kathy and Bobby Slaton have become great friends.

USA Swimming, the USA Swimming Foundation, and the swimming community have always been so supportive: Tim Hinchey, Frank Busch, Lindsay Mintenko, the late Chuck Wielgus, Rowdy Gaines, Scott

Leightman, Jim Fox, Stacy Michael-Miller, Jennifer Thomas, Russell Mark, Jack Roach, Keenan Robinson, Kaitlin Pawlowicz and family, and many others. Jon Urbanchek has played a special role in my swimming career since 2012. Alicia Glass, Sean McCann, the medical staff, and many others behind the scenes make sure every athlete gets what they need leading up to race day. Thank you to everyone who generously contributes to the USA Swimming Foundation.

Mike Unger, in his great work for both USA Swimming and World Aquatics, has always been so thoughtful and helpful.

The U.S. Olympic & Paralympic Committee and its leaders, such as Sarah Hirshland, Lawrence Probst, and Susanne Lyons, have been a pleasure to work with at various events and are always thinking of ways to improve Team USA's success on the biggest stage. I am appreciative of all the resources and people I can call on when I have a question or idea. Thank you to Brett Nowicki and colleagues at World Aquatics, and to Travis Tygart and colleagues at USADA.

I have been so honored to carry on the tradition of Team USA Swimming, with so many champions who have been especially kind to me along the way. Chris and Bob Olmstead are dear friends. I have been honored to receive support from distance swimming legends Debbie Meyer and Janet Evans. Kate Ziegler and Katie Hoff were two Olympians I looked up to from a young age. Donna de Varona, Kaitlin Sandeno, Dara Torres, Missy Franklin, Maya DiRado, and Lia Neal have all shown me friendship and support. Summer Sanders is a Stanford legend and was one of the first to welcome me into the Olympic family after I qualified for the Olympics in 2012. I have had so many remarkable National Team teammates over the years—those who have been supportive, those who have been relay teammates, those who looked out for me when I was a rookie, those who have inspired me with their performances, and those who have become friends. If I started listing out every name here, it would look like one long Team USA roster from 2012 to the present. Nathan Adrian, Elizabeth Beisel, Natalie Coughlin, Anthony Ervin, Matt

ACKNOWLEDGMENTS

Grevers, Brendan Hansen, Cullen Jones, Kara Lynn Joyce, Jason Lezak, Ryan Lochte, Michael Phelps, Allison Schmitt, Rebecca Soni, and Dana Vollmer were some of the experienced swimmers on the 2012 Olympic Team, and I learned a lot by observing them.

On the international scene, Rebecca Adlington and Lotte Friis were classy standouts in my early years on that stage, and I consider them friends.

I appreciate sportswriters and other media members who have taken great pains to cover the sport of swimming, many of whom have made long journeys to do their jobs.

Finally, thanks to you—and to all fans of swimming—for your support.

ABOUT THE AUTHOR

Katie Ledecky is a record-breaking swimmer who has represented Team USA at three Olympic Games and six World Championships; she won her first Olympic gold medal in 2012 at the age of fifteen. Her combined seven Olympic gold medals and twenty-one World Championship gold medals are the most ever won by a female swimmer. She was the most decorated U.S. female athlete at the Rio and Tokyo Olympic Games, and she is widely regarded as one of the greatest Olympians and sportswomen of all time. Born in Washington, D.C., and a longtime resident of Bethesda, Maryland, Katie is a graduate of Stanford University and is currently training in Gainesville, Florida, in an attempt to qualify for the Olympic Games in Paris in the summer of 2024.